D1242071

Travel industry economics

A Guide for Financial Analysis

Spending on travel and tourism accounts for well over $1 trillion of the world's total gross domestic product and translates into direct and indirect employment of more than 300 million people, around one-tenth of the global work force. In this path-breaking book Harold L. Vogel examines the business economics of each of the major travel industry segments with coverage of airlines, hotels, cruise lines, railroads, buses, automobiles, casinos, amusement/theme parks, and tourism. The result is a concise, up-to-date reference guide for financial analysts, economists, industry executives, journalists, and teachers and students interested in the economics, finance, production, and marketing of travel-related goods and services in the United States and overseas. Its approach closely parallels the highly successful perspective the author takes in *Entertainment Industry Economics* (Fourth Edition, 1998, Cambridge University Press; Fifth Edition, 2001, forthcoming).

Readers are introduced to the basic economic concepts employed to analyze each of the travel segments, bringing together valuable data from a wide variety of sources. Each chapter also provides a brief historical overview and a systematic discussion of the particular economic, production, financial, and accounting issues related to each segment. A glossary, "time-line" diagrams, and technical appendices enhance the book's appeal as a reference tool. Its fully integrated assessment of the business of travel makes the work unique in the marketplace.

Harold L. Vogel is the author of all four editions of Entertainment Industry Economics: A Guide for Financial Analysis (Cambridge University Press), which Cambridge will publish in a fifth edition in 2001. He was ranked as top entertainment industry analyst for a record ten years by Institutional Investor magazine and served for seventeen years as senior entertainment industry analyst at Merrill Lynch & Co. A chartered financial analyst and member of the New York Society of Securities Analysts, Mr. Vogel formerly served on the New York State Governor's Motion Picture and Television Advisory Board. He is a frequent writer and speaker on investment topics related to leisure, entertainment, and travel, serves as adjunct professor of media economics at Columbia University's Uris Graduate School of Business, and is author of the novel Short Three Thousand (2000). Mr. Vogel currently works as an independent investment manager and venture capitalist in New York City.

Travel industry economics
A Guide for Financial Analysis

HAROLD L. VOGEL

CAMBRIDGE
UNIVERSITY PRESS

PUBLISHED BY THE PRESS SYNDICATE OF THE UNIVERSITY OF CAMBRIDGE
The Pitt Building, Trumpington Street, Cambridge, United Kingdom

CAMBRIDGE UNIVERSITY PRESS
The Edinburgh Building, Cambridge CB2 2RU, UK
40 West 20th Street, New York, NY 10011-4211, USA
10 Stamford Road, Oakleigh, VIC 3166, Australia
Ruiz de Alarcón 13, 28014 Madrid, Spain
Dock House, The Waterfront, Cape Town 8001, South Africa

http://www.cambridge.org

First published 2001

Printed in the United States of America

Typeface Times Roman 10.75/12 pt.   *System* LaTeX 2_ε [TB]

A catalog record for this book is available from the British Library.

Library of Congress Cataloging in Publication Data
Vogel, Harold L., 1946–
      Travel industry economics / Harold L. Vogel.
          p.   cm.
      Includes bibliographical references.
      ISBN 0-521-78163-9
      1. Tourism–Economic aspects.   I. Title.
      G155.A1 V64   2000
      338.4′791 – dc21
                                  00-023674

ISBN 0 521 78163 9 hardback

TO MY BEAUTIFUL MOM
– WHOSE LOVE AND SPIRIT KNEW NO BOUNDS

Contents

Preface

We are all born, it seems, with an natural curiosity – with an urge to travel. What normal infant, confined to crib or playpen, doesn't soon want to explore the world beyond? What normal teenager doesn't want to explore a new neighborhood or city or country? And what person hasn't at one time or another dreamt of how it would feel to travel across the boundaries of time or space?

The urge to travel is universal. And this makes travel, as broadly defined, a very big business indeed. In the United States, for example, travel and tourism is estimated to account for approximately 5% of gross domestic product and to be the third largest retail industry after automobile dealers and food stores. Clearly, in getting from here to there and back again, we need lots of goods and services. In fact, including everything, the travel industry turns out to be the world's largest in terms of numbers of people employed and in terms of total direct and indirect revenues generated. Three hundred million people – one of every ten employees world-wide – and more than US$1.5 trillion out of a total world economic output of around US$40 trillion are probably good estimates for those numbers at the start of the twenty-first century.

With an industry so large, it is difficult to even know where to begin. There are texts relating to hotel or restaurant or casino management policies. There are tomes and stock brokerage house reports and consultants' papers providing forecasts for the various travel-related business segments. Statistics of all types abound.

Yet what seems to be missing is a concise treatment that ties together all the major industry segments from the perspective of a potential investor and financial economist. That is indeed the ambition of the text you currently hold. As such, anyone who analyzes or manages or writes about travel-related investments ought to be interested in this book. Its mission is to broadly cover the financial and economic dynamics of the businesses that service the needs of people who, whether for pleasure (tourism) or commerce, require physical transportation: travel, in other words.

In contrast, the underlying concept of my previous work, *Entertainment Industry Economics: A Guide For Financial Analysis*, involves a different kind of transportation – that of people's emotions. Fortunately, the previous work has been well-enough received to have gone into a fourth edition in 1998 (and soon, a fifth). The style of that work, as well as the chapters providing an economic overview and coverage of casinos and theme parks, has been largely carried over from that volume.

But also, as in that volume, only those industry segments that have clearly defined boundaries and reliable data histories are examined. Accordingly, the topics, following the early economic overview chapter, are broken down into segments aimed at the level of advanced undergraduate or graduate students. Financial analysts, economists, industry executives, managers and consultants, journalists, and general readers would, however, also likely find the material to be of interest and to be user-friendly. The minimum requirement is for the reader to have a degree of familiarity with general economics and financial terminology, although a little knowledge of advanced mathematics would undoubtedly make the selected readings and footnotes somewhat easier to fully grasp. With this in mind, and for convenience, a glossary section has been appended.

Nevertheless, to stay focused, it has been necessary to omit the larger aspects of transportation industries that could, for example, further include studies of airports, urban public transit, trucking, shipping, and cargos and freights. The separate but closely related topic of *tourism* economics, covered in Chapter 7, is also only sketched, as an in-depth analysis would take the text into areas (e.g., trade and regional development) that would only distract from the primary purpose without giving those topics the full treatments they deserve. And, for much the same reason, coverage of subjects that are commonly discussed in transport economics – externalities, infrastructure investment criteria, peak-load pricing, regulation, and social cost-benefit analysis, to name a few – is tangential.

In the preparation of this text, I am indebted to the transportation and travel industry economists upon whose academic shoulders this work rests.

Particularly noteworthy for making the task of exposition a lot easier than it would have otherwise been are Kenneth Boyer's *Principles of Transportation Economics*, Adrian Bull's *The Economics of Travel and Tourism*, Kenneth Button's *Transport Economics*, Rigas Doganis's airline economics masterpiece, *Flying Off Course*, and J. P. (Pat) Hanlon's *Global Airlines*. Also proving invaluable were Morrell's text on airline finance, Block's on REITs, Dickinson and Vladimir's on cruise ships, Meyer and Oster's on intercity passenger travel, and both Friedman's and Scarne's pioneering work in the casino gaming field.

I would also like to thank Michael Lenz, Director of Investor Relations at American Airlines, for taking time to review a draft of the airline chapter. Similarly, I thank Erin Williams, Manager of Investor Relations at Royal Caribbean, for reviewing the cruise ship section, and Laura Paugh, Vice President for Investor Relations at Marriott International for reviewing the hotel chapter. And I am grateful to Cambridge University Press and especially to Scott Parris, economics editor, for support of this project.

In addition, the book has benefited greatly from data made available by the various industry trade groups including the Airline Transport Associations (ATA and IATA) and the International Civil Aviation Organization (ICAO). Similar benefit was derived from data of the Cruise Lines International Association (CLIA), the World Tourism Organization (WTO), and the International Association of Amusement Parks and Attractions (IAAPA).

Of course, responsibility for any errors that may inadvertently remain is mine alone.

In all, I hope and expect that readers will find *Travel Industry Economics* to be a truly enjoyable and moving experience.

All aboard!

New York City Harold L. Vogel

Part I
Introduction

1
Economic perspectives

Travel broadens the mind.

It also costs money and takes up time.

In this chapter we examine the fundamental economic factors that affect all aspects of the travel and tourism business. The perspectives provided by this approach will enable us to see how travel industries are defined and fit into the larger economic picture. They will also form a framework for understanding the financial features that guide investments in this field.

1.1 Time concepts

Alternatives

You need time to get from here to there. And given that time-transport machines are still to be seen only in science fiction films, it is worth our while to spend a little time to understand the economic value of time.

Time for leisure or business travel comes out of a budget that includes time for work, time for play, and time for taking care of the necessities of life. But in recent years the boundaries between these categories have become increasingly blurred. For instance, we associate what is loosely known as "leisure time," as time in which people are free from having any sense of obligation or compulsion to do anything.[1] Yet we could just as easily characterize the term *leisure* as simply time not spent at work. No matter what the definitional preference, however, the essential economic fact is that time has a cost in terms of alternative opportunities foregone.

Because time is needed to use or to consume goods and services as well as to produce them, economists have attempted to develop theories that treat time as a commodity with varying qualitative and quantitative cost features. As Sharp (1981) notes in his comprehensive coverage:

> Although time is commonly described as a scarce resource in economic literature, it is still often treated rather differently from the more familiar inputs of labor and materials and outputs of goods and services. The problems of its allocation have not yet been fully or consistently integrated into economic analysis. (p. 210)

Nevertheless, investigations into the economics of time, including those of Becker (1965) and DeSerpa (1971), have suggested that the demand for leisure is affected in a complicated way by the cost of time to both produce and consume. For instance, according to Becker (see also Ghez and Becker 1975),

> The two determinants of the importance of forgone earnings are the amount of time used per dollar of goods and the cost per unit of time. Reading a book, taking a haircut or commuting use more time per dollar of goods than eating dinner, frequenting a night-club or sending children to private summer camps. Other things the same, forgone earnings would be more important for the former set of commodities than the latter.
>
> The importance of forgone earnings would be determined solely by time intensity only if the cost of time was the same for all commodities. Presumably, however, it varies considerably among commodities and at different periods. For example, the cost of time is often less on week-ends and in the evenings. (Becker 1965, p. 503)

Availabilities

Most of us do not normally experience sharp changes in our availability of leisure time (except on retirement or loss of job). Nevertheless, there is a fairly widespread impression that leisure time has been trending steadily higher ever since the Industrial Revolution of more than a century ago. Yet the evidence on this is mixed. Figure 1.1 shows that in the United States the largest increases in leisure time – workweek reductions – for agricultural and nonagricultural industries were achieved prior to 1940. But more recently, the lengths of average workweeks, as adjusted for increases in holidays and vacations, have scarcely changed for the manufacturing sector and have also stopped declining in the services sector (Table 1.1 and Figure 1.2). By comparison, average hours worked in other major countries, as illustrated in Figure 1.3, have declined markedly since 1970.

Although this suggests that there has been little, if any, expansion of leisure time in the United States, what has apparently happened instead is that work schedules now provide greater diversity. As noted by Smith (1986), "A larger

Table 1.1. *Average weekly hours at work,*
1948–1995,[a] and median weekly hours at work
for selected years[b]

	Average hours at work		Median hours at work	
Year	Unadjusted	Adjusted[c]	Year	Hours
1948	42.7	41.6	1973	40.6
1956	43.0	41.8	1975	43.1
1962	43.1	41.7	1980	46.9
1969	43.5	42.0	1984	47.3
1975	42.2	40.9	1987	46.8
1986	42.8		1995	50.6

[a]Nonstudent men in nonagricultural industries. *Source:*
Owen (1976, 1988).
[b]*Source:* Harris (1995).
[c]Adjusted for growth in vacations and holidays.

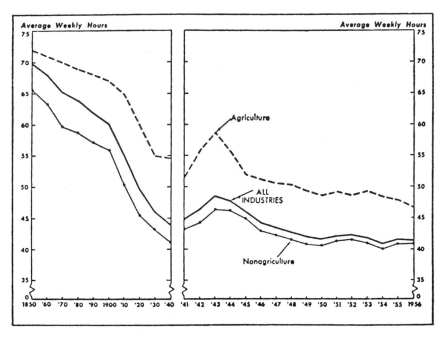

Figure 1.1. Estimated average weekly hours for all persons employed in agricultural and
nonagricultural industries, 1850–1940 (10-year intervals) and 1941–56 (annual averages
for all employed persons, including the self-employed and unpaid family workers).
Source: Zeisel (1958).

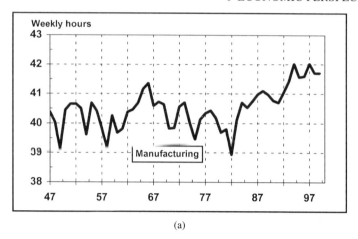

(a)

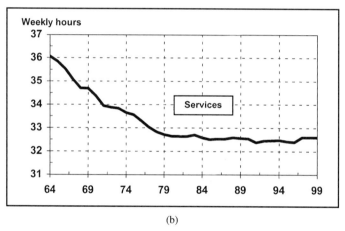

(b)

Figure 1.2. Average weekly hours worked by production workers in: (a) manufacturing industries, 1947–97; and (b) service industries, 1964–99. *Source:* U.S. Department of Commerce.

percentage of people worked under 35 hours or over 49 hours a week in 1985 than in 1973, yet the mean and median hours (38.4 and 40.4 respectively, in 1985) remained virtually unchanged."[2]

But if findings from public-opinion surveys of Americans and the arts conducted in 1995 and earlier years by Louis Harris and Associates, Inc. are to be believed, the number of hours available for leisure may actually be declining.[3] This view has also been supported by Schor (1991, p. 29), with an estimate that between 1969 and 1987, "the average employed person is now on the job an additional 163 hours, or the equivalent of an extra month a year. . . and that hours have risen across a wide spectrum of Americans and in all income categories."[4]

However, these data also appear suspect, and some evidence to the contrary is provided by Robinson (1989, p. 34), who has measured free time by age

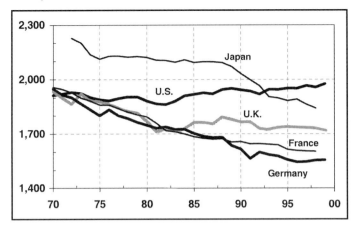

Figure 1.3. Average annual hours worked in the United States versus other countries, 1970–99. *Source: OECD Employment Outlook.*

categories and found that "most gains in free time have occurred between 1965 and 1975 [but] since then, the amount of free time people have has remained fairly stable." By adjusting for age categories, the case for an increase in total leisure hours available becomes much more persuasive.[5] In addition, Roberts and Rupert (1995) found that total hours of annual work have not changed by much but that the *composition* of labor has shifted from home work to market work with nearly all the difference attributable to changes in the total hours worked by women.[6] A similar conclusion as to average annual hours worked was also reached by Rones, Ilg, and Gardner (1997).[7] Yet, as Jacobs and Gerson (1998, p. 457) note, "even though the average work week has not changed dramatically in the U.S. over the last several decades, a growing group of Americans are clearly and strongly pressed for time."

In all, it seems safe to say that for most middle-aged and middle-income Americans, leisure time is not expanding.[8] However, no matter what the actual rate of expansion or contraction may be, there has been a natural evolution toward repackaging the time set aside for leisure into more long holiday weekends and extra vacation days, rather than in reducing the minutes worked each and every week.[9] Particularly for those in the higher-income categories – conspicuous consumers, as Veblen would say – the result is that personal-consumption expenditures (PCEs) for leisure activities are likely to be intense, frenzied, and compressed instead of evenly metered throughout the year. Moreover, with some adjustment for cultural differences, the same pattern is likely to be seen wherever large middle-class populations emerge.

Estimated apportionment of leisure hours among various activities in the United States, and the changes in such apportionment between 1970 and 1995, are indicated in Table 1.2.[10] In addition, many of the time and cost concepts that apply specifically to travel and tourism can be tied together in what has been dubbed a distance-decay function as shown in Figure 1.4. The

Table 1.2. *Time spent by adults on selected leisure activities, 1970 and 1995 estimates*

Leisure activity	Hours per person per year[a]		% of total time accounted for by each activity	
	1970	1995	1970	1995
Television	1,226	1,575	16.5	46.2
Network affiliates		836		24.5
Independent stations		183		5.4
Basic cable programs		468		13.7
Pay cable programs		88		2.6
Radio	872	1,091	33.1	32.0
Home		442		13.0
Out of home		649		19.0
Newspapers	218	165	8.3	4.8
Records & tapes	68	289	2.6	8.5
Magazines	170	84	6.5	2.5
Leisure books	65	99	2.5	2.9
Movies: Theaters	10	12	0.4	0.4
home video		45		1.3
Spectator sports	3	14	0.1	0.4
Video games: arcade		4		0.1
home		24		0.7
Cultural events	3	5	0.1	0.1
Total	2,635	3,407	100.0[b]	100.0[b]
Hours per adult per week	50.7	65.5		
Hours per adult per day	7.2	9.3		

[a] Averaged over participants and nonparticipants.
[b] Total not exact due to rounding.
Source: CBS office of Economic Analysis, Wilkofsky Gruen Associates, Inc.

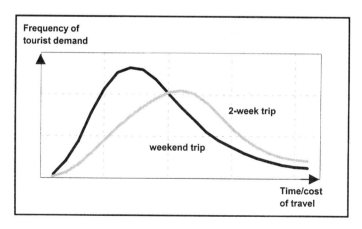

Figure 1.4. Distance-decay function for tourist travel.

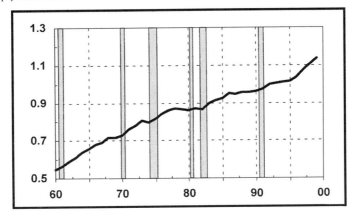

Figure 1.5. Nonfarm business productivity in the United States, shown by output per hour index (1992 = 100), 1960–99. Bars indicate periods of recession.

function captures the fact that while traveling, an opportunity cost of time rather spent doing something else is incurred. As Bull (1995, p. 45) suggests, a good proxy for physical distance is a composite variable that includes the opportunity cost of time *and* of the money-cost for a trip. Such a variable is inversely related to demand for tourist travel.

1.2 Supply and demand factors

Productivity

Ultimately, however, more leisure time availability is not a function of government decree, labor union activity, or factory-owner altruism. It is a function of the rising trend in output per person-hour – in brief, rising productivity of the economy. Quite simply, technological advances embodied in new capital equipment and in the training of a more skilled labor pool enable more goods and services to be produced in less time or by fewer workers. Thus long-term growth in leisure-time related industries depends on the rate of technological development throughout a nation's economy.

Information concerning trends in productivity, as well as other aspects of economic activity, may be derived from the National Income and Product Accounting (NIPA) figures of the U.S. Department of Commerce. According to those figures, overall productivity between 1973 and 1990 rose at an average annual rate of approximately 1.2% as compared with a rate averaging 2.8% between 1947 and 1973 (Figure 1.5). But in the 1990s, productivity growth rebounded to an average annual rate of 2.0%, thereby implying that the *potential* for leisure-time expansion remained fairly steady in the last quarter of the twentieth century.[11]

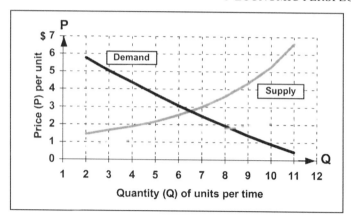

Figure 1.6. Supply and demand schedules.

Demand for leisure

All of us can choose to either fully utilize our free time for recreational
purposes (defined here as being inclusive of entertainment and leisure-travel
activities) or use some of this time to generate additional income. How we
allocate free time between the conflicting desires for more leisure and for
additional income then becomes a subject that economists investigate with
standard analytical tools.[12] In effect, economists can treat demand for leisure
as if it were, say, demand for gold, or for wheat, or for housing. And they
often estimate and depict the schedules for supply and demand with curves
of the type shown in Figure 1.6. Here, in simplified form, it can be seen
that as the price of a unit rises, the supply of it will normally increase, and
the demand for it decrease, so that over time, price and quantity equilibrium
in an openly competitive market will be achieved at the intersection of the
curves.[13]

    It is also important to note that consumers normally tend to substitute
less expensive goods and services for more expensive ones and that the
total amounts they can spend – their budgets – are limited or constrained by
income. The effects of such substitutions and changes in income as related
to demand for leisure have been extensively studied by Owen (1970), who
observed:

An increase in property income will, if we assume leisure is a superior good, reduce hours
of work. A higher wage rate also brings higher income which, in itself, may incline the
individual to increase his leisure. But at the same time the higher wage rate makes leisure
time more expensive in terms of forgone goods and services, so that the individual may
decide instead to purchase less leisure. The net effect will depend then on the relative
strengths of the income and price elasticities. . . .It would seem that for the average worker
the income effect of a rise in the wage rate is in fact stronger than the substitution effect
(p. 18).

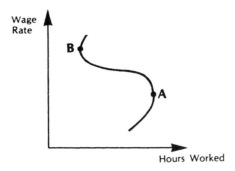

Figure 1.7. Backward-bending labor-supply curve.

In other words, as wage rates continue rising, up to point A in Figure 1.7, people will choose to work more hours to increase their income (income effect). But they eventually begin to favor more leisure over more income (substitution effect, between points A and B), resulting in a backward-bending labor-supply curve.[14] Although renowned economists, including Adam Smith, Alfred Marshall, Frank Knight, A. C. Pigou, and Lionel Robbins have substantially differed in their assessments of the net effect of wage-rate changes on the demand for leisure, it is clear that "leisure does have a price, and changes in its price will affect the demand for it" (Owen 1970, p. 19). Indeed, results from a Bureau of Labor Statistics survey of some 60,000 households in 1986 suggest that about two thirds of those surveyed do not want to work fewer hours if it means earning less money.[15]

As Owen (1970) has demonstrated, estimation of the demand for leisure requires consideration of many complex issues including the nature of "working conditions," the effects of increasing worker fatigue on production rates as work hours lengthen, the greater availability of educational opportunities that affect the desirability of certain kinds of work, government taxation and spending policies, market unemployment rates, and several other variables.[16]

Expected utility comparisons

Individuals differ in terms of the sense of psychic gratification experienced from consumption of different goods and services. Consequently, it is difficult to measure and compare the degrees of satisfaction derived from, say, eating dinner as opposed to buying a new car. To facilitate comparability, economists have adapted an old philosophical concept known as utility.[17] As Barrett (1974, p. 79) has noted, utility "is not a measure of usefulness or need but a measure of the desirability of a commodity from the psychological viewpoint of the consumer."

Of course, rational individuals try to maximize utility – in other words, make decisions that provide them with the most satisfaction. But they are hampered in this regard because decisions are normally made under conditions of uncertainty, with incomplete information, and therefore with risk of an undesired outcome. People thus tend to implicitly include a probabilistic component in their decision-making processes – and they end up maximizing *expected utility* rather than utility itself.

The notion of expected utility is especially well applied in thinking about demand for travel goods and services. It explains, for example, why people may be attracted to gambling, or why they are sometimes willing to pay premiums for certain hotel services. Its application also sheds light on how various travel and entertainment activities compete for the limited time and funds of consumers.

To illustrate, assume for a moment that the cost of an activity per unit of time is somewhat representative of its expected utility. If the admission price to a two-hour movie is $6, and if the purchase of video-game software for $25 provides six hours of play before the onset of boredom, then the cost per minute for the movie is 5 cents whereas that for the game is 6.9 cents. Now, obviously, no one decides to see a movie or buy a game based on explicit comparisons of cost per minute. Indeed, for an individual, many qualitative (nonmonetary) factors, especially fashions and fads, may affect the perception of an item's expected utility. However, in the aggregate and over time, such implicit comparisons do have a significant cumulative influence on relative demand for travel (and other) products and services. In the case of the distance-decay function of Figure 1.4, for example, expected utility thinking is what makes travelers behave as they do in terms of balancing the opportunity cost of time and money (distance) against frequency of travel.

Demographics and debts

Over the longer term, the demand for leisure goods and services can also be significantly affected by changes in the relative growth of different age cohorts. For instance, teenagers tend to be important purchasers of recorded music; people under the age of 30 are the most avid moviegoers. Accordingly, a large increase in births following World War II created, in the 1960s and 1970s, a market highly receptive to movie and music products. In terms of travel and tourism, this generation is currently into or just past its years of family formation and peak earnings power, and it would be natural to expect a rising demand for visits to amusement/theme parks, casinos, and resort destinations.

The broad demographic shifts most important to travel industry prospects in the United States include (1) a projected increase of the numbers of 18- to 34-year-olds in the early 2000s (4.8 million more in 2010 than in 2000), (2) a projected rapid growth in the large group of 35- to 64-year-olds (up from 105 million in 1990 to 118 million in 2010), and (3) a significant expansion of the population over age 65 (Table 1.3). In particular, the rapid upcoming

Table 1.3. *U.S. population by age bracket, components of change and trends by life stage, 1970–2010*

Components of population change

Age	Percentage distribution					Change (millions)		
	1970	1980	1990	2000[a]	2010[a]	1980–90	1990–2000[a]	2000–2010[a]
Under 5	8.4	7.2	7.6	6.9	6.6	2.4	0.0	0.8
5–17	29.3	24.6	18.2	18.8	17.6	−1.9	6.5	0.5
18–34	15.1	18.2	28.1	23.1	23.0	2.0	−6.4	4.8
35–65	33.2	34.3	33.6	38.5	39.5	13.7	21.7	12.3
65 and over	14.0	15.7	12.5	12.7	13.3	5.5	3.7	4.8
Total	100.0	100.0	100.0	100.0	100.0	21.7	25.5	23.2

Population trends by life stage (millions)

Life stage	1970	1980	1990	2000[a]	2010[a]
0–13 Children	53.8	47.6	50.9	55.0	55.2
14–24 Young adults	40.6	46.5	40.1	41.9	46.9
25–34 Peak family formation	25.3	37.6	43.1	37.4	38.4
35–44 Family maturation	23.1	25.9	37.8	44.7	38.9
45–54 Peak earning power	23.3	22.8	46.3	37.1	43.7
55–64 Childless parents	18.7	21.8	21.1	24.0	35.4
65 and retirement	20.1	25.7	31.2	34.9	39.7
Total	204.9	227.9	249.4	275.0	298.1

[a]Forecast.
Source: U.S. Department of Commerce, series P25.

expansion of the over-65 generation would seem to presage a large increase in demand for tourism and resort-destination trips designed for retired people.

That the number of people in the 45 to 64 age group will be gaining rapidly in proportion to the number of people in the 18 to 34 age group is of particular importance given that those in the younger category are generally apt to spend a large portion of their income when they enter the labor force and form households. Those in the older category, however, are already established. They are thus more likely to be in a savings mode to perhaps finance college educations for their children, or to prepare for retirement, when earnings are lower. But they are also more likely to have the time and money to indulge in travel and tourism.

Depending on the specific industry component to be analyzed, proper interpretation of long-term changes in population characteristics may also require that consideration be given to several additional factors, including dependency ratios (Figure 1.8a), fertility rates, number of first births, number of families with two earners, and trends in labor-force participation rates for women (Figure 1.8b).[18]

Indeed, two paychecks have become an absolute necessity for many families as they have attempted to service relatively high (to income) installment and mortgage debt obligations that have been incurred in the household-formative years. As such, elements of consumer debt (Figure 1.8c), weighted by the aforementioned demographic factors, probably explain why, according to Louis Harris surveys, leisure hours per week seem to have declined noticeably since the early 1970s. However, as the median age rises, these very same elements may combine and begin to abate pressures on time availability.

As can be seen from Figure 1.9, aggregate spending on transportation is concentrated in the middle-age groups, which are the ages at which income usually peaks even though free time may be relatively scarce.

Barriers to entry

The supply of travel and tourism products and services offered would also depend on how readily prospective new businesses can overcome barriers to entry and thereby *contest* the market. Barriers to entry restrict supply and fit broadly into the following categories, listed in order of importance to travel service industries:

Capital
Know-how
Regulations[19]
Price competition

A decision to begin operating an airline, hotel, railroad, bus company, cruise line, or travel agency cannot be made without considerable planning and expertise. To compete effectively, even large corporations must invest considerable time and capital to acquire technical knowledge and experience.

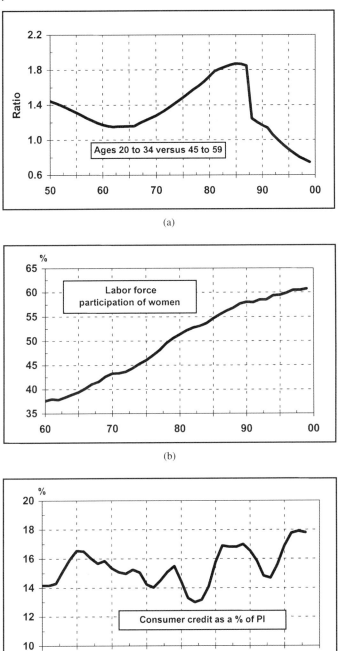

Figure 1.8. (a) Ratio of spenders to savers, 1950–99. (b) Labor force participation rate for women, 1960–99. (c) Consumer credit as a percentage of personal income, 1960–99.

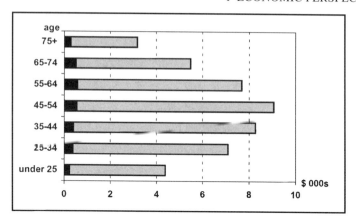

Figure 1.9. Average annual spending on total and public transportation (black bar) per person by age category, 1998. *Source:* U.S. Department of Commerce survey.

Government regulations such as those applying to the airline and casino businesses often present additional hurdles for potential new entrants to surmount. Furthermore, in most industries, established firms would ordinarily have some ability to protect their positions through price competition.

1.3 Primary principles

Marginal matters Microeconomics provides a descriptive framework in which to analyze the effects of incremental changes in the quantities of goods and services supplied or demanded over time. A standard diagram of this type, Figure 1.10, shows an idealized version of a firm that maximizes its profits by pricing its products at the point where marginal revenue (MR) – the extra revenue gained by selling an additional unit – equals marginal cost (MC), the cost of supplying an extra unit. Here, the average cost (AC), which includes both fixed and variable components, first declines and is then pulled up by rising marginal cost. Profit for the firm is represented by the shaded rectangle (price $[p]$ × quantity$[q]$ − cost$[c]$ × quantity$[q]$).

In analyzing the pricing of airline tickets, for instance, the so-called competitive-monopolistic model of Figure 1.10a, in which many firms produce slightly differentiated products, is not far-fetched. The objective for such profit-maximizing firms is to both rightward-shift and to also steepen the demand schedule idealized by line D. By thus making the schedule of demand more vertical – that is, quantity demanded becomes less sensitive to change in price (i.e., more price-inelastic) through promotional and advertising efforts – a firm would be able to reap a potentially large proportionate increase in profits as long as marginal costs are held relatively flat (Figure 1.10b).

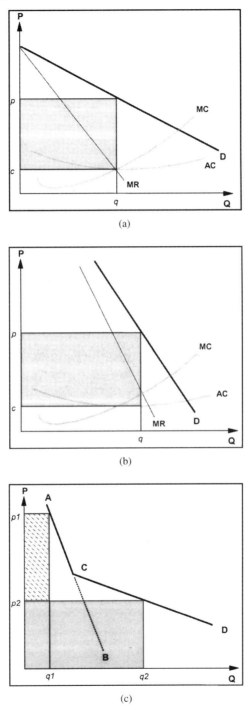

(a)

(b)

(c)

Figure 1.10. Marginal costs and marginal revenues.

Nonetheless, no matter what the elasticities or the ultimate demand functions turn out to be, the costs of building airports and airplanes and hotels, which are large compared to other, later costs, are mostly borne upfront. Come what may, these costs here are *sunk*. In travel and tourism, the cost of generating an incremental unit is normally quite small as compared to other operating (and also sunk) costs. Accordingly, it often makes sense for a travel service distributor to take a chance on spending a little more on marketing and promotion in an attempt to shift the demand schedule into a more price-inelastic and rightward position. Such inelastic demand is characteristic of products and services that:

- are considered to be necessities
- have few substitutes
- comprise a small part of the budget
- are consumed over a relatively brief time
- are not used often.

Economists use estimates of elasticity to indicate the expected percentage change in demand if there is a one percent change in prices or incomes (or some other factor). All other things being equal, demand would be normally expected to rise with an increase in income and decline with an increase in price. In theory, cross–elasticities of demand between goods and services that are close substitutes for each other (a trip to Venice versus a trip to Florence), or complements to each other (a trip and a suitcase), might also be estimated.

Price discrimination If, moreover, a market for, say, airline seats or hotel rooms can be segmented into first and economy classes, profits can be further enhanced by capturing what is known in economics as the *consumers' surplus* – the price difference between what consumers actually pay and what they would be willing to pay. Such price discrimination models extract, without adding much to costs, the additional revenues shown in the cross-hatched rectangular area of Figure 1.10c. The conditions that enable discrimination include:

- existence of monopoly power to regulate prices
- ability to segregate consumers with different elasticities of demand
- inability of original buyers to resell the goods or services

Public good characteristics Public goods are those that can be enjoyed by more than one person without reducing the amount available to any other person. Spending on national defense or on programs to reduce air pollution would be of this type. In travel, also, it is not unusual to find goods that have near public good characteristics. The marginal cost of allowing an extra visitor to a theme park is not measurable.

1.4 Personal-consumption expenditure relationships

There is a close relationship between demand for leisure and demand for recreational products and services that would include those provided to the tourist and leisure traveler. Demand for business travel services would be similarly related to overall business conditions as measured through growth of the economy and corporate profits.

As may be inferred from Table 1.4, National Income and Product Account (NIPA) data classify spending on transportation and on recreation as subsets of total personal-consumption expenditures (PCEs). This table is particularly important because it allows comparison of the amount of transportation and leisure-related spending to the amount of spending for shelter, food, clothing, national defense, and other items.[20] For example, percentages of all PCEs allocated to selected major categories in 1999 were as follows:

Medical care services	15.1%	
Housing	14.4	
Hotels & motels		0.40
Food	14.4	
All Transportation	11.4	
Purchased intercity transportation		0.53
Railway		0.012
Bus		0.033
Airline		0.48
Foreign travel by U.S. residents		1.16
All recreation	8.7	
Clothing	4.9	

In taking just the sum of those categories directly related to travel – hotels and motels, purchased intercity transportation, and foreign travel by U.S. residents – we can see that in 1999 the percentage of total personal-consumption expenditures for travel amounted to approximately 2.1%. But if indirect spending for restaurant meals, private-car gasoline, and similar items were to be also included the percentage would be significantly (and arbitrarily) higher. Indeed, total expenditures for travel and tourism including such items has been estimated by the United States Bureau of Economic Analysis to account for approximately 5% of United States gross domestic product (GDP) and 3.3% of employment.[21]

Another way to visualize the longer term shifts in spending preferences is provided in Figure 1.11, in which it can be seen that spending for transportation services as compared to some other major categories has held to a fairly stable percentage of all PCEs whereas the percentage spent on medical services clearly has risen and that on clothing and food has declined.

However, because travel is a composite activity involving elements of both transportation and recreation, the close-up view provided in Figure 1.12 is,

Table 1.4. *PCE by major type of product personal consumption expenditures in billions of current dollars*

	1970	1980	1990	1995	1999
PCE by type of product or service	648.9	1,762.9	3,831.5	4,969.0	6,257.3
Services	292.0	852.7	2,117.8	2,882.0	3,655.6
Total transportation services	23.7	64.7	141.8	197.7	255.0
Transportation services as a percentage of total PCEs	3.7%	3.7%	3.7%	4.0%	4.1%
User-operated transport svcs	16.7	44.6	105.3	155.3	204.4
Auto repair, rental & other	12.3	34.0	84.9	122.2	160.9
Other user-op transport svcs	4.4	10.5	20.5	33.1	43.5
Purchased local transportation	3.0	4.8	8.4	10.4	12.5
Mass transit systems	1.8	2.9	5.8	7.1	8.8
Taxicab	1.2	1.9	2.6	3.2	3.8
Purchased intercity transportation	4.0	15.4	28.1	32.1	38.0
Intercity railways	0.2	0.3	0.7	0.6	0.7
Intercity buses	0.5	1.4	1.3	1.6	2.0
Airline	3.1	12.8	22.7	25.5	30.0
Other transportation services	0.2	0.9	3.3	4.3	5.3
Recreation services	15.1	42.8	120.8	176.0	246.2
Net foreign travel	2.8	1.7	(8.9)	(21.4)	(15.6)
Foreign travel by US residents	5.4	13.3	42.7	54.1	72.7
Less: exp in US by foreigners	2.7	11.6	51.6	75.4	88.3

Source: US Bureau of Economic Analysis.

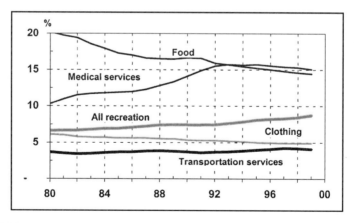

Figure 1.11. Trends in percent of total personal consumption expenditures in selected categories, 1980–99.

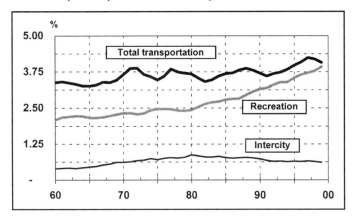

Figure 1.12. Transportation services (total and intercity) and recreation services as a percent of total PCEs, 1960–99.

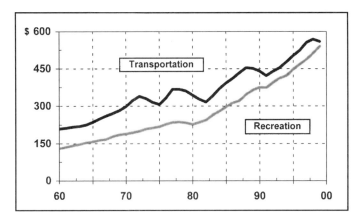

Figure 1.13. Real per capita PCE on transportation services and recreation services, 1960–99.

in some respects, more revealing. For instance, it is interesting to also see that the percent of PCEs spent on *intercity* transportation – the component of total transport services that practically defines travel – has recently declined slightly. Yet the time around 1980 appears to be pivotal, reflecting the price-lowering effects of things such as global airline deregulation (beginning in the late 1970s), declining oil prices, and the introduction of wide-bodied planes (i.e., new technologies) all while the relative costs of commuting to work (a large part of spending for *total* transport services) has continued to rise.

Measuring real (adjusted for inflation) per capita spending on total trans-portation and recreation *services* provides yet another long-term view of how Americans have allocated their travel-related dollars. These data are presented in Figure 1.13, where once again we can see that the time around

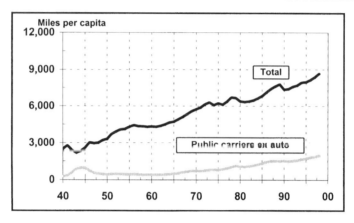

Figure 1.14. Miles traveled per capita, 1940–98. *Source: Transportation in America*, 1999 and Census Bureau.

1980 marks the beginning of a steeper uptrend in spending for travel and recreation services, both of which have pretty much risen in parallel.[22]

Still, various travel industry sectors will have markedly different responses to changing conditions, and travel-sector time series comparisons against components of Gross National Product (GNP) or Gross Domestic Product (GDP) accounts are fairly limited in what they can tell us about the degree of recession resistance or cyclicity of travel relative to that of the economy at large.[23]

What we can, however, say with virtual certainty is that the positive relation between income and travel is seen globally. As Schafer and Victor (1997) note:

throughout the world, personal income and traffic volume grow in tandem. As average income increases, the annual distance traveled per capita by car, bus, train or aircraft. . . rises by roughly the same proportion. The average North American earned $9,600 and traveled 12,000 kilometers (7,460 miles) in 1960; by 1990 both per capita income and traffic volume had approximately doubled.

But, as Button (1993, p. 40) suggests, in addition to a budget for income, there is also a budget for *time*, and at the aggregate level, "time expenditure on travel per head increases roughly proportionally to income budgeted for travel."

The data depicted in Figure 1.14, while not the same as Schafer and Victor's (but still validating their point), indicate that, since 1950, growth of per-capita passenger-miles – a measure of the quantity of transportation services demanded – has risen at a compound annual rate of approximately 2.2%. In other words, the average American of the late 1990s each year traveled more than 9,000 miles by air, rail, bus, and private automobile as compared to 3,000 miles a half a century ago. Of this recent total, however, only around 1,800 miles were by public carriers. Americans now not only drive a lot more than they used to, but each person is also on the average taking more trips and longer trips.

1.5 Industry structures and segments

Structures

Microeconomic theory suggests that industries can be categorized according to how firms make price and output decisions in response to prevailing market conditions. In the model assuming *perfect competition*, firms all make identical products and each firm is so small in relation to total industry output that its operations have a negligible effect on price or on quantity supplied. At the other idealized extreme is a *monopoly* structure, in which there are no close substitutes for the single firm's output, prices are set by the firm, and there are barriers that prevent potential competitors from entry.

However, in the real world, the structure of most industries cannot be characterized as being perfectly competitive or as monopolistic, but as somewhere in between. One of those in-between structures is known as *monopolistic competition*, in which there are many sellers of somewhat differentiated products and in which some control of pricing and competition through advertising is seen. An *oligopoly* structure is similar, except that in oligopolies, there are only a few sellers of products that are close substitutes and pricing decisions may affect the pricing and output decisions of other firms in the industry.

In travel, industry segments fall broadly into the following structural categories:

Monopoly:	Oligopoly:	Monopolistic Competition:
Major airports	Airlines	Buses
Some intercity routes	Car rental agencies	Hotels and motels
	Cruise ships	Restaurants
	Major hotel chains	Travel agencies
	Major gaming chains	Local casinos
	Theme parks	

These categories can then be further analyzed in terms of the degree to which there is a concentration of power among rival firms. A measure that is sensitive to both differences in the number of firms in an industry and differences in relative market shares – the *Herfindahl–Hirschman Index* – is then frequently used by economists to measure the concentration of markets.[24]

Segments

The relative economic importance of selected industry segments is illustrated in Figure 1.15, the trendlines of which provide long-range macroeconomic

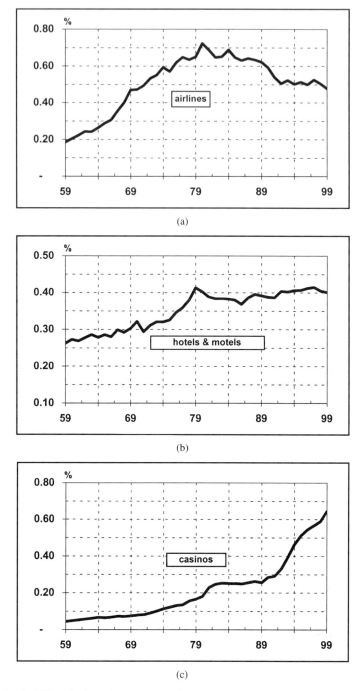

Figure 1.15. PCEs of selected travel categories as percentages of total PCEs for (a) airlines, (b) hotels and motels, and (c) casinos, 1959–99.

Table 1.5. *Travel industry composite sample, 1993–98*

Compound annual growth rates (%): 1993–98

Industry segments	Number of companies in sample	Revenues	Operating income	Assets	Cash flow
Airline	9	4.9	51.6	6.2	20.3
Bus	2	14.7	28.6	22.4	25.0
Car rental	3	16.8	32.5	20.4	25.1
Cruise line	3	15.9	20.6	20.1	20.1
Gaming	37	9.4	6.4	17.7	8.4
Hotels	6	15.8	27.8	21.3	19.6
Theme parks	4	6.7	11.9	15.0	11.1
Total	64				

Total Composite

	Pretax return(%) on		Revenues[b]	Operating income[b]	Assets[b]	Operating cash flow[b]
	Revenues	Assets				
1998	11.4	8.5	141,933	16,150	189,820	25,563
1997	11.1	8.9	133,877	14,829	166,868	22,884
1996	10.2	8.8	122,804	12,473	141,806	19,768
1995	8.5	7.5	111,202	9,425	125,448	16,842
1994	6.7	5.9	104,168	6,984	118,362	14,293
1993	5.0	4.5	99,117	4,967	109,238	11,374
CAGR:[a]			7.4	26.6	11.7	17.6

[a]Compound annual growth rate (%).
[b]In $millions.
Source: Company reports.

perspectives of travel industry growth patterns relative to personal-consumption expenditures. These patterns then translate into short-run financial operating performance, which is revealed in Table 1.5, where revenues, pretax operating incomes, assets, and cash flows for a selected sample of major public companies are presented. The sample includes an estimated 70% of the domestic transactions volume in travel-related industries and provides a means of comparing efficiencies and growth rates in various segments. For example, airline segment operating income has grown nearly twice as fast as hotel segment operating income between 1993 and 1998. Figure 1.16, meanwhile, shows how airlines have come to account for the major share of intercity travel at the expense of travel by cars, buses, and rail.

More immediately, we can further estimate that major travel industry segments generated revenues of at least $200 billion (70% of sample

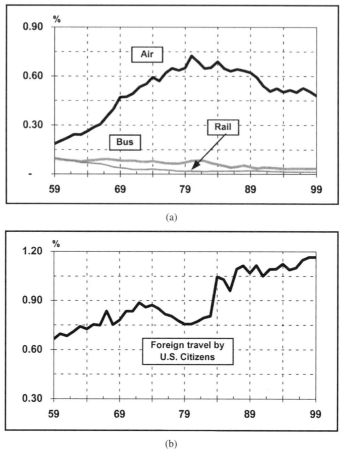

(a)

(b)

Figure 1.16. Percent of PCEs for travel by (a) air, bus, and rail, and (b) foreign travel by U.S. citizens, 1959–99.

totals $142 billion) in 1998 and that annual growth between 1993 and 1998 averaged approximately 7.4%. We can also see from Table 1.5 that over the same span, operating income rose at a compound rate of 26.6%, whereas assets have increased at a rate of 11.7%. Operating cash flows, rising at a rate of 17.6%, have more than kept pace with the growth of assets and, by and large, it has not been necessary to finance new asset additions through borrowings and/or sales of equity (i.e., shares of stock).

Indeed, the long-lasting economic upturn that began in 1991 has provided a solid basis for rising returns on composite industry assets, which have increased from an average of 4.5% in 1993 to 8.5% in 1998. A parallel improvement is also evident in pretax returns on revenues (margins), which rose from 5.0% to 11.4% over this span. However, a thorough analysis of the

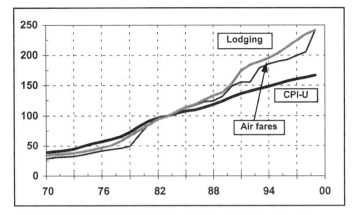

Figure 1.17. Consumer Price Index inflation-rate comparisons for all urban consumers (CPI-U) and selected industry segments, 1970–99. *Source:* Bureau of Labor Statistics.

composites shown in Table 1.5 would further require consideration of many business-environmental features, including interest rates, antitrust policy attitudes, the trend of dollar exchange rates, and relative pricing power.

This last factor is illustrated by Figure 1.17, which compares the rise of the Consumer Price Index for the airfare and lodging segments against the average of all items for all urban consumers (CPI-U). From this, we can see that since the early 1980s, prices in both segments have been rising faster than the average rate of inflation.

However, perhaps the most important data are presented in the comparisons of operating cash flow. Cash flow is important because it can be used to service debt, acquire assets, or pay dividends. Representing the difference between cash receipts from the sale of goods or services and cash outlays required in production of the same, operating cash flow is usually understood to be operating income before deductions for interest, depreciation, and amortization. Cash flow, so defined, is the basis for valuing all kinds of hotel, airline, media, and entertainment assets because the distortionary effects of differing tax and financial structure considerations are stripped away. A business property can thus be more easily evaluated from the standpoint of what it might be worth to potential buyers. As we can see, operating cash flows for the airline, bus, car-rental, cruise-ship, and hotel industry segments have grown much faster than for the gaming or theme-park segments.

1.6 Valuation perspectives

Important as it is to understand the economic perspectives, it is ultimately the role of the financial analyst to condense this information into an asset valuation estimate. The key question for investors is whether the assets of an industry or of a company are being priced correctly by the market. In attempting to arrive at an answer, we find that valuation of assets often involves as much art as science.

Valuation methods fall into three broad categories of approach, using discounted cash flows, comparison methods, and options. Sometimes all three approaches are suitable and the results of each are compared. At other times the characteristics of the asset to be valued are such that it makes sense for only one approach to be used. In most cases, however, discounted cash flow is the central concept that takes account of both the time value of money and risk.

Discounted cash flows

Given that the primary assets of travel industry companies are composed of both tangible assets such as buildings and equipment and intangible assets embodied in the form of brand names and reservation systems, it is reasonable to base valuations on the expected future profits that the control of such assets might be expected to convey over time. Although it is not a flawless measure, estimated cash flow (EBITDA) – which was discussed in Section 1.5 – discounted back to a present value will usually provide a good reflection of such profit potential.

Essentially, the discounted cash flow approach takes the value of any asset as the net present value (NPV) of the sum of expected future cash flows as represented by the following formula:

$$NPV = \sum_{\tau=1}^{\tau=n} CF_t/(1+r)^t$$

where r is the risk-adjusted required rate of return (tied to current interest rates), CF_t is the projected cash flow in period t, and n is the number of future periods over which the cash stream is to be received.

To illustrate most simply, assume that the required rate of return is 9%, that the projected net cash flows of a new theme-park attraction in each of the next three years are $3 million, $2 million, and $1 million, and that the attraction has no value beyond the third year.

The NPV of the attraction would then be

$$3/(1.0+0.09) + 2/(1.0+0.09)^2 + 1/(1.0+0.09)^3$$
$$= 2.75 + 1.683 + 0.7722 = \$5.205 \text{ million.}$$

Comparison methods

Comparisons of various company financial ratios and characteristics will also often provide important valuation insights. These comparisons will frequently include current price-multiples of cash flows and estimates of earnings, shareholders' equity, and revenue growth rates relative to those of similar properties.

Of course, a ratio of price to cash flow, earnings, revenues, or some other financial feature should already reflect inherently the estimated discounted cash flow and/or salvage (terminal) values of an asset or class of assets. Thus, if hotels are being traded at prices that suggest multiples of ten times next year's projected cash flow, it is likely that most other hotels with similar characteristics will also be priced at a multiple near ten.

This comparative-multiple approach is often used in valuations of travel industry properties even though it is not particularly good in capturing what economists call *externalities* – those factors that would make a hotel property, for example, especially valuable, say, as a "trophy" to a specific buyer. Prestige, potential for political or moral influence, or access to certain markets are all externalities that commonly affect transaction prices.

Options

For assets that have optionlike characteristics or that are not traded frequently, neither the discounted cash flow nor the price and ratio comparison approaches can be readily applied. Instead, option-pricing models (e.g., the Black–Scholes model) that use contingent claim valuation estimates (of assets that pay off only under certain contingencies) are usually employed.

However, this approach is not normally used in travel industry practice unless the asset to be valued is an option contract (e.g., a warrant, call, or put) or is a contract for marketing or distribution rights or for some form of intellectual property right, such as for a patent. Some other variations on these valuation concepts are discussed in Appendix B.

1.7 Concluding remarks

This chapter has sketched the economic landscape in which all travel industries operate. It has indicated how hours at work, productivity trends, expected utility functions, demographics, and other factors can affect the amounts of time and money we spend on leisure-related goods and services. And it has also provided benchmarks against which the relative growth rates and sizes of different industry segments or composites can be measured.

Technological development has obviously played an important role too. It, of course, underlies the very growth of productivity and thus of the relative supply of leisure time, but just as significantly, technological development has changed the way in which we think of travel and leisure services. Figure 1.18 provides an overview of travel industry milestones. Greater detail appears in the milestone illustrations in each of the industry chapters that follow.

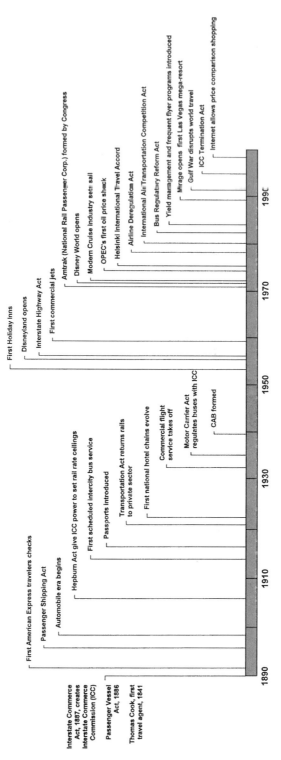

Figure 1.18. Travel industry milestones, 1890–2000.

Selected additional reading

Aron, C. S. (1999). *Working at Play: A History of Vacations in the United States*. New York: Oxford University Press.

Brealy, R. A., and Myers, S. C. (1996). *Principles of Corporate Finance*, 5th ed. New York: McGraw-Hill.

Cooke, A. (1994). *The Economics of Leisure and Sport*. London: International Thomson Publishing Company.

Elliott, J. (1997). *Tourism: Politics and Public Sector Management*. London and New York: Routledge.

Han, X., and Fang, B. (1998). "Measuring Transportation in the U.S. Economy," *Journal of Transportation Statistics* (June). Washington, D.C.: U.S. Department of Transportation, Bureau of Transportation Statistics.

Lundberg, D. E., Stavenca, M. H., and Krishnamoorthy, M. (1995). *Tourism Economics*. New York: John Wiley & Sons.

Marano, H. E. (1999). "The Power of Play," *Psychology Today*, 32(4)(August).

McDowell, E. (1997). "The Abbreviated Tourist: Americans Are So Busy with So Many Places to Go," *New York Times*, July 31.

Naisbitt, J. (1994). *Global Paradox*. New York: Morrow.

Reilly, R. F., and Schweihs, R. P (1999). *Valuing Intangible Assets*. New York: McGraw-Hill.

Scott, J. (1999). "Working Hard, More or Less," *New York Times*, July 10.

Smith, G. V., and Parr, R. L. (1994). *Valuation of Intellectual Property and Intangible Assets*, 2nd ed. New York: John Wiley & Sons.

"Study of Travel and Tourism," *The Economist*, March 21, 1991.

"Survey of Travel and Tourism," *The Economist*, January 10, 1998.

Winston, C. (1985). "Conceptual Developments in the Economics of Transportation: An Interpretive Survey," *Journal of Economic Literature*, 23.

Part II
Getting there

2
Wings

I'll teach you how to jump on the wind's back, and then away
we go. – *Peter Pan* by J. M. Barrie

The dream has always been to fly. Icarus, the famous flyer of Greek mythology, flew too close to the Sun and his wax wings melted. The Wright Brothers of North Carolina managed in 1903 to fly their *Kitty Hawk* a few hundred feet across a field and just barely above the ground.

Nowadays, though, travel by air is so common that, on a global basis, 1.5 billion passengers a year take 20 million flights over more than 1.3 billion miles (2 billion km). This volume of traffic, growing globally at an estimated rate of 5%, makes the airline business one of the largest of any in the world economy. Despite its enormity, as will be seen in this chapter, the airline industry, while increasingly complex and technologically sophisticated, is guided by relatively simple and readily analyzed economic principles.

2.1 Onward and upward

The principles of flight had, by the late 1800s, already been demonstrated (Figure 2.1). However, it required another 100 years or so before the oligopolistic structure of the global airline industry had been solidly established through a spate of mergers and acquisitions. That the industry should evolve

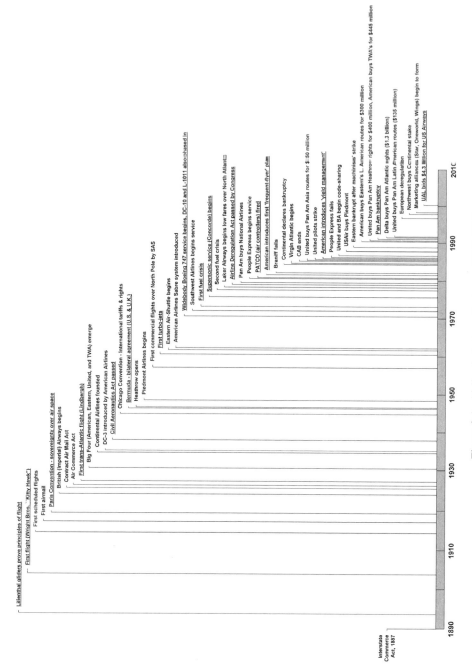

Figure 2.1. Airline industry milestones, 1890–2000.

in this way should come as no surprise given the tremendous amounts of capital investment required to launch and maintain airline equipment and services.

Technology and early history

Twelve seconds. That's how long the first powered airplane, the *Kitty Hawk*, designed by the Wright brothers, stayed aloft on its first flight in December 1903. Much development was still required before the first scheduled air service began in Florida in 1914, but ever since, technological progress and growth of passenger volume has been onward and upward.

Still, commercial aviation was slow to catch on with the general public. In those early days people could travel as fast and more comfortably by rail and perceived flight as dangerous. But the value for military purposes quickly became clear in World War I, especially as evolution of more powerful motors enabled aircraft to reach higher speeds and altitudes.

Airmail came next. Using a large number of war-surplus planes, the U.S. Post Office began airmail service in 1917, and by 1919 it had begun to provide segments of transcontinental service by air. The government then moved to transfer airmail service to the private sector through the 1925 Contract Air Mail Act (Kelly Act), which provided the impetus for creation of a private U.S. airline industry. And the core of several of today's major carriers, including United Airlines, American Airlines, and TWA (as well as the ultimately defunct Pan Am and Eastern), grew from the roots of the winners of the initial five contracts. Also in 1925, the predecessor of the Federal Aviation Authority (FAA), the Morrow Board, was established to recommend national civil aviation standards. Congress adopted the Morrow Board recommendations in passing the Air Commerce Act of 1926. With this, the government began to pay private mail carriers according to the weight carried rather than a percentage of the postage paid.

It was, however, Charles Lindbergh's historic first nonstop flight from New York to Paris across the Atlantic Ocean in 1927 that fully captured the public's imagination and began to attract to this industry many millions of dollars of private investment. With capital now being injected more rapidly, technological development of aircraft and aviation systems accelerated. Airlines began to attract more passengers away from the railroads, engines and cockpit instruments improved, and better radio communications equipment made it possible to fly at night or in poor weather conditions. Radio beacons became operational in 1932 and the first air traffic control tower was constructed at Newark International Airport in 1935.

The 1930s also brought political scandal in the form of the Watres Act passed by Congress in 1930 and the subsequent "spoils conference" based on this Act. In the spoils conference, smaller airlines were purposely shut out of bidding for government airmail contracts in the expectation that promotion of larger, stronger airlines would be in the national interest. But the issue of unfairness to the smaller lines raised political pressure that led to the Air Mail Act of 1934 and a more competitive structure for the private carriage of mail.

Modern passenger aircraft also advanced rapidly at this time, with United Air Lines in 1933 buying sixty Boeing 247s, each of which could accommodate ten passengers and cruise at 155 miles per hour. Not to be outdone, TWA bought an alternative model from Douglas aircraft, the DC-1, which was equipped with the first efficient wing flaps and autopilot. Rapid improvements on the initial model then led to the DC-3, which American Airlines introduced in 1936 and which – being the first aircraft that enabled airlines to make money carrying passengers – became the workhorse of the industry. The DC-3 had twenty-one seats, was equipped with hydraulic landing gear, and could go coast-to-coast in sixteen hours, an impressive speed for that time. By 1940, however, the Boeing Stratoliner, a derivative of the B-17 bomber, provided another technological leap, with its pressurized cabins allowing flights to go as high as 20,000 feet and at speeds of 200 miles per hour.

Things also began to move faster on the regulatory front with the establishment of the Civil Aeronautics Authority (CAA) by way of the Civil Aeronautics Act of 1938. The Act was unusual from today's perspective in that the airlines actually *wanted* greater government regulation through an agency empowered to regulate airline tariffs, airmail rates, mergers, and routes while sheltering them from unbridled competition. Congress then also created, in 1940, a separate agency, the Air Safety Board, which was combined with the CAA into an agency known as the Civil Aeronautics Board (CAB).

Aviation also played an important role in World War II, a time of especially rapid technological progress in systems and equipment development. The fighter and bomber planes and radar designs that came out of the war were soon applied to the civilian segment, with an early-model British-made passenger jet, the Comet, flying from London to Johannesburg in 1952 at speeds up to 500 miles per hour. But the true coming of the passenger-jet age didn't appear until 1958, when Boeing introduced its 707 model, flown by Pan Am. The 707 could carry 181 passengers at a speed of up to 550 miles per hour.

Regulation and deregulation

With travel by air becoming more popular and the skies too crowded for existing systems to properly handle, Congress also saw, in 1958, the need to pass the Federal Aviation Act. This Act created the predecessor to the current Federal Aviation Administration (FAA), which is now contained within the Department of Transportation. The FAA is responsible for maintaining safe operating conditions for all commercial aircraft through all phases of flight within the air traffic control system. It also assumes jurisdiction over all other aviation safety matters such as certification of aircraft designs, airline training, and maintenance programs.

Introduction of wide-bodied aircraft such as the Boeing 747 in 1969, and the Douglas DC-10 and Lockheed L-1011 in 1970, further revolutionized the economics of civilian aviation. The planes could seat as many as 450 passengers and, as such, had the potential to significantly lower the cost of carrying each passenger per mile of service. Yet it was not until after 1978, when the CAB was disbanded and competitive air travel pricing strategies could be implemented, that the public could truly reap the benefits of relatively low-cost travel by air. The Airline Deregulation Act of 1978 made all the difference; passenger demand soon afterward began rising quickly as flying became a common mode of transportation for the public at large. Only the supersonic Concorde, introduced in 1969 and flown by British Air and Air France (until 2000), had remained limited to those few who could afford the steep price of a ticket.

Nevertheless, the one thing that the traffic growth and deregulation of this era could not easily offset was the adverse effect on airline profits that came from formation of the OPEC oil cartel in the 1970s. Two steep hikes in the price of jet fuel (oil) – always a significant component of total operating cost and at the time comprising 20% of the total – suppressed nascent industry profitability and gave airline investors an especially bumpy ride.[1] As Figure 2.2a illustrates, it was not until after the economic recessions of the early 1980s that profitability was briefly restored. Thereafter, another recession beginning in mid-1990, the Gulf War of early 1991, and a highly competitive pricing environment once again restrained profitability to the point that cumulative industry profits were wiped out (Figure 2.2b). But finally, the record-long economic expansion of the 1990s took hold, with the airline industry becoming a major beneficiary of the rising demand thereby created. Such demand was further sustained by continuing the long-term decline of the *average* real price (now around fifteen cents) that passengers paid to fly a mile (Figure 2.2c).

Although the public-utility style regulation that characterized the airline business until the late 1970s no longer exists, some restrictions and regulations concerning the award of landing rights and other privileges to carriers of foreign countries remain. Such international landing agreements and privileges are negotiated bilateral between nations and specify which cities can be serviced, how many flights each airline may operate, and the prices that each carrier may charge. Bilateral negotiations involving the United States are led by the State Department, with active participation from the Department of Transportation (formed in 1967).[2] The International Air Transport Association (IATA) – founded in 1945 to represent the interests of the airlines and to operate a clearinghouse for inter-airline debts arising from inter-airline traffic – may also still set fares and cargo rates (although with much diminished influence since the late 1970s).[3] Figure 2.3 displays the key trends of airline passenger growth of recent decades.

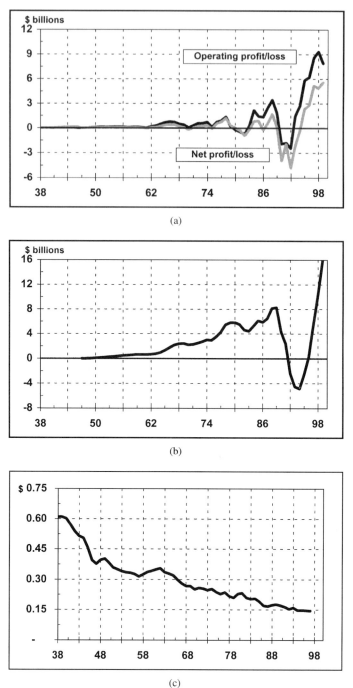

Figure 2.2. (a) Airline industry operating profit/loss ($ billions) and net profit/loss
($ billions), (b) cumulative net profit/loss ($ billions), and (c) average price to consumer
to fly a mile in constant (1999) dollars 1938–99. *Source:* ATA and (c) W. M. Cox, Federal
Reserve Bank of Dallas.

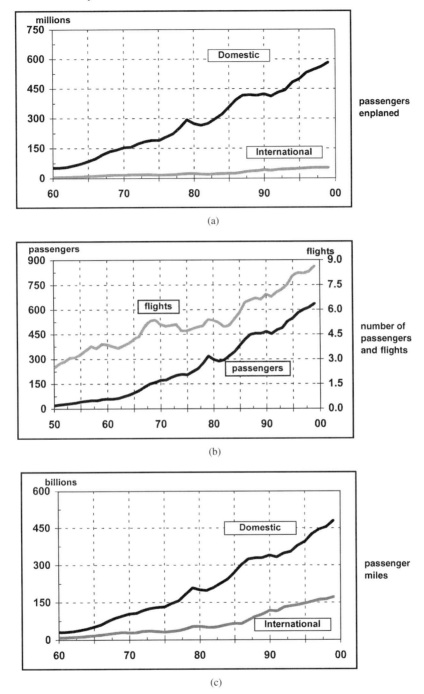

Figure 2.3. Plots of (a) passengers enplaned (in millions), (b) number of passengers and flights (in millions), (c) passenger-miles (in billions), (d) available seat-miles (in billions), (e) load factor (%), (f) yield, and (g) average number of passengers per departing flight and average miles per departure. *Source:* ATA.

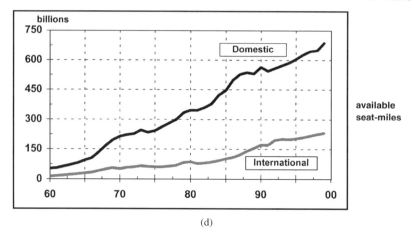

(d)

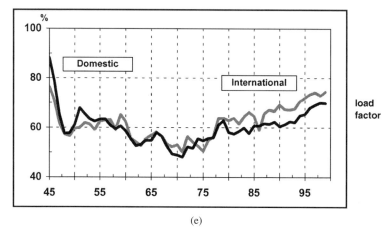

(e)

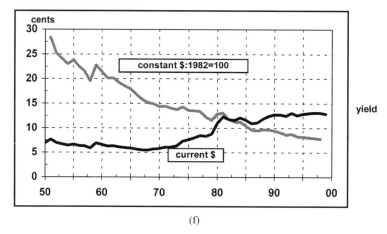

(f)

Figure 2.3. *(cont.)*

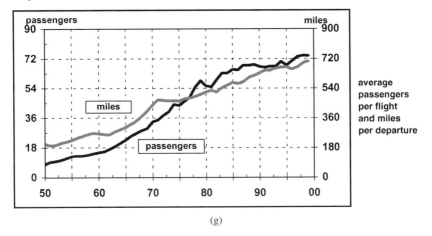

(g)

Figure 2.3. *(cont.)*

2.2 Operational characteristics

Structural features

The industry has evolved to the point where several large carriers in the United States and a few large national carriers elsewhere capture an estimated 75% of all revenues generated. This structure clearly takes advantage of economies of scale in which purchases of everything from aircraft equipment to fuel, food, maintenance, insurance, financing, and advertising and marketing are less per mile flown and passenger served than if the industry operated with many smaller independent companies unable to pare down average unit costs.

Majors The industry defines major airlines, also known as trunk carriers, as those companies generating revenues of more than $1 billion annually from provision of scheduled nationwide or worldwide services. Though the number seems bound to shrink as the industry consolidates into an oligopoly dominated by a few mega-carriers, as of the end of the 1990s, there were twelve major U.S. airlines: Alaska, America West, American, Continental, Delta, Federal Express, Northwest, Southwest, TWA, United, UPS, and US Airways. For these airlines, more than 90% of aggregated revenue is generated from passenger traffic and less than 10% from cargo carriage. Also, approximately 75% of the flights are between domestic destinations.

All of the majors are required to hold two certificates issued by the federal government. The first, a fitness certificate, is issued by the Department of Transportation (DOT) under Section 401 of the Federal Aviation Act. It establishes that the carrier has the financial and management wherewithal in place to provide scheduled service with large aircraft, those with sixty-one or more seats and a payload of more than 18,000 pounds. The second, an operating certificate, is issued by the FAA under Section 121 of the Federal

Aviation Regulations and specifies for aircraft with ten or more seats numerous requirements including those pertaining to the training of flight crews and to aircraft maintenance programs.

Nationals and regionals National carriers are defined as scheduled airlines generating annual revenues of between $100 million and $1 billion, but they may sometimes provide long-haul and even international service. Like the majors, nationals operate mostly medium and large size jets and are thus subject to the same certification requirements as the majors. As of the late 1990s, the nationals included Aloha, American Trans Air, Emery, Evergreen, Hawaiian, Midwest Express, and Polar airlines.

Regionals are among the fastest growing companies and, as the name implies, are those carriers that for the most part provide service to only one region of the country and generate revenues of under $100 million. The largest regionals, with revenues of more than $20 million, must also comply with FAA and DOT certification requirements, although smaller, so-called commuter airlines are only required to file certain annual reports according to DOT's Section 298 regulations. These small carriers are exempt from Section 401 fitness certificate requirements because their aircraft have less than thirty seats.[4]

Charters Nonscheduled airline operators, known as charter airlines, are more frequently found serving the European than the U.S. tourism markets (see Chapter 7). Such airlines organize their operations by chartering aircraft equipment, often on a temporary basis, for the purpose of flying to specific tourist locations in season. But Section 401 certification regulations for any aircraft operating within the U.S. are largely the same as for the major scheduled carriers.

Labor relations Labor accounts for a significant part, usually at least 20%, of any airline's operating cost. As such, the industry has always found it important to contain labor costs because even small savings in this area may often translate into the difference between profit and loss. For many companies, margins are already narrow to begin with.

As a consequence, the industry has had a long history of labor strife, with work slowdowns or strikes being not all that uncommon. This history of labor dissent, expressed in frequent union–management clashes, has extended across-the-board from pilots (e.g., the Airline Pilot's Association, ALPA), to machinists (e.g., the International Association of Machinists and Aerospace Workers, IAM), and to flight attendants (e.g., the Association of Flight Attendants, AFA).[5] In attempts to relieve tensions and to combine the interests of labor and management, several airlines have – through union governance and in lieu of larger pay raises – given their workers equity stakes in the companies. For example, as of 1999, at United 55% of the holding company's UAL shares were employee owned and at TWA, 45%. To date,

Table 2.1. *Airline scheduled-service carriage of passengers, freight, and mail, domestic and international routes, 1998*

Type of service	Passengers carried (millions)	Passenger-km performed (millions)	Freight tons carried (millions)	Freight ton-km performed (millions)	Mail ton-km performed (millions)	Total ton-km performed
International	452	1,510,770	15.8	87,180	2,470	231,240
Domestic	1,010	1,119,600	10.4	15,090	3,270	117,540

Source: "Annual Review of Civil Aviation," *ICAO Journal*, July/August 1999 (www.ICAO.org).

experience is mixed as to whether such arrangements will prove viable over the long term. Whether they are or aren't, however, does not change the fact that labor unions are an important part of the airline industry's operating structure.

Basics

The airline industry long ago developed its own descriptive terminology of operational features. For instance, it is important for an airline and also other types of public carriers to be able to compare revenues and costs per mile that are respectively earned and incurred in carrying each passenger (or cargo) unit. The standard measurements are thus stated in terms of *revenue passenger-miles* (RPM) – the number of revenue-paying passengers multiplied by the number of miles flown. In economic terms, RPMs are a measure of an airline's or the industry's output.

Similarly, in freight and mail carriage, the analogous units on scheduled routes would be ton-miles or ton-kilometers. Although it is not the purpose of this text to provide an analysis of the cargo-hauling aspects of airline operations, it should be noted that on a worldwide basis, freight accounts for roughly one fourth of total airline output and perhaps up to an eighth of total operating revenues (Table 2.1).[6] This means that for many airlines, especially those with international routes, cargo carriage will contribute significantly to profitability.[7]

From these definitions it is then a simple step to calculate what is known as the *yield*, which is total revenue divided by the total number of passenger-miles flown (or in the case of cargo, tons flown). Yield is thus an arithmetic mean that indicates on the average how much revenue is generated per unit of output. It is usually stated in terms of cents per passenger-mile (Table 2.2).

As such, in the determination of airline profits, yield is normally more important than the actual passenger fares charged. But yield also tends to vary widely from one route to another and from one airline to another because of differences in average sector length flown, geographic territory covered,

Table 2.2. *Comparative yields, selected sample of major airlines, 1998*

	Yield (cents)
American	13.49
Continental	12.79
Delta	12.75
Northwest	11.26
Southwest	12.62
United	12.40
US Airways	17.02

Source: Company reports.

currency fluctuations, and so forth. In other words, yield is a price index rather than a price, and it is sensitive to changes in the composition of traffic. As an index, it does not directly reflect demand because it does not reference the variation of quantity along with a variation of price; it is instead a derived statistic.

It is also important to know how much of a system's total potential capacity for carriage is being used at any given time. Capacity would of course be determined by multiplying the number of seats by the distances flown. *Load factors* (LFs) are a way of expressing the amount of potential capacity that is being sold.[8] For most airlines on most routes, passenger load factors, taken as a percentage of total seats available, would generally have to average above 55% for the flight to be profitable. For a whole system of routes, such load factors could also be arithmetically expressed in terms of *available seat-miles* (ASM) (i.e., the number of available seats times the number of miles flown on designated routes). In other words,

$$LF = RPM/ASM.$$

Again, a similar measure for cargo operations would be the weight load factor – ton-kilometers sold as a percentage of available ton-kilometers.

Both yield and load factors are important profit determinants and both will immediately reflect competitive conditions on a local, if not a global basis. Usually, however, projected yields on routes are used to calculate breakeven load factors, although an airline might still find a route to be profitable if its low yield is in practice offset by a relatively high load factor. On an industry-wide basis, experience has shown that in almost any year it is difficult to increase available seat capacity by more than 5% without having to cut prices.[9]

Other terms used frequently in the industry are fairly obvious in meaning. *Hubs* are the centers of the hub-and-spoke route networks that airlines operate out of a few important regional cities (e.g., United uses Chicago and San Francisco as hubs, American uses Dallas–Ft. Worth, Northwest uses

Minneapolis, Delta uses Atlanta, and TWA uses St. Louis). Also, through *code-sharing* arrangements, flights on one line use the same airline code-designation as that of another in order to feed passengers into the other line's routes. A domestically based line might, for instance, share its code with an international line, to the presumed benefit of both. And *cabotage*, a term used by international airlines, is the right to carry traffic between two points in the same country.

Marketing features

Airlines must fight their relentless battles on many different fields and at many different levels: market-by-market, price-by-price, and sometimes even down to flight-by-flight. In so doing they must protect brand image and maintain good relations with their primary customer and local-community constituencies all while minimizing costs. The primary marketing tools are implemented through advertising campaigns, reservation systems, frequent-flyer programs, travel agencies, clustered alliances between domestic and foreign camers (e.g., Star, Oneworld, Wings), and yield management/price discrimination strategies that could conceivably include selling spare off-peak capacity *en bloc* to charter or tour market operators.

Advertising and reservation systems To succeed over the long run, airlines need to be sharp on many fronts: equipment and fuel purchasing, bidding for routes, labor and government relations, safety maintenance procedures, and flight scheduling. All other things being equal, however, none of these things matters unless customers can be convinced to fly the same route on one line instead of another. Given the normally competitive-monopolistic nature of most (but not all) airline route operations, advertising plays a key front-line role used both offensively and defensively. Many airlines will in the normal course of business have to allocate at least 2% of revenues toward advertising, but they will need to spend much more if launching a new service, entering a new market, or trying to gain share against entrenched competitors. Economists call this measure of advertising-to-revenues the *advertising intensity ratio*. More formally, it can be expressed as:

advertising intensity $=$ (advertising expenditure)/(sales revenue)
$$= A/(P \times Q) = E_a/E_p$$

where A is advertising expenditure, P is price, Q is quantity, E_p is the price elasticity of demand, and E_a is the advertising elasticity of demand. The notions of elasticity here are similar in concept to those discussed in Section 1.3 (Primary principles) and below in Section 2.3 (Economic characteristics).[10]

Because a reservation system is one of the first things that a prospective passenger comes into contact with, the reservation system is now as much a powerful advertising and marketing medium as it is a data bank. American

Airlines most visibly demonstrated this through shrewd use of its SABRE reservation system (versus United's APOLLO), which, in the 1980s, notably boosted share of market through the simple expedient of listing American's scheduled flights ahead of competing flights on every reservation screen. However, such biases are no longer permitted under current DOT rules.[11]

These computer-based reservation systems can sift data banks of mind-boggling size and complexity, as they keep constant track of billions of pieces of information – everything from flight schedules, passenger names, and seat assignments to fares that change almost by the minute. But such systems can do much more. Indeed, perhaps the most useful aspect of a comprehensive reservation system is that it can be used to predict passenger bookings and price and departure-time sensitivities. Airlines have come to depend on these systems to manage the yield that they derive from every flight. In the post-1978 deregulated environment, *yield management* has become an essential price-setting tool, without which most airlines would likely be perennially unprofitable.[12]

Since most business travelers usually care more about convenient departure times than about ticket prices and they also book closer to departure time than leisure travelers, airlines can maximize yield based on forecasted booking patterns. Such patterns run pretty close to those formed for the same day of the week and time of the year as in prior years and allow operators to engage price discrimination strategies (as described in Chapter 1) to the utmost. In other words, prices can be set just high enough to fill a flight with a maximum number of high-paying passengers.

Frequent-flyer programs These major marketing tools, along with the advent of sophisticated reservation systems, came into prominence in the early 1980s. Frequent flyers, those making more than ten trips a year, are worthy customers who account for only 8% of passengers but 45% of trips flown. These programs had the intended effect of bonding the passenger's loyalty to one line in preference to another flying the same route at the same or at perhaps even lower prices and more convenient departure times.

In offering free flights to passengers frequenting an airline's routes, the operators may be arguably providing a special type of quantity discount to their best customers. But in the process, they are also surely building brand loyalty and, as explained in Chapter 1, are attempting to shift the demand curve to the right and to make it more price inelastic (i.e., vertical). So effective, indeed, have these frequent-flyer programs become, that people have been known to fly far out of the way and to spend much more time in transit than necessary just to qualify for additional mileage points.

Having taken on a life of their own, these programs have thus turned out to be essential in building a brand. To implement them, airlines incur administrative costs (perhaps 1% of total costs) and create deferred long-term liabilities on their balance sheets. For major carriers, this might amount to 10% to 13% of total current liabilities. However, brand-building effects and potentially firmer pricing structures largely offset added costs. And the incremental revenues from affiliated consumer merchandising partners such as hotel, car rental, credit-card issuer, and telephone companies that pay the airlines an average of 2 cents per mile-point may actually add up to more than the price of a discounted-fare ticket on the typical route flown (e.g., for 25,000 redemption mile-points sold to marketing partners, the airline receives $500).

Travel agencies With the implementation of yield management practices and deregulation, passengers in the 1980s began to face a vast array of ever-changing prices and scheduling choices. And travel agencies, long functioning both as an indirect marketing arm of the airlines (and the other modal carriers) as well as product and service rationalizers, helped to turn chaos into order. The number of agencies in the United States more than doubled to 27,000 between 1977 and 1985, a period that included a large increase in demand related to airline deregulation and the Civil Aeronautics Board's (CAB) lifting of restrictions on travel agency commissions. For the airlines in particular, tickets written by agencies came to account for approximately three fourths of air carrier revenues.

The great volume of business transacted through agencies should not be surprising in view of the long history of development between airlines and these independently owned distributors who were originally required to be officially accredited in a plan devised by the Air Traffic Conference (ATC) of 1945. However, throughout the postwar period leading up to the early 1980s, the travel agency business was inherently fraught with various potential or actual conflicts of interest that did not begin to be addressed until the CAB voted in 1980 to eliminate fixed commissions. After that, relations between agencies and airlines were never quite as cozy, with United and then other carriers in 1997 reducing their commission rates from 10% to 8% (and then to 5% in 1999), and with commission caps being placed on both domestic and international flights. In contrast, cruise package commissions can range as high as 15%.[13]

Although air carriers still derive about two thirds of their bookings through tickets sold by travel agents, the agencies are seeing their roles diminished through a disintermediation effect as price-comparison information and discounts become increasingly available on the Internet and through other sources.[14] Carriers have also become less dependent on agents as they themselves implement electronic ticketing technology and direct marketing campaigns tied to frequent-flyer programs.

Agencies remain an important link to the carriers in that they create value to travelers in customizing vacation tours and developing fly/drive/cruise packages, often in conjunction with charter airline operators. But it seems inevitable that agency profits will grow more slowly, if at all, and that a wave of consolidation into a few large national and international agencies will not soon be ending. The peak in the number of full-service retail travel

Table 2.3. *Estimated percent of volume booked*

Airlines:	
Domestic	52
International	80
Hotels:	
Domestic	25
International	85
Cruise lines	95
Rail	37
Bus	under 10
Rental cars	50
Packaged tours	90

Source: Travel Industry World Yearbook 1998.

agent locations (excluding satellite ticket printer locations) was probably seen in 1996 at 33,715 as compared to 27,193 in 1985. Although airline tickets sales by agents in the United States were $70.5 billion in 1997 as compared to $49.5 billion in 1990, as Table 2.3 shows, the share of total domestic airline business, which had long held at 80%, had by 1997 already been eroded down by Internet services to around 50%. International airline bookings had been 85% and fell to 80%.

Finally, agencies might also be affiliated with or act as passenger consolidators who book the seats and inclusive tour (IT) packages for charter airlines at fares below those of scheduled flights on similar routes. Even with their low fare schedules, charters can be profitable because their unit costs are also below those at scheduled airlines. Charter flights have high load factors, use secondary airports at off hours, have tight seating configurations, use fewer cabin attendants, offer few in-flight amenities, have significantly lower general and administrative costs, and save on ticketing, sales, promotions, and reservation systems. For charter companies, the main cost of ticket distribution and promotion is reflected in commissions that are paid to travel and tour operators.

2.3 Economic characteristics

Macroeconomic sensitivities

Demand for travel services depends on factors such as the purpose for which a trip is made, the distance traveled, and the cost of the service. Implicit in these factors is the value of time and the cost of opportunities foregone. Business travelers would, for example, presumably value their time more highly than leisure travelers and would therefore be more likely to travel by air, the normally faster means of transportation. A traveler's valuation of time savings would also appear to be roughly correlated with income.[15] This would

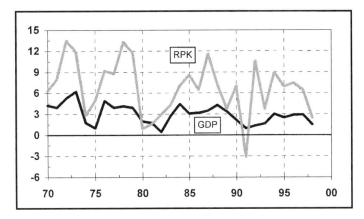

Figure 2.4. Percentage change in GDP versus revenue passenger-km, 1970–98.

suggest that, all other things being equal, rising real incomes ought to increase demand for the most rapid forms of transportation, which in most cases would be by air. Indeed, studies suggest that the income elasticity of demand for travel by air (a concept explained in the following section) is usually in the range of 1.5 to 2.5.[16] It also suggests that, from an economic standpoint, the fastest modes – the Concorde supersonic service, for instance – can justifiably charge significant fare premiums.

As a result, we can be secure in the expectation that air-travel demand is normally sensitive to changes in business cycle conditions, rising easily when the economy is growing and falling when it is not. Figure 2.4 illustrates the correlation between percent changes in gross domestic product (GDP) and percent changes in air passenger-kilometers traveled.

Microeconomic matters

Cost categories Airline managements have considerable leeway in the supply of services, whether passenger or cargo, that they offer. They have considerably less control over demand. They can advertise and market and cut fares and offer new frequent-flyer programs all day and night. But in view of the industry's consolidation into just a few mega-carriers, so can their competitors. Because of this, airline managements can have the greatest effects on prospective profitability through their attempts to control costs, normally about half of which are variable (and dependent on definition). It is thus imperative in deregulated markets to operate with average costs per passenger-mile or ton-kilometer as low as possible. Otherwise, long-run survival becomes an open question. In fact, studies such as those by Straszheim (1969) and White (1979) suggest that (except in marketing and perhaps in terms of the mix of fleet equipment) the industry does not tend widely toward significant cost economies of scale.

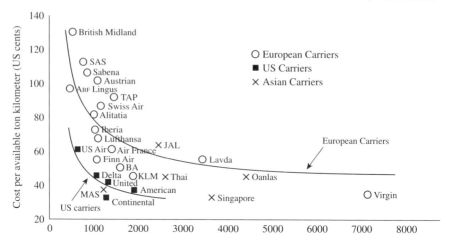

Figure 2.5. Unit operating costs as a function of stage length. *Source:* Comité des Sages (1994). *Expanding Horizons, Civil Aviation in Europe: An Action Programme for the Future.* Brussels: European Commission. (See also, Hanlon, 1996, p. 20).

Airlines nevertheless tend to benefit from what are known as *economies of density* that appear when passenger traffic through hub airports is aggregated. By establishing hub-and-spoke traffic networks that combine passengers from different markets, airlines derive two main advantages: They can serve passengers with larger aircraft – which lowers the cost per seat-mile – and load factors are higher, which also enhances profitability. The economies of density occur because, as traffic increases, not all input factors (e.g., vehicles or fixed facilities) need be scaled proportionally upward.

However, such networks require that more miles be flown. Furthermore, hub costs are higher because passengers making connections increase their use of hub-airport facilities, with arrivals and departures unevenly scheduled, in waves. The use of hubs may therefore not necessarily lower total operating costs.[17] With sufficiently high traffic, direct service between two cities will be less expensive than would be a hub-and-spoke arrangement.

From a larger systemic point of view, though, it may also be important to recognize that hub-and-spoke systems also exhibit behavior consistent with the *Law of Connectivity*, the basis of the Internet's exponential growth.[18] This law states that the utility (value) of a network rises by at least the number of users (or nodes) squared. More formally, the relationship can be stated as:

$$V = aN^2 + bN + c$$

where V is the value, N is the number of nodes, and the other terms are constants.

Still, as Doganis (1991, p. 129) notes, there is a wide variation of unit costs among airlines, especially those of the international foreign-flag carriers. In the early 1990s, for example, Lufthansa and Swiss Air had unit costs (as shown in Figure 2.5) twice that of Singapore Airlines (which flies

Table 2.4. *Operating cost per average ton-kilometer (ATK) by item, 1998 IATA International Scheduled Services*

	US cents/ATK	% of total
Cockpit crew	2.8	7.2
Fuel and oil	4.9	12.5
Flight equipment, insurance, depreciation, rentals	5.0	12.7
Maintenance and overhaul	3.9	10.0
Landing charges	2.1	5.4
En-route charges	1.8	4.6
Station and ground costs	4.7	12.0
Cabin crew and passenger service	5.3	13.6
Ticketing, sales and promotion	6.4	16.4
General and administrative	2.2	5.6
Total	39.1	100.0

Source: IATA Annual Report, 1999.

predominantly what are known as "long, thin" routes). When defined by the degree to which these costs can be affected by management decisions, costs can be categorized into three groups.

In the first category are costs such as those for fuel, prevailing wages, landing, navigation, and other user fees and taxes. In the second category are costs over which an airline has somewhat greater, but still limited, control. Costs of this type are to a degree determined by the geographic location and predominant conditions (mountainous, flat, foggy, sunny, snowy, etc.) at the carrier's home base, by the average length of routes (stages or sectors, i.e., the distance between two airports) flown, by bilateral agreements reached with other lines, and by decisions concerning the class of aircraft to be used and the frequency of schedules on which the equipment is to be operated. In the third category, however, are the costs over which management has potentially the greatest amount of control. Such costs might include those for marketing, financial leverage, and acquisitions and expansions.

As is apparent from the long history of airline-business failures, cumulative errors in judgment on these variable costs, that is, costs that are escapable over the short run, can be just as debilitating as errors in judgment on fixed costs, those that do not vary over the short run if a particular flight or series of flights were to be canceled. From Table 2.4, we can see that for international scheduled services, fuel and oil at 13% of total cost is second to personnel costs (cockpit and cabin crews), which combined amount to 20.8% (7.2% + 13.6%). With fuel, passenger service, en route, and landing costs being primarily variable or semivariable, a total of at least 35% and perhaps as much as 50% of all costs may be considered as being of a variable nature.

Productivity factors In analyzing the determinants of airline costs there are, in addition, a few that are not quite as obvious as the price of fuel and labor's wage rate. The size of aircraft and their cruising speed and range significantly affect the airline's average hourly productivity. Generally, the larger the aircraft, the less it will cost to operate per unit of output, whether a passenger-mile or a ton-kilometer. However, the higher trip costs of flying large aircraft can potentially offset any lower average cost per passenger-mile or ton-kilometer produced.

Any analysis of productivity would also not be complete without considering the effect of aircraft speed, which is also a measure of output per hour. A faster plane will by definition be able to transport more passengers or tons per hour than a slower one even though landing fees, flight crew, and other costs might be almost the same for each aircraft. In this regard, additional cost considerations such as engine performance (fuel burn rates) at different average flight speeds, *stage length* – the typical length of route between airports over which a particular aircraft is flown – as well as frequency of service will come into play. Of these factors, stage length is the most important determinant of relative productivity. Indeed, it has been the matching of stage-length to airport and airplane size that has led to development of hub-and-spoke networks (such as American's Dallas–Ft. Worth hub). Airlines feed shorter stage-length flights from smaller cities using smaller planes into their hubs and then fly the longer stage-length flights from such hubs.[19]

For an airline thinking of buying new equipment or changing that which is already being used on a particular route, potential market demand growth is always a key consideration. However, the range capability of the aircraft being used (or to be used) on that route will also ultimately affect the buy or change decision. Obviously, the less time spent on the ground loading and unloading relative to distance covered, the greater the productivity per hour. But productivity should also be further measured in terms of the many costs associated with ticket sales, reservations, and baggage handling, which are related to the number of passengers hauled, rather than distances covered. For example, since the unit costs of ticketing and baggage handling are the same no matter what the distance flown, on a total cost per flight basis, the airline would be better off hauling fewer passengers on longer flights than more passengers on shorter ones.

Last, but not least, are the productivity considerations of fleet size. Generally, the larger the fleet, the greater the efficiency and flexibility in the scheduling of crews and aircraft and the greater the likelihood that the type of aircraft and size of crew will be properly matched to the needs of a particular market. Also, although most areas of airline operations generally have constant returns to scale (i.e., they provide no important cost economies as size increases), fleets that are standardized using the same type of aircraft will normally have lower maintenance and training costs for mechanics and crews and higher productivity than if the fleet were a mongrel lot.

At the margin At its core, microeconomic analysis describes what happens to costs and prices when an extra unit is bought or sold at the margin. Economists will look for responses to small changes in terms of what are known as price or income elasticities. For airlines and also other travel-related segments such as hotels and theme parks, these elasticities practically become defining characteristics of the underlying businesses. Once the air network or hotel or theme park is up and running, it costs virtually nothing to allow an extra traveler onto the flight or guest into the hotel or theme park. Estimates of elasticities in relation to changes in prices and incomes are thus central, not only to the care and feeding of economists on the whole, but also to an understanding of how the travel industries intrinsically operate.

The basic idea is, for example, to estimate how much a change of income or a change in price – either up or down – will change demand for air travel. In the case of income, this can be stated as:

income elasticity = (% change in demand)/(% change in income).

Therefore, if a 4% increase in personal income causes an 8% increase in demand for airline tickets, the elasticity is +2.0. In other words, for every 1% percent increase in income, the industry should expect to see a 2% rise in ticket sales. Of course, the same type of calculation would be made in determination of price elasticities:

price elasticity = (% change in demand)/(% change in price).

Here, however, a negative elasticity would be expected since price increases are likely to lower demand, and vice versa. If prices rise 4% and demand declines 8%, the price elasticity of demand would be −2.0.

Calculations of what are known as cross-elasticities of demand are also important considerations in travel economics. Assuming all else remains constant, such cross-elasticities measure the change in demand for one service or product when the price of another substitutable or complementary service or product changes. A cross-elasticity greater than zero – meaning that a price rise in one mode of travel causes the other mode's traffic to rise – indicates that the modes are substitutes for each other (e.g., car rentals and taxis). Conversely, a negative cross elasticity – wherein a rise in the price of one mode causes the other mode's traffic to decline – indicates that the modes are complementary (e.g., air travel and car rentals).[20]

In all, the main determinants of travel income or price elasticity can be stated as:

- *Competition*, where the more competition, the greater the demand elasticity
- *Distance*, where long-haul flights tend to be more demand-elastic than those for the short haul

- *Business versus pleasure*, where business flyers tend to be less responsive to price changes than are individuals on personal trips or vacations
- *Time*, where the more time available for a trip to be planned in advance, the greater the elasticity

Unfortunately, the theory is easier to state than the practice is to apply because, when making estimates, many other variables will come into play and the relevant economic data on income or prices may not be so obviously isolated. For instance, is the relevant income that of the nation, of a region, or of a city? For estimates of demand for a single route out of a small midwestern city to another small city, the choice may be relatively unambiguous. For an estimate of routes out of New York, Los Angeles, or Atlanta (a major transfer hub), the possible income-data set choices are overwhelming.

Per capita income series are also imperfect because income is never evenly distributed over populations and traveler age profiles are not taken into account. Moreover, the elasticities for business travelers are surely different than those for leisure travelers, even when both are of the same age, live in the same cities, and earn the same incomes. And problems in the estimation of price elasticities also abound, in part because there are so many different fares for the same routes on the same days. In addition, people react differently to price changes over the long run than over the short run – sometimes adjusting by altogether moving their homes or business locations.

The moral of the story is that both income and price elasticity estimates, whether made in terms of airlines or any other travel-related industry segments, are, in and of themselves, imprecise and changeable over time. That said, most income elasticity estimates for airlines suggest that such elasticities generally range between 1.2 and 2.3, with short-haul leisure being near the upper end of the range and long-haul business near the lower end.

As for price elasticities, it should come as no surprise that business travelers, who generally do not pay for their own travel expenses, are less sensitive to price changes than are leisure travelers, who do mostly pay their own way. Business travelers – who in the late 1990s accounted for 40% of the flyers but 60% of domestic airline revenues – should thus have lower price elasticities of demand. As Doganis (1991, p. 225) notes, "An examination of price elasticities in some studies shows this to be true. Whereas nonbusiness travel tends to have price elasticities greater than minus 1.0, the price elasticity of business travel is less than minus 1.0 and in the case of first-class travel on the North Atlantic it was as low as minus 0.65."

Although it is impossible in most situations to estimate elasticity precisely, it is still possible to get a sense of whether a certain class of potential travelers' demand is elastic or inelastic with respect to price and/or income.[21] The estimates are important because proper implementation can make a significant difference in an airline's (or hotel's or theme park's) profitability.

Table 2.5. *Demand elasticity estimate ranges for selected modes of transportation*[a]

Mode	Time series	Cross-section	Other
Air passenger			
Leisure travel	0.40–1.92	1.52	1.40–4.60
Business travel	0.65	1.15	0.9
Mixed or unknown	0.82–1.81	0.76–4.51	0.53–1.90
Intercity rail			
Business travel	0.67–1.00	0.70	0.15
Mixed travel	0.37–1.54	1.4	0.12–1.50
Urban transit	0.01–1.32	0.05–0.34	0.06–0.70
Automobile usage	Short run	Long run	Unspecified
United States	0.23	0.28	0.13–0.45
Australia	0.09–0.24	0.22–0.31	0.22–0.34

[a] All elasticity estimates are in negative values.
Source: Oum, Waters, and Yong (1992).

Indeed, the elasticity estimates provide the basis for price-discrimination strategies, from which (as shown in Chapter 1) revenues can be maximized by charging different market segments markedly different prices. Comparisons of estimated elasticities for different modes of transportation are shown in Table 2.5.

Finally, assuming that most airlines (and hotels too) will find that they commonly operate in structural environments that can be characterized as being either monopolistic competitive or oligopolistic, the standard microeconomic diagrams can be applied as in Figure 2.6a (short-run equilibrium in monopolistic competition) and Figure 2.6b (classical profit maximization in an oligopoly). As in all such idealized representations, the *short-run equilibrium price, P*, is the one at which marginal revenue (MR) equals marginal cost (MC)*, a rising *MC* intersects the long-run average cost (*LAC*) curve at its low, and the demand schedule is represented by line *D*. Maximum industry profit under the assumption that all firms work together toward this objective is then indicated by rectangle *P*ABC*. In addition, the cost effects of congestion, applicable to the economics of all modes of transportation, is illustrated in Figure 2.7.

However, as neat and clean as this all seems, in practice, it is often difficult to make as sharp a distinction between short-run and long-run costs or between fixed and semifixed variable costs as the theory would have us believe is possible: A degree of arbitrariness of definition in an accounting and economic sense is inevitable.[22]

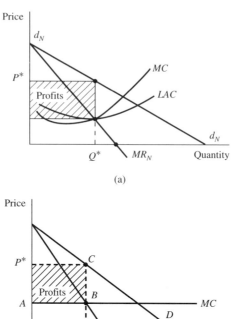

(a)

(b)

Figure 2.6. (a) Monopolistic competition and short-run equilibrium, and (b) classical profit maximization in an oligopoly.

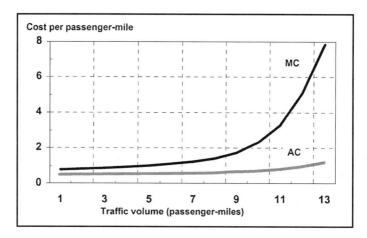

Figure 2.7. Marginal and average costs per passenger-mile versus traffic volume.

In practice, it is also especially difficult in transport operations to readily substitute one factor input for another as relative prices change. Nonetheless, over the long run, demand schedules – and therefore marginal revenues – can in fact be shifted by changes in pricing and in the technological development of travel services by other modes such as buses, trains, and cars or whatever else might evolve in the future. In sophisticated models, such changes would then have to be reflected in estimated technical change coefficients.

Pricing considerations In the pricing of transportation and travel services, the concept of economic efficiency is paramount. That is because economic efficiency requires that producers make the best use of the available resources. For instance, airlines or hotels that do not set their prices correctly will find, if they price too low, that they incur the costs of congestion shown in Figure 2.7. Or, if they price too high, their assets will be underutilized. From the standpoint of economic efficiency, the price charged for any transportation service should under all conditions be equal to the opportunity cost of producing it.

Opportunity costs are the costs of foregoing doing something else. In other words, the cost of an action is the value of other opportunities that are not taken. For example, a sales person could decide to make a presentation in Denver, foregoing the possibility of making the same presentation in London. The sales person has foregone the opportunity to make the pitch in London and must view this as a cost, a fact that becomes especially evident if the pitch fails in Denver when it might have succeeded in London. In the case of tourists, the opportunity cost of vacationing in Italy might be foregoing a trip to Spain. The cost becomes more evident if it rains every vacation day in Italy, while the sun shines every day in Spain. As translated into economics terminology, this means that the opportunity cost of an individual making a single trip is the short-run marginal cost, which for purposes of economic efficiency ought to be the price charged for the trip.

A related concept is that of *subsidy-free pricing*, which begins with the idea that users of transportation facilities must collectively cover all of the costs of the facilities that they use. Otherwise, someone else is subsidizing the users.

The economic efficiency criteria is most helpful in the setting of prices (fees or tolls) for the use of infrastructure (fixed facilities) under congestion (peak-load) conditions, which is when marginal costs rise sharply (Figure 2.7).[23] In the airline business, this might apply, for instance, to takeoff and landing slots at the busiest times of the day. Subsidy-free pricing considerations would, however, be mostly used in determining which users or user groups should pay for particular fixed system facilities such as airports.[24]

Traffic forecasting Except perhaps for specific purposes in the course of touring (e.g., a nostalgic train trip), people usually do not directly demand to be transported from one point to another just for the sake of riding in a plane, bus, car, or train. The demand is instead for a bundle of transport services that is derived from other needs and objectives such as to engage in business, to vacation, or to visit friends and relatives (VFR). Given the difficulties of estimating the derived demand for intercity business and leisure travel – each of which is driven by different passenger objectives – economists have sought other approaches that might provide a logical basis for forecasting traffic. Time-series (i.e., noncausal) estimation, using traffic as the dependent variable and time as the independent one, is the approach that most readily comes to mind. As usual, equations of this type can be couched in terms of linear or exponential forms. In the linear version, traffic (i.e., the anticipated number of passengers carried) increases by a constant absolute amount with each unit of time and is simply

traffic $(y) = a + bt$,

where a and b are constants and t is time. The comparable exponential form is

traffic $(y) = a(1 + b)^t$

For example, if traffic on the New York–Baltimore route in 1995 was 200,000 passengers, and the average annual growth rate has been 5%, then the exponential form would predict 1998 traffic as 231,525.

The basic problem with such simplistic models, however, is the assumption that traffic growth is merely a function of time. As Witt and Witt (1992, p. 7) note, "a great problem with forecasting by extrapolation is that it presupposes that the factors which were the main cause of growth in the past will continue to be the main cause in the future." Obviously, many other factors might affect traffic growth, including changes in local industry prospects, demographics, and regional incomes. To make sense of all this, most economists would then resort to standard regression (i.e., causal) forecasting techniques that give weight to many different variables and that also, in effect, estimate factor elasticities. The form of one such simple regression equation might be as follows:

$$T = f(F, Y, t)$$

where traffic, T, is the number of passengers on a route taken as a function of average real fares, F, Y is a measure of real personal consumption expenditures per capita, and t is the time trend. As usual, many additional variables (including the cost of travel time) can be added to this type of model. With all other things being equal, most forecasting models of this kind would probably include at least the following variables (and would also be applicable in studies of other modes of transportation):

- *Population*, wherein the higher the number of people resident in a country, the larger the number of trips likely to be taken
- *Income*, which measured as real per capita income in the originating region affects demand

- *Own price of service*, which is the cost of travel to the destination
- *Prices of substitutes*, which would obviously affect demand

However, neither time-series nor regression models are useful when trying to forecast traffic on new routes, for which most, if not all input data do not yet exist. An approach that to a degree solves this problem uses what is known as the *gravity model*, which was suggested as early as 1885. As discussed by Kanafani (1983, p. 165) and by Boyar (1997, p. 84), the gravity model is analogous to the one used in physics to describe the attraction between two objects. In the case of travel, the model predicts that the number of trips between any two origins and destinations will be distributed according to the formula:

$$t_{ij} = \alpha A_i B_j \, c_{ij}^{-\sigma}$$

where

t_{ij} = the number of trips taken between origin i and destination j
A_i = number of total trips taken from origin i
B_j = number of total trips taken to destination j
c_{ij} = distance between i and j or a measure of cost of transportation between them
α and σ = parameters whose values are estimated for each particular city.

The underlying concept in this model is that the number of people moving between cities seems proportional to the sizes of the cities and inversely proportional to the distance between them. Indeed, some empirical estimates have found that values of σ are approximately 2.0 (i.e., the same value of σ as found in physics), which suggests "that trips between any pair of localities will increase with the product of the trips generated at those places and decline with the square of the distance between them."[25]

In addition to the gravity model, economists have also sometimes adapted from physics models based on statistical mechanics (entropy) and electrical systems. All such models may, of course, be applied not only to the study of airlines but also to demand estimation for intercity travel by rail, bus, and private car. However, to be useful, all such models must somehow incorporate the fundamental characteristics of transportation service demand, which is derived, tends to fluctuate on daily and seasonal as well as long-term macroeconomic cycles, and is sensitive not only to the fare charged but also to the cost of time over which the transport service is used.

Financial features

At first glance, one would think that it should be relatively simple to compare profitability parameters among different airlines. But because of substantially different policies regarding asset depreciation, mix of leased versus owned equipment, and degree of government subsidy (if any), it is difficult to derive an independent, internally consistent estimate of something even as simple

Table 2.6. *U.S. major airlines' operating performance: Composite of nine companies, 1993–98*

	Revenues	Operating income	Operating margin[a] (%)	Assets	Operating cash flow
CAGR (%)[b]	4.9	51.6	44.4	6.2	20.3

[a] Average margin, 1993–98 = 6.3%.
[b] Compound annual growth rate.

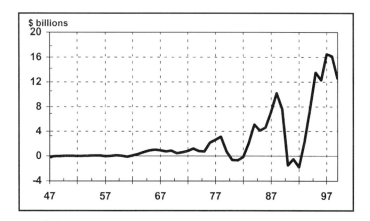

Figure 2.8. ICAO-member operating profits, 1947–99. *Source:* ICAO.

as a return on assets for the industry as a whole. The closest that we can come is to use operating (pretax) and net income (after tax) data compiled by the Air Transport Association (ATA) for U.S. carriers and the International Civil Aviation Organization (ICAO) for most of the world's airlines organized by country of operation.

Such data for the ATA are illustrated in Figure 2.2a, from which we see that over most of the time since 1938, when operating statistics were first compiled, the domestic industry produced cumulative losses. In fact, the industry has only recently moved into a cumulative profit position, supported by the booming economy of the 1990s, relatively low fuel prices, and firm ticket prices. ICAO data of Figure 2.8, which are the most globally inclusive, are comparable, with volatility of results (huge swings from up to down to up) again being the most salient feature. Figure 2.9 presents additional ICAO operating statistics. However, domestic financial operating performance in the 1990s is better revealed by the data of Table 2.6.

Another important industry feature is reflected in the industry's balance sheet, which has traditionally been, relative to other industries, high on the proportion of debt relative to equity. As in other industries, the relative

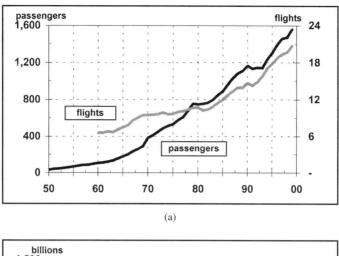

(a)

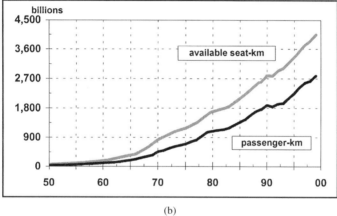

(b)

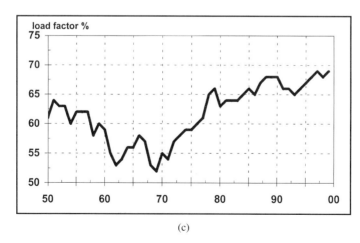

(c)

Figure 2.9. ICAO-member (a) flights and passengers (in millions), (b) available seat-kilometers (in billions), and (c) load factors, 1950–99. *Source:* ICAO.

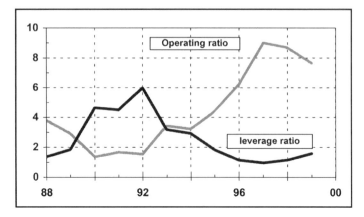

Figure 2.10. Major domestic airline passenger carriers, estimated leverage and operating ratio comparisons for 1992–99. *Source:* Office of Airline Information, U.S. DOT.

burden of debt, or financial leverage, would be reflected in a leverage ratio defined as debt to cash flow (earnings before interest, taxes, depreciation and amortization, EBITDA):

leverage ratio = total net debt (long-term debt minus cash)/EBITDA.

The similar operating ratio would show how well covered by cash flows are gross interest payment expenses (i.e., including capitalized interest and not net of interest income)

operating ratio = EBITDA/interest cost.

Both ratios are often subject to small definitional refinements (e.g., sometimes EBITDA is measured before subtracting rental and/or lease payments, which is EBITDAR), but the basic features are retained. Companies with a leverage ratio of, say, more than 5.0 to 1 would be rather financially risky as even a small downturn in cash flow due to an economic recession, rising fuel costs, or more competition would likely put the company on the road to bankruptcy.[26] By contrast, in the case of the operating ratio, the higher the better. Any company that can barely cover its interest costs with operating cash flow (EBITDA) (i.e., showing a ratio close to 1 : 1) is risking ruin.[27]

As can be seen in Figure 2.10, major domestic airline profits have been strong enough in recent years to restore the industry's financial health; the industry's leverage ratio fell from an extreme of nearly 6 : 1 at the beginning of the 1990s to a normal 1.8 : 1 at the end of the decade and the operating ratio rose from approximately 1.5 : 1 to about 7 : 1 over the same span. However, as this period only suggests the change from an economic low point (the recession of 1990–91) through a decade of the longest U.S. economic expansion, it is probably atypical.

2.4 Financing and accounting issues

Financing

Airlines finance their operations in much the same ways as do other capital-intensive companies. They try to tap the bond markets more aggressively when interest rates are low, and they are inclined to sell equity or convertible debt when the equity markets favor the company's shares with a high price-to-earnings or price-to-cash flow valuation. The goal is to find a mix wherein the weighted average cost of capital (*WACC*), including debt and equity components (or variants), is as low as possible. Without going into greater detail, the province of pure texts on finance, we can state the *WACC* as

$$WACC = \text{debt}/(\text{debt} + \text{equity}) \times r_d + \text{equity}/(\text{debt} + \text{equity}) \times r_e$$

where r_d is the cost of debt expressed as an interest rate, and r_e is the cost of equity, as estimated using risk premiums and risk adjustment factors (known as betas).

Nevertheless, all of the capital-intensive transport industries also use other means of equipment finance to shift debt off their balance sheets and also to gain potential tax advantages. With this in mind, it is quite common for airlines or railroads, for example, to sell their equipment or have other parties buy their equipment for them in a sale-leaseback type of arrangement (the accounting implications of which are discussed below). By shifting some of the equipment-related debts and assets off the balance sheet, not only do the companies appear less financially risky to potential investors, but they also provide financial companies specializing in these areas with annuity income and tax advantages that might otherwise go unused.

Issuance of plain-vanilla common and preferred shares would be as typical a way for this industry to finance itself as it would be for any other. The same holds for convertible bonds of various flavors. But companies that have a need to finance large and expensive pieces of movable equipment (for instance, airplanes, ocean tankers, rail cars and locomotives, and trucks) have found that equipment trust certificates (ETCs) are advantageous. Such certificates first evolved in the rail industry and are a form of secured debt, which means that the trustee, as the formal owner of the equipment, can upon default immediately repossess the equipment that has been pledged as collateral. In this structure, legal ownership is vested in the trustee (who leases the equipment to the company) and an investor has a claim rather than a mortgage lien.

The advantage to the company using the equipment is that it can conserve cash over the near term, making only a down payment in the range of 10%–25% of the cost of the equipment and paying the balance on a scale of maturities that could be between one to fifteen years. Moreover, debt-ratings agencies such Moody's will often rate the trust certificate debt one grade higher than the company's other debts, thereby making comparative financing through issuance of such debt certificates a little less costly.[28] ETCs are often also created as much for tax reasons as for the spreading of risk and the lowering of borrowing costs.

A modified version of the ETC is the Enhanced Equipment Trust certificate (E-ETC). Such certificates are a type of debt securitization in which the plain ETC is divided up into several readily tradable pieces, each with a different risk/reward profile in terms of security and access to lease rental cash flows. As Morrell (1997, p. 186) notes, "a structure of this type will give the senior (lower risk) certificates a much higher credit rating than under the ETC."[29]

Accounting

Operating items In all business accounting systems there is a need to separate financial statement items into operating and nonoperating categories. For airlines, uniform categorization of this kind has been provided by the ICAO, which identifies nonoperating items as:

- Gains and losses derived from sale of retired property and equipment
- Interest paid on loans
- All profits or losses arising from an airline's affiliated companies
- Gains or losses arising from foreign exchange or securities transactions
- Direct government subsidies

However, as in other complex businesses, questions of definition remain in terms of what is considered operating revenue and operating cost. Direct operating cost, for example, should in theory include all costs associated with and dependent on the operation of aircraft, which would include fuel, flight crew salaries, maintenance and overhaul, and depreciation expenses. Other costs, including those for ticketing, administration, passenger service, administration, and ground costs, would be indirect. In practice, though, the distinction is not as clear, with some companies categorizing costs of administration or for cabin crews as direct while others assign them as indirect.

Leases Equipment leasing is another area in which there may be accounting ramifications that are of analytical importance. According to U.S. generally accepted accounting principles (GAAP), leases are classified as being either of the operating or of the capital (finance) type. Both types are governed by rules spelled out in Financial Accounting Standards Board (FASB) Statement 13. The finance lease gives priority to the concept of economic ownership of the lease asset, accounting for it on the balance sheet as if it were purchased. In contrast, the operating lease prioritizes the concept of legal ownership of the asset. The difference between the two types may have a substantial impact on reported earnings.

For example, in the case of an operating lease, as lease payments become payable by the lessee, they are charged as a period expense over the term of the lease. Following FASB 13, "if rental payments are not made on a straight-line basis, rental expense nevertheless shall be recognized on a straight-line basis unless another systematic and rational basis is more representative of the time pattern in which use benefit is derived from the leased property."

In the case of a capital lease, however, FASB 13 says that "the leasee shall record a capital lease as an asset and an obligation at an amount equal to the present value at the beginning of the lease term. . . [and]. . . the asset shall be amortized in a manner consistent with the lessee's normal depreciation policy except that the period of amortization shall be the lease term." To be classified as a capital lease, the lease must meet one or more of the criteria listed below. Otherwise, it is an operating lease. Also, sale-leaseback transactions may be of either type depending on the criteria met by the lease.

- A capital lease transfers ownership of the property to the lessee by the end of the lease term.
- It contains a bargain purchase option
- The lease term is equal to 75% or more of the estimated economic life of the leased property.
- The present value of the minimum lease payments, including certain adjustments, is 90% or more of the fair value of the leased property at the inception of the lease.

A capital lease will thus transfer substantially all the benefits and risks inherent in the ownership of a property and will directly appear as an asset and a related liability on the balance sheet and with financial statement footnotes providing details on minimum obligations. In contrast, with an operating lease, which is cancelable and requires the regular payment of rent, equipment assets and liabilities do not appear on the balance sheet (although information about minimal obligations would appear in financial statement footnotes). And lease rentals are charged evenly to the income statement over the lease term.[30]

This difference may materially affect the comparability of transportation service company balance sheets and financial ratios. For example, in the first year, expenses for a lessee under a capital lease (i.e., interest expense and depreciation) are greater than expenses under an operating lease (i.e., rent expense). But in later years, as the interest component on a capital lease diminishes, annual expense becomes greater with operating leases. Reported period net earnings would, all other things equal, then depend on a company's mix of leasing versus asset-purchasing strategies. However, for companies that have already encumbered much of their free cash flow, leasing allows the company to hold onto more cash over the near term than would otherwise be possible.[31]

One last complication – as if there aren't enough already – is that international treatments for leases may differ from those in the U.S. even though the finance/capital lease approach, based on a concept of economic ownership of the asset, is the treatment suggested by International Accounting Standard-Accounting for Leases (IAS 17). As Morrell (1997, p. 49) notes, in Europe and Japan "finance leases were often excluded from the balance sheet because the airline did not have legal title or ownership. In the U.K. and U.S., however, these leases are capitalized and placed on the balance sheet."[32]

Sale-leasebacks The sale and subsequent leaseback of aircraft is a commonly used airline financing strategy that can generate cash, realize economic gains, and increase fleet flexibility. According to the International Accounting Standards Statement 17 (see IATA Airline Accounting Guide No. 6), if a sale-leaseback transaction results in a capital (finance) lease, any profit or loss should not be recognized immediately through income but should be deferred and amortized over the lease term. However, if such a transaction results in an operating lease and it is clear that the transaction is established at fair value, any profit or loss should be recognized immediately. It should further be noted that this treatment is not consistent with U.S. GAAP (Generally Accepted Accounting Principles), which requires that all gains arising on operating leasebacks be deferred and amortized over the minimum lease term in proportion to the gross rental charged as an expense.

In summary, for airlines, the advantages of leasing (which may, in part, also be derived from outsourcing of other major equipment assets and services) are:

- Volume discounts for aircraft purchases can be obtained and passed on to the airline.
- The airline conserves working capital and credit capacity.
- Up to 100% of the equipment is financed with no deposits or pre-payments required.
- The airline shifts the burden of risk of obsolescence to the lessor.
- It is sometimes possible to exclude leasing finance commitments from the balance sheet.
- The tax status might become more favorable.

The disadvantages of leases are:

- The cost may be higher than for straight-debt financing.
- The profit from eventual sales of the equipment accrue to the lessor, not the airline.
- Higher debt-equity (gearing) ratios may result.
- Aircraft equipment specifications may not be fully compatible with the airline's needs.

Other elements Other elements specific to the airline business include accounting for frequent-flyer programs and acquired gates, routes, and airport landing slots. Airlines will generally record, under an accrual approach (also known as the *incremental cost method*) an estimated liability for the incremental cost associated with providing the related free transportation at the time a free travel award is earned. The liability will then be periodically adjusted for awards redeemed and earned or for changes in program require-ments.[33] Indeed, most airlines utilize the incremental cost method.

However, as noted in IATA Airline Accounting Guideline No. 2, a *deferred revenue approach* may also be used. With the deferred revenue approach, a proportion of passenger revenue generated from the sale of tickets conferring frequent-flyer benefits is deferred until such time as a ticket associated with the use of the frequent-flyer award is granted and used.[34] The same approach pertains to revenues generated from mileage credits that have been sold to other companies participating in such programs; the deferred revenue is amortized as transportation is provided.

Routes will be normally amortized on a straight-line basis over forty years, gates over the stated term of the related leases, and slots over twenty years.

Then there are tax considerations. As with cruise lines (Chapter 3), foreign-registered corporate income from aircraft operation is exempt from U.S. federal taxation if the country in which the firm is registered offers equivalent exemptions to American firms. Under these provisions, major airlines such as British Airways or Lufthansa thus do not pay U.S. taxes but pay substantial taxes in their home countries.

2.5 Valuing airline properties

In the valuation of airline assets, projected cash flow forecasts provide only a starting point. The difference between what the shares of the company are selling for on the open market and what they might fetch in a takeover may be a function of the following factors, which are not all necessarily well captured in discounted cash flow projections.

Economic forecasts on a regional, national, or global basis
Brand-name value
Prospective reservation-system and frequent-flyer program capabilities
Amount of prospective competition
Age of equipment and facilities
Demographic and income profiles of business and leisure travelers in terri-
  tories covered
Current and prospective rights to fly routes
Number and quality of gates at airports served
Number and time of day for current and prospective acquisitions of landing
  slot rights[35]

For the financial analyst, the objective is to take all of these factors into account and to then compare such private market acquisition-value estimates to public share price valuations. In this regard, computation of what is known as the enterprise value (EV) of a company is a related and helpful concept.

$$EV = (\text{number of shares outstanding} \times \text{price of the shares})$$
$$+ \text{outstanding value of net debt}$$

where

net debt = long-term debt + current liabilities − cash and cash equivalents.

This EV is often further modified by deducting the estimated value of off-balance sheet, nonoperating, assets to arrive at an adjusted enterprise value (AEV).

$AEV = EV -$ off-balance sheet assets.

These *AEV* estimates, which reflect public market prices, are then in turn used to compute a ratio to cash flow (*EBITDA*) that allows for relatively clean and simple comparisons to be made among similar firms in an industry (be it airlines, hotels, or media):

valuation ratio = $AEV/EBITDA$.

In the airline industry, for example, such valuation ratios will normally cluster around five to six times *EBITDA*. However, private market values, which include an implicit control premium, are normally much higher than are seen in public market trading of shares. The securities of a company would become attractive for purchase when the public share price is at a sizable discount (perhaps 20% or more) to such private value estimates.[36]

For many assets, private market multiples would typically range between 8 and 15 times the cash flow that is *projected* for the next year (Table 2.7). This multiple would also be more precisely determined by comparing to cash-flow multiples on similar, recently traded, airline properties and to estimates of the potential for generating new revenue streams – economic value added (EVA) – on already invested capital. In such EVA models, share valuations key off of the difference between the weighted-average cost of debt and equity capital (WACC) and the returns in excess of the WACC.[37] Appendix B discusses such valuation concepts in more detail.

2.6 Concluding remarks

Travel by air is a comparatively recent convenience that has forever changed the way we think about the size of the world and the way we conduct our business and leisure activities. The systems that have been developed are complex and could not operate without the important advances in computing technology that have come out of the twentieth century.

Many of the financing and operating methods are tailored to the specific needs of this industry, in which technological obsolescence is much more of a factor than it is perhaps in rails or buses. However, the analytical methods used to study economic sensitivities here are generally also applicable to other travel-related segments. From a microeconomic standpoint, the rules of operations basically boil down to what Petzinger (1995) has

Table 2.7. *Public and private market valuation methods: Examples*

Public market values	
Public market values	
Price per share	$11.50
Shares outstanding	60
Total market value of equity* plus	690
Total long term debt	1,200
Total	1,890
less	
Cash	150
Other off-balance-sheet assets	250
Enterprise value (EV)	1,490
EBITDA	165
Cash-flow multiple (EV/EBITDA):	9.0
Private market values	
EBITDA	165
times assumed multiple**	10
Unadjusted value	1,650
plus	
Cash	150
Other off-balance sheet assets	250
less	
Long-term debt	1,200
Net asset value	850
Shares outstanding	60
Net private market asset value per share	$14.17

*If preferred stock is in capitalization, its market value must also be included.
**Derived by comparison with recent transfer-price multiples for similar assets.

described as:

- Every additional passenger is almost pure profit.
- Whoever has the most flights from a city gets a disproportionate share of passengers.
- You can fill some, but not all, of the seats at low fares.[38]

Airlines will constantly have to battle pressures on margins and will always be affected to a notable extent by the ups and downs of the overall economy. Although opportunities to realize significant cost economies of scale are probably limited, airlines will continue to combine and to consolidate operations – if not through outright acquisitions then through sharing of flight codes and frequent-flyer programs and other such arrangements. In this regard, pricing power, market share, and brand dominance are more the motivating elements than are potential cost savings. Still, over time, new regional carriers can and do emerge. That is the nature of the business.

Selected additional reading

"A Survey of the Airline Industry," *The Economist*, June 12, 1993.

Alperovich, G., and Machnes, Y. (1994). "The Role of Wealth in the Demand for International Air Travel," *Journal of Transport Economics and Policy*, 28(2)(May).

Ashford, N., and Moore, C. A. (1992). *Airport Finance*. New York: Van Nostrand Reinhold.

Brannigan, M., and De Lisser, E. (1996). "Cost Cutting at Delta Raises the Stock Price but Lowers the Service," *Wall Street Journal*, June 20.

Bryant, A. (1997). "No Longer Flying in Formation: Labor Rifts Return to Employee-Owned United Airlines," *New York Times*, January 17.

Button, K. (1999). "The Usefulness of Current International Air Transport Statistics," *Journal of Transportation and Statistics* (May). Washington, D.C.: U.S. Department of Transportation, Bureau of Transportation Statistics.

Cappelli, P., ed. (1995). *Airline Labor Relations in the New Global Era: The New Frontier*. Ithaca, NY: Cornell University Press.

Carey, S. (1999). " 'I'm Opening a Door!' 'No, No, Don't Do It!' 'How About a Valium?'," *Wall Street Journal*, April 28.

   (1998). "Aided by Its Shuttle, United Air Is Taking Los Angeles by Storm, *Wall Street Journal*, January 16, 1998.

   (1997). "How Alaska Airlines Beat Back Challenges from Bigger Rivals," *Wall Street Journal*, May 19.

Carey, S., and McCartney, S. (1998). "Northwest's Older Jets Tax Maintenance, Lead to Service Disruptions," *Wall Street Journal*, June 12.

Carley, W. M. (2000). "New Cockpit Systems Broaden the Margin of Safety for Pilots," *Wall Street Journal*, March 1.

   (1999). "FAA Sparks Criticism with Efforts to Speed Traffic at Airports," *Wall Street Journal*, September 9.

Carley, W. M., and Pasztor, A. (1999). "Korean Air Confronts Dismal Safety Record Rooted in Its Culture," *Wall Street Journal*, July 7.

Cole, J. (1999). "Airbus Prepares to 'Bet The Company' as It Builds a Huge New Jet," *Wall Street Journal*, November 3.

Cole, J., and Carey, S. (1994). "Airlines Are Keeping Aging Planes Aloft, Testing Repair Rules," *Wall Street Journal*, November 3.

Cole, J., and Pasztor, A. (1996). "Airlines Are Grappling with a Complex Task: Avoiding Catastrophe," *Wall Street Journal*, May 13.

Daniel, J. I. (1995). "Congestion Pricing and Capacity of Large Hub Airports: A Bottleneck Model with Stochastic Queues," *Econometrica*, (March).

DeVany, A. S. (1974). "The Revealed Value of Time in Air Travel," *Review of Economics and Statistics*, 56.

Goldsmith, C. (1996). "No-Frills Flying Gains Altitude Inside Europe as Barriers Fall Away," *Wall Street Journal*, December 17.

Hale, S. (1999). "Kansas City Thrives Despite Not Boasting a Major Airline Hub," *Wall Street Journal*, July 2.

Heppenheimer, T. A. (1995). *Turbulent Skies: The History of Commercial Aviation*. New York: John Wiley.

Guyon, J. (1999). "British Airways Takes a Flier," *Fortune*, 140(6)(September 27).

Ingersoll, B. (1999). "Gateless in Detroit, Low-Fare Spirit Docks at Rivals' Convenience," *Wall Street Journal*, July 12.

Jenkins, D., ed. (1995). *Handbook of Airline Economics*. Washington, DC: Aviation Week (McGraw-Hill).

Komons, N. A. (1989). *Bonfires to Beacons: Federal Civil Aviation Policy Under the Air Commerce Act, 1926–1938.* Washington, DC: Smithsonian Institution Press.

Labich, K. (1999). "Fasten Your Seat Belts," *Fortune*, 139(9)(May 10).

Landler, M. (1998). "Bad Timing for Some Epic Projects: Asia's Financial Crisis Leaves New Airports Scrambling for Passengers," *New York Times*, July 2.

Lieber, R. B. (1995). "Turns Out This Critter Can Fly," *Fortune*, (132)(11)(November 27).

Mathews, A. W., and Cooper, H. (2000). "U.S. Airlines Pull Out the Stops in Lobbying for New China Route," *Wall Street Journal*, April 28.

McCarthy, M. J. (1996). "Major Airlines Find Their 'Fortress' Hubs Aren't Impenetrable," *Wall Street Journal*, February 6.

(1995). "No.19603 Still Flies After 27 Years' Service to a Number of Airlines," *Wall Street Journal*, August 9.

McCartney, S. (2000a). "How the Pilots Fly the Plane Varies a Lot From Airline to Airline," *Wall Street Journal*, March 14.

(2000b). "American Plays Hardball With a Start-up Over All-First-Class Flights," *Wall Street Journal*, March 9.

(2000c). "Airlines Find a Bag of High-Tech Tricks to Keep Income Aloft," *Wall Street Journal*, January 20.

(1999a). "A Crush of Air Traffic, Control-System Quirks Jam the Flight Lanes," *Wall Street Journal*, September 1.

(1999b). "Feeling Confined? You May Be Flying in One of Boeing's New 737s," *Wall Street Journal*, August 2.

(1999c). "At American Airlines, Pilots Trace Grievances to Deals in Lean Years," *Wall Street Journal*, February 11.

(1999d). "Continental Is Winning the Battle for Share in New York Market," *Wall Street Journal*, February 9.

(1997a). "Business Fares Increase Even as Leisure Travel Keeps Getting Cheaper," *Wall Street Journal*, November 3.

(1997b)."How Renegade Pilots at American Airlines Upset the Union's Pact," *Wall Street Journal*, February 10.

(1996a). "Free Airline Miles Become a Potent Tool for Selling Everything," *Wall Street Journal*," April 15.

(1996b), "Why Airline Fare Sales Aren't Always a Bargain," *Wall Street Journal*, March 11.

(1995). "Why Are Big Airlines Considering Mergers? Look in the Cockpit," *Wall Street Journal*, November 9.

McCartney, S., and Adair, B. (2000). "Merger Talk Fills Skies and Airline Regulators Have a Juggling Act," *Wall Street Journal*, June 8.

McCartney, S., Carey, S., and Brannigan, M. (1998). "How Northwest Beat the Top Contender to Control Continental," *Wall Street Journal*, January 27.

McCartney, S., and Friedland, J. (1998). "How American Airlines Is Building Dominance in the Latin Market," *Wall Street Journal*, January 9.

McDowell, E. (1999). "Two New Airline Alliances Are Aimed at Sharpening Competition," *New York Times*, June 23.

Michaels, D. (2000), "No-Frills Irish Airline Flies High," *Wall Street Journal*, September 6.

Morrison, S. A. (1996). "Airline Mergers: A Longer View," *Journal of Transport Economics and Policy*, 30(3)(September).

Morrison, S. A., and Winston, C. (1990). "The Dynamics of Airline Pricing and Competition." *American Economic Review (Papers and Proceedings)*, 80.

Morrow, D. J. (2000a). "Twilight of Turboprops?" *New York Times*, February 18.

(2000b). "Bed Is Latest Weapon in Airline Perk Wars," *New York Times*, January 29.

Murphy, M. E. (1986). *The Airline that Pride Almost Bought: The Struggle to Takeover Continental Airlines*. New York: Franklin Watts.

Nomani, A. Q. (1990). "Fare Game: Airlines May Be Using Price-Data Network to Lessen Competition," *Wall Street Journal*, June 28.

Nomani, A. Q., and Blackmon, D. A. (1998). "How Maneuvering by Airlines Shaped U.S.-Japan Accord," *Wall Street Journal*, February 2.

O'Brian, B. (1995). "Continental's CALite Hits Some Turbulence In Battling Southwest," *Wall Street Journal*, January 10.

(1994). "Ticketless Plane Trips, New Technology Force Travel Agencies to Change Course," *Wall Street Journal*, September 13.

O'Reilly, B. (1999). "The Mechanic Who Fixed Continental," *Fortune* 140(12)(December 20).

Oum, T. H., Park, J. H., and Zhang, A. (1996). "The Effects of Airline Codesharing Agreements on Firm Conduct and International Air Fares," *Journal of Transport Economics and Policy*, 30(2)(May).

Palmer, J. (1994). "The Empire Strikes Back," *Barron's*, December 14.

Pasztor, A. (1996). "An Air-Safety Battle Brews Over the Issue of Pilots' Rest Time," *Wall Street Journal*, July 1.

Petersen, B. S., and Glab, J. (1994). *Rapid Descent: Deregulation and the Shakeout in the Airlines*. New York: Simon & Schuster.

Sampson, A. (1984). *Empires of the Sky: The Politics, Contests, and Cartels of World Airlines*. New York: Random House.

Smith, T. K. (1995). "Why Air Travel Doesn't Work," *Fortune*, 131(6)(April 2).

Starkie, D. (1994)."The U.S. Market in Airport Slots," *Journal of Transport Economics and Policy*, 28(3)(September).

Taylor, A., III. (1999). "Blue Skies for Airbus," *Fortune*, 140(3)(August 2).

(1998). "Pulling Delta Out of Its Dive," *Fortune*, 138(11)(December 7).

(1996). "United We Own," *Business Week*, March 18, 1996. No. 3467.

Tully, S. (1996). "Northwest and KLM: The Alliance from Hell," *Fortune*, 133(12)(June 24).

Wald, M. L. (1999). "Canada's Private Control Towers," *New York Times*, October 23.

Wardman, M. (1998). "The Value of Travel Time: A Review of British Evidence," *Journal of Transport Economics and Policy*, 32(3)(September).

Zhang, A. (1996). "An Analysis of Fortress Hubs in Airline Networks," *Journal of Transport Economics and Policy*, 30(3)(September).

Zuckerman, L., and Wald, M. L. (2000). "Crisis for Air Traffic System: More Passengers, More Delays." *New York Times*, September 5.

3
Water and wheels

A tourist is a fellow who drives thousands of miles so that he can be photographed standing in front of his car. – Emile Ganest

Not everyone flies. Sometimes it may, in fact, still be more convenient, more fun, and less expensive to go by car, bus, or train – or to take a cruise. This chapter provides background about travel on vehicles that move on water or wheels.

3.1 Wetting the whistle

Modern cruise ships are arguably the one mode of transportation that are also, to some, a destination in and of themselves. No one, for example, would think of a modern airplane in quite this way, not even while encamped in the plushest of first-class cabins or aboard the Concorde. On a cruise, the ambiguity of purpose, however, is not coincidental. It is instead an important aspect and also the desired outcome of earnest marketing campaigns designed to stimulate in the middle-class traveler's mind the most Sybaritic of fantasies. As such, the modern cruise ship operates as much as a floating hotel as it does as a means of carriage.

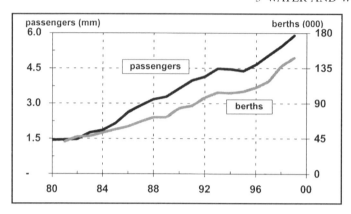

Figure 3.1. Cruise-line industry passengers and berths, 1980–99. *Source:* CLIA and company reports.

Fantasy islands

Although ships have been transporting passengers since the beginning of time, the first cruises were, according to Dickinson and Vladimir (1997, p.1), conducted by the Penisula and Oriental Steam Navigation Co., which ran vessels from Britain to Spain and Portugal and to Malaysia and China beginning in 1844. However, the modern industry only dates back to the early 1970s, when rising consumer disposable income opened up the possibility of cruising on a giant ship purely for pleasure and not necessarily for the purpose of going anywhere. Prior to that time, the giant ships – the *Titanic* and *Queen Elizabeth*, for instance – were, until the appearance of jet aircraft, the only way for most people to traverse the oceans. And prior to the 1960s, cruises were characterized by their long duration and distances covered as opposed to the relatively brief, "movable resort" cruises of today.

Ted Arison, a Miami-based entrepreneur was among the first to see the sea of opportunities, forming Carnival Cruise Lines in 1972 with the purchase of a Canadian vessel that he renamed the *Mardi Gras*. Using this as a base, he quickly embellished and aggressively promoted the concept of fun and frolic aboard ship to people of all ages and backgrounds.[1] Meanwhile, Royal Caribbean, a competitor founded in 1968, reinforced the concept by being the first to design ships specifically for warm water year-round cruising.[2] As of the end of the 1990s, Carnival accounted for approximately 40% of all industry revenues and Royal Caribbean, 30%.

Competitors to Carnival, including companies such as Viking, Princess, and Royal Caribbean, soon developed cruise packages of their own, boosting industry growth to a compound annual rate of 8.9% from 1970 through 2000. Over this span, the number of passengers carried by the industry rose to more than 6 million in 2000 as compared to one-tenth as many in 1970 (Figure 3.1).

Table 3.1. *Large cruise ships, selected sample, circa 2000*

Name	Year built	Passenger capacity	Approximate gross registered tons
Carnival Cruise			
Victory	2000	2,758	101,000
Triumph	1999	2,758	102,000
Destiny	1996	2,642	101,000
Royal Caribbean			
Voyager of the Seas	1999	3,114	142,000
Explorer of the Seas	2000	3,114	142,000

Source: Company reports.

Even so, cruise ships account for only an estimated 3% to 5% of the North American vacation market, defined as persons who travel for leisure purposes on trips of three nights or longer involving at least one night's stay in a hotel. Also, Cruise Line International Association (CLIA) data suggest that only 11% of the North American population has ever taken a cruise.

In recent years passenger unit growth has been sustained if not accelerated by the industry's shift toward use of larger ships that have allowed efficiencies to be gained and prices to be lowered. The strategy is similar to that implemented by airlines in their transition to using wide-bodied jumbo jets for long-distance flights. Indeed, the size of the ships has continued to burgeon, with the largest of them several football fields long and able to feed and shelter the population of sizable village. For example, the *Carnival Destiny*, built in 1996, sails with 101,353 tons, a length of 893 feet, and a passenger capacity of 2,642. And *Voyager of the Seas*, launched in 1999 by Royal Caribbean, is the world's largest at 142,00 tons and makes aircraft carriers seem small. Vessels of this size typically cost well in excess of $400 million.[3]

A list of some of the largest cruise ships built in recent years appears in Table 3.1. Nearly all of those listed are registered outside of the United States, where the cost of shipyard construction is often subsidized by foreign governments. Also, foreign-flag ships, having greater flexibility in hiring, are likely to have lower average unit labor costs than those flying the American flag. This can be an important profitability enhancement factor since the ratio of crew to passengers may be as high as 50%.[4] As noted by Frantz (1999), many cruise companies further benefit from a loophole in the Federal tax code that exempts from taxation a foreign-registered firm's income from ships and aircraft if the country in which the firm is organized (e.g., Panama, Liberia, and the Bahamas) offers equivalent exemptions to American companies.[5] These rules were initially established to promote international shipping and trading by air.

Operational aspects

As of the year 2000, the North American cruise industry had approximately 164,000 berths on 156 ships and generated revenues of approximately $8 billion. To reflect demand versus supply, the industry prefers to measure occupancy rates, which, for the three major players (Carnival, Princess, and Royal Caribbean), all typically run at over 100%.[6] Of course, as in any other capital-intensive businesses, occupancy rates (which implicitly reflect capacity utilization) are important in the setting of prices and in the determination of the returns on invested capital that are to be ultimately generated. Indeed, the lower the expected long run occupancy rate, the more short-run pricing volatility is likely to be seen.[7]

From the standpoint of perishibility of product, cruise ships are more like airlines than hotels.[8] An unused hotel room at 6 PM might still be sold to a late-arriving traveler by 10 PM, but once a cruise ship sails or the airplane lifts off, there can be no additional passengers boarded. For a ship, this may mean that berths remain unsold for at least three and as much as seven days. Yield is accordingly defined as the average gross revenue per available berths. And occupancy rates are the equivalent of occupancy rates in hotels, only with the assumption that there are two passengers per room.[9] One other measure of growth and of capacity utilization is the number of guest-cruise days, which is the number of guests times the number of days cruised.

The *space ratio* of a ship, however, is measured in terms of gross registered tons (GRT), which has nothing to do with weight. GRT is instead a measure of the amount of usable space per passenger on a ship. By definition, 1 gross registered ton is 100 cubic feet of volume, which means, for example, that a ship of 18,000 GRT carrying 750 passengers provides a space ratio of 24 tons per passenger. On modern ships, the space ratio averages more than 44 and may range as high as 50 on luxury-class services. As in the hotel industry, ship service categories are segmented into markets that fall broadly from luxury to premium to contemporary to budget to economy classes, the precise definition of each depending on the cruise line's marketing targets and the amenities and service levels provided in each category.

Although cruise revenues are generated from many different sources, the on-board sale of beverages usually ranks high in contribution to profits. Other large sources of on-board revenue would also normally include sale of shore excursions, retail sales from shops, and promotions of photo, beauty salon, and health spa services. With only 30% of passengers typically interested in gambling, casino revenues often do not contribute proportionately as much to total income (perhaps 10%) as is frequently assumed.

Also, as might be expected, the costs of providing various on-board services vary by type of market segment. For instance, excluding labor and overhead, food costs on a per diem or per passenger-day basis might be as high as $25 to $30 on the luxury end, as low as $8 to $11 for the mass market segment, and somewhere in between for so-called premium segment cruises.

Table 3.2. *1994 estimated average industry
economic profit per passenger*

Gross ticket revenue	$2,200
Discounts	−600
Less (Agency) Commission (@ 13%)[b]	−200
Air cost	−320
Transfers	−17
Credit card fees	−16
Plus on-board revenues	+250
Less on-board cost	−100
Less other variable cost:	
Reservation/documentation	−40
Food (7-day cruise)	−97
Economic profit per passenger[a]	$1,000

[a]Economic profit is defined as net total revenue less variable
cost.
[b]Travel agencies are the most important source of cruise line
bookings and most agencies derive a large and growing share
of their revenues from the cruise business (Section 2.2).
Source: Dickinson and Vladimir (1997, p 135).

However, because the operating (variable) costs of a cruise do not rise
proportionally with the number of passengers, the industry has moved to
increase the average ship-carrying capacity. Indeed, as ship size rises from
around 1,500 berths to 2,600 berths and with occupancy levels of around
100% (and ranging as high as 110% when more than two people are in a
cabin), the cash flow (EBITDA) margin before corporate expenses can move
up from 45% to 55%. The breakeven occupancy level for the larger ships
meanwhile tends to decline to 50% as compared to 60% for the smaller
ones.[10] But once a ship reaches the size of about 2,000 berths, the benefits
from further scaling up begin to rapidly diminish.

Table 3.2 shows the estimated average industry economic profit per passenger. Table 3.3 meanwhile provides a view of the cruise industry's recent
aggregate financial performance.

Economic aspects

Economic sensitivities Demand for cruise line services, like those for other
travel services, must ultimately be somewhat dependent on the overall health
of the economy, particularly as measured in terms of such factors as unemployment rates, interest rates, and the growth potential and availability of
disposable income. However, the industry has not been around long enough
in its current form to display a full range of potential change, and it cannot

Table 3.3. *Major cruise line operating performance: Composite of three companies, 1993–98*

	Revenues	Operating income	Operating margin[a] (%)	Assets	Operating cash flow
CAGR (%)[b]	15.9	20.6	4.0	20.1	20.1

[a] Average margin, 1993–98 = 20.2%.
[b] Compound annual growth rate.

yet be demonstrated that consumers of cruise ship services do indeed scale back the number of trips demanded during recession periods.

Marketing and price discrimination strategies The basics of marketing cruise ship vacation packages are similar to what they would be for any other consumer service with mass-market appeal. The emphasis, however, would likely be on the entertainment aspects of a cruise. Moreover, as in any other entertainment-related business, the percent of total operating budget spent on marketing and advertising as a percent of total costs per unit is rather high.

In economic terms, the objective in spending so much per unit on promotion is, as described in Chapter 1 (Figure 1.10), to shift the demand curve to the right of where it would otherwise be and to make the demand schedule more price-inelastic. In so doing, the ship operator can then also take better advantage of profit-enhancing price discrimination strategies that are similar to what airlines do by selling different seats at different prices (coach, business, first-class) even though all travelers arrive at the same destination at the same time. For the largest companies, advertising as a percent of revenues can range above 4.5%, and combined marketing, selling, and administrative expenses can top 13.5%.[11]

Sunk cost As in movie making, to use an example, the large capital costs of first building the ship are what economists would call – pardon the expression – "sunk costs." This means that once a vessel is ready to float, all further strategic decisions by management must be based on prospective returns in the future (i.e., the original cost of the ship then becomes irrelevant). In this respect, *Titanic* the movie and *Titanic* the ship were the same even though the movie ultimately stayed afloat much longer than the ship.

3.2 Automobiles

Jamming

Commercial production of automobiles began around the year 1900. As with most consumer products that are born of new design and manufacturing technologies, they were at first curiosities affordable only by the wealthiest people. Yet it didn't take long for costs to decline and for passenger cars to be priced so that people of average means could buy them. In the first decade alone, half a million cars were sold, and by 1930, 27 million were registered, with more than half of all U.S. families owning at least one car. Although growth slowed during the middle, war, and Depression-filled years of the twentieth century, by 1980, postwar prosperity pushed the incidence of car ownership to one in two persons, from one in five fifty years before.

Technology, of course, played a role in making cars more user-friendly and easier to manufacture. And as more of them were registered, political pressures for highway improvements rose accordingly, with the percentage of roads having paved surfaces increasing rapidly after 1920, when states adopted various registration fee and gasoline tax structures to finance road improvements. The extraordinary growth in automobile registrations combined with road improvements then had the effect of dramatically increasing the number of miles traveled – with much of the increase coming at the expense of the railroads (Figure 3.2a). As Meyer and Oster (1987, p. 177) noted:

total intercity travel by all modes (but excluding commuting) grew from 42 billion passenger miles in 1916 to 198 billion in 1929, with the automobile accounting for all the growth and its share increasing from less than 20 percent to over three quarters of the market in 1929. By 1940 intercity travel had increased to 330 billion passenger miles, and auto's share had reached 89 percent.

Although construction of Connecticut's Merritt Parkway and Pennsylvania's Turnpike in the late 1930s first enabled traffic to flow faster, it was not until the Interstate Highway system was initiated by an Act of Congress in 1956 that the quality of the road system had caught up with the capabilities of the cars. Once that had happened, intercity travel by automobile rose several-fold to over one trillion passenger-miles by 1970. However, the automobile's share of market also peaked around that time: Jet aircraft were beginning to take an increasing percentage of intercity traffic volume (Figure 3.2b).

Meanwhile, as Table 3.4 shows, Federal government spending on highways has been consistently greater on a proportional basis (representing about half of total outlays) than for any other mode of transportation. Despite these expenditures, traffic jams are today probably no less common than they were years ago. No matter what, Americans, and most other people as well, still love to travel in their cars.

Car rentals

The car rental business, with approximately 80% of its volume originating at airports, sits at the intersection of travel, where wings change into wheels. Yet the business has long been structured as an oligopoly in which four companies – Hertz, Avis, National, and Budget – dominate with a combined 80% share of a market that in the late 1990s generated nearly $15 billion

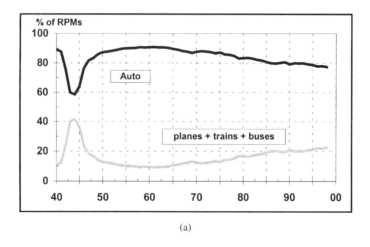

(a)

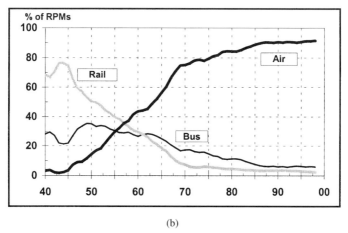

(b)

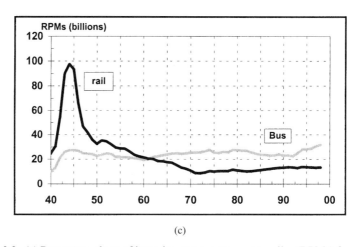

(c)

Figure 3.2. (a) Percentage share of intercity revenue passenger-miles (RPMs) for private carriers (automobile) versus public carriers (planes, trains, and buses), 1940–1998. (b) Percentage share of total public carrier intercity RPMs, 1940–98. (c) Bus and rail revenue passenger-miles, 1940–98. *Source:* U.S. Department of Transportation and *Transportation in America*, 1999. Washington, DC.: Eno Transportation Foundation, Inc.

Table 3.4. *Federal transportation outlays by mode (millions of current dollars), 1980–95*

	1980	1985	1990	1995
Air	3,762	4,947	7,305	10,389
Highway	11,706	15,031	15,452	20,082
Transit	3,307	3,427	3,832	4,474
Rail	2,170	1,057	534	1,034
Water	2,837	3,065	3,069	3,675
Total[a]	23,961	27,715	30,391	40,031

[a] Also includes outlays for pipelines and general support.
Source: U.S. Dept. of Transportation.

in revenues.[12] In the United States, this market is funneled through approximately 7,000 airport locations and another 20,000 others routinely located at car dealers or service stations. For many locations outside the United States, franchise arrangements are also used. Depending on location, a typical agreement might call for between 5% and 7.5% of gross rental revenues to go to the franchisor.

At first glance, the business of renting cars to travelers seems simple enough. The price paid by the renter is somewhat proportionate to the length of time for which the car is rented and the value of the car. The priced paid would, of course, also be sensitive to local-market competitive conditions. And revenues per transaction are higher from leisure than from business rentals because leisure rentals are generally for longer periods. Profit would result when the rental price received exceeds the all-in costs of buying and holding the vehicle and of administration and marketing to customers. Travel agencies, which book between one fourth and one half of all rental agreements, would be entitled to earn 5% of sales for corporate bookings and 10% for other types of bookings.

Nevertheless, a significant part of a rental company's profit may be derived from the difference between prices paid for cars (whether leased or bought outright) and the prices for which they are sold after being used by customers. In dominant companies such as Hertz, with a 30% share of the U.S. market, it is not unusual to find that most of the cars acquired (80%+) will be bought under manufacturer repurchase agreements wherein the repurchase price is subject to mileage, repair, and depreciation-schedule charges. Because such arrangements tend to limit the rental company's residual risk, cars acquired under these conditions are referred to in the industry as "nonrisk".[13] Thus the cost and the availability of suitable cars are important variables in the determination of profits.

Underlying this, however, is a trade-off between the length of time that a car is owned by the rental company and the car's ultimate depreciated

Table 3.5. *Major U.S. car rental company operating performance: Composite of three companies, 1993–98*

	Revenues	Operating income	Operating margin (%)[a]	Assets	Operating cash flow
CAGR (%)[b]	16.8	32.5	13.4	21.1	25.1

[a] Average margin, 1993–98 = 6.1%.
[b] Compound annual growth rate.

value on resale. The longer the vehicle is owned, the more rental turns it can potentially generate, with the average fixed cost per rental declining over time even as the variable costs of maintenance and repairs inevitably begin to rise. The larger companies will usually hold a car for an average of around six to seven months, although some may be kept for up to a year.

From a macroeconomic standpoint, the rental business is somewhat sensitive to general economic conditions and also more specifically to airline industry prospects and prices. Almost by definition, in prosperous times, both airlines and rental companies will benefit from strong pricing of their services and relatively benign behavior of fuel, borrowing, and labor costs – all of which are important to both of these similarly capital- and labor-intensive industries. Because of the close linkages between them, with one segment largely feeding the other, capacity utilization trends (fleet utilization in cars and load factors in airlines) must track, up and down, more or less in tandem. This implies that car rental company profitability is apt to be cyclically volatile, with operating and financial leverage relatively high.

From a microeconomic standpoint, the goal of the car rental company is to maximize fleet utilization at the highest possible price. Again, here, marketing and price-discrimination (i.e., yield management) strategies and reservation systems retain their importance in the overall scheme of operations. Yet the analytical framework remains comparable to that applied to other oligopolistic, capital- and labor-intensive industry segments. Table 3.5 shows the composite financial operating performance of several major car rental companies: Table 3.6 provides a comparison of major company attributes.

3.3 Kings of the road

The first scheduled intercity bus service in the United States began in 1913 in Minnesota using a seven-passenger Hupmobile that frequently broke down and whose arrival time was unpredictable.[14] However, even without a network of good roads at the time, travel by bus flourished and, by the mid-1920s, over 4,000 companies were competing.

Table 3.6. *Major U.S. car rental company attributes, 1998*

	Fleet size U.S./foreign	% of revenues at airport locations	Locations worldwide[a]	% business/leisure
Hertz	263,000/168,000	82	5,500	54/46
Avis	206,000/N.A.	85	4,200	64/36
Budget	95,000/N.A.	74	3,200	50/50

[a]Owned & franchised, N.A. = not available.
Source: Company reports.

Nevertheless, regulations soon began to spread and almost every state had some, with the earliest regulations focused primarily on issues of passenger safety and highway maintenance. Later regulations evolved into protection from competition on intrastate routes, and it took a Supreme Court ruling in 1925 to break the monopoly patterns that were being established. The turbulent conditions that came with the opening of interstate routes to competition then led to passage of the Motor Carrier Act in 1935. At that point, the Interstate Commerce Commission (ICC) became the regulator of interstate bus fares, safety, routes, mergers, and financial fitness.[15]

Such fitness was especially important given that the government had begun to see the industry as a capital-intensive public utility deserving overview similar to that which had already been long applied to the railroads.[16] As a result, the government did not object to the many mergers and consolidations between carriers that occurred starting in the mid-1920s. Formation of national bus systems ensued and demand for long-distance services then increased rapidly. Already by 1930, Greyhound had emerged as the dominant carrier, operating major routes and holding many intrastate as well as all major transcontinental rights. The only significant competition to Greyhound was fostered by the ICC, which certified new interstate bus operators and the creation of many railroad-owned bus subsidiaries. In 1936 several of these subsidiaries formed the National Trailways System, a company that eventually evolved into Continental Trailways.[17]

As can be seen in Figure 3.2c, the bus industry's carriage volume still amounts to approximately 28 billion revenue passenger-miles a year. It had, however, been as high as 27 billion passenger-miles in 1945, at the end of World War II. Since then, however, bus ridership has steadily lost share of the intercity travel market, from nearly 10% in the mid-1940s to 2.5% by 1960, and to around 1% currently. Rising disposable income of the population at large combined with declining relative prices and technological improvements in other modes of travel had early on begun to shift ridership over to planes, to cars, and even to trains once the government-subsidized Amtrak began (in the 1970s) to compete on price in the Northeast.

With industry operating costs as a percent of revenues rising to 95% in the late 1970s from an average of between 85 to 88% during the postwar period, profit-pinched industry managements began to seek the regulatory relief that Congress provided in 1982 with passage of the Bus Regulatory Reform Act. The significantly loosened controls that followed have allowed operators such as Greyhound to extend their brand names and to lower costs through implementation of franchising arrangements with local carriers. Bus operators have also developed charter services that now account for about half of all intercity revenue passenger miles. Nevertheless, intercity buses are now used mostly for trips of under 200 miles and/or between cities not served well or at all by air and rail transportation.

Because growth has remained sluggish and profits have been largely evanescent, the industry has evolved into a bifurcated structure, being almost monopolistic on some routes and monopolistic-competitive on others. As with other transportation modes, the costs of fuel, labor, and capital are important variables in the determination of profitability. Indeed, the industry's profile of capital intensity is similar enough to that of the airline and rail industries that many of the equipment leasing and other tax-advantaged financing methods discussed in Chapter 2 apply here as well.

3.4 Iron and steel

One hundred years ago passenger trains, accounting for almost all intercity travel, were the only effective means of high-speed travel suitable for long distances. But throughout the twentieth century, technological advances, particularly in the form of internal combustion and jet engines, worked to the relative disadvantage of the railroads just as such change had worked to their benefit in the century before. Consequently, the market share of long-distance intercity travel carried by rail has currently slipped to below 1% of revenue passenger-miles as compared to nearly 100% at the dawn of the automobile's era circa 1900. Still, even today, there remain times and places in which travel by rail retains not only its peculiar charm but an efficiency advantage as well.

Although rail regulations served as a model for later regulations applied to the airline and bus industries, governments were initially little involved in the early development of railroads. In fact, the emerging railroads had competed successfully against the many government owned and sponsored canal and turnpike companies of the mid-1800s and had bankrupted most of them.

By the 1870s, however, overcapacity had sparked rate wars among competing freight carriers and peace was not restored until monopolistic rate and revenue-pooling agreements between carriers had been negotiated. Ultimately, complaints against these agreements led Congress to pass, in 1887, what is known as the Interstate Commerce Act. The Act created the Interstate Commerce Commission (ICC) and required that rates be set at reasonable levels while also outlawing discriminatory pricing and pooling practices among carriers. The Hepburn Act of 1906 (followed by the Mann–Elkins Act in 1910) then gave the ICC legal power to set rate ceilings and to issue more stringent regulations against alleged monopolistic practices.

The first peak for rail ridership came in 1920 at 47 billion passenger-miles. After that came a series of events and technological developments – the recession of 1921, the Great Depression, and most significantly, buses, cars, and planes – that caused a persistent drop-off in ridership. The railroads tried to stem the decline by replacing older equipment with new, air-conditioned trains with sleeping cars, but any gains in ridership were short-lived. In fact, after 1945, the year of a second (wartime) peak (Figure 3.2c), demand for passenger rail service began to fall progressively faster each year.

Although there was some controversy as to how railroad companies allocated their costs between freight and passenger services, there was no doubt that, by the 1950s, passenger service deficits were large enough to offset an estimated 30% to 40% of the rail industry's operating profits derived from carriage of freight. At the time, shippers had also begun to complain that the ICC was forcing them to subsidize passenger service by allowing high rates for freight. And in those years, the financial strain on rail companies became so great that there was no recourse but for them to cut back on passenger services.

The trouble was that when such service cutbacks were attempted, local political pressures were often sufficient to deny the railroads' abandonment petitions. Congress was finally forced to provide some regulatory relief measures in the Transportation Act of 1958. But service abandonments nevertheless remained as much a political as an economic issue through the 1960s. And it was not until 1970, when Congress created the National Rail Passenger Corporation, commonly known as Amtrak, that a potentially more viable solution to this problem was devised. Although Amtrak was founded as a quasi-governmental for-profit corporation that has survived into the twenty-first century, it has yet to earn a profit and it remains dependent on annual operating subsidies (nearly $1 billion annually in the late 1990s) that come out of Federal budget appropriations (Table 3.4).[18]

In all, rail is now competitive on an operating and capital cost basis only over a few short-haul, high-density routes (which are typical of those between European cities). However, in the United States, travel by rail is unlikely to totally disappear because the public is still willing to provide subsidies of various types.[19] Travel by air, car, or bus is usually much more cost effective on a per passenger or per mile operating basis. Table 3.7 compares average passenger revenue per passenger-mile by mode.[20]

3.5 Finance and accounting issues

Financial and accounting issues for companies providing services on land or sea are much the same as for airlines. The initial cost of each equipment

Table 3.7. *Average passenger revenue per passenger-mile (current cents) by mode, 1960–97*

Year	Air carrier, domestic, scheduled service	Class I bus, intercity[a]	Commuter rail	Intercity/Amtrak
1997	13.9	11.9	14.1	17.3
1995	13.5	12.2	13.1	14.6
1990	13.4	11.6	13.5	14.1
1985	12.2	9.9	12.1	11.3
1980	11.5	7.3	6.7	8.2
1975	7.7	4.9	4.6	5.7
1970	6.0	3.6	3.8	4.0
1965	6.1	2.9	3.3	3.1
1960	6.1	2.7	2.9	3.0

[a] Regular route intercity service.
Source: Bureau of Transportation Statistics, National Transportation Statistics 99.

unit, be it a locomotive, a cruise ship, or a fleet of cars is enormous, and the securities markets for debt and equity are both usually tapped at least to some degree. Equipment trust certificate financing and sale-leaseback arrangements (as detailed in Chapter 2) are also frequently encountered as there are normally purely financial or other companies that can take better advantage of tax and financing conditions than can the operators of such travel businesses. This is particularly evident when, as happens in a period of economic recession, cash flows are skimpy compared to needs, public equity and debt are relatively expensive, and tax-loss carry-forwards are so large that the value of a depreciation tax shield to the operating company is minimal.

Equipment depreciation schedules will otherwise follow Internal Revenue Service guidelines (Section 168) for the particular class of asset. For instance, cars are allowed to be depreciated on an accelerated basis over 5 years (so-called 5-year property), whereas a jet plane is usually 20 years and a ship or vessel up to 30 years.

In the case of car rental companies, purchases of cars are financed through funds from operations and borrowing programs. At-risk cars as well as those nonrisk cars not returned to the manufacturer are sold through auctions and at used-car dealer locations. At Hertz, for example, upon sale of a car, the difference between the net proceeds from sale and the remaining book value is recorded as an adjustment to depreciation in the period when sold.

3.6 Concluding remarks

One hundred or so years ago, rail was the only way to really travel in style over long distances. And the only way to cross the oceans was by large steamship.

The trips were surely adventuresome and exciting for the passengers of those days, but no one would think of a long train ride or ocean crossing as a vacation or as a form of entertainment. Travelers of the time didn't have a choice: Airplanes, cars, buses, and cruise ships hadn't yet been sufficiently developed for carriage of high-volume commercial traffic.

Today we take all of these forms of carriage for granted, with travel by air the dominant mode for carriage over medium to long distances. For the foreseeable future, it is likely that current modes of transportation will be improved upon in small increments that are more evolutionary than revolutionary. Technologically enhanced (e.g., magnetic levitation) high-speed intricate rails have, for example, been conceptualized for many years and may one day become cost effective. And a new generation of supersonic planes is nearly certain to be in service within a decade or two.

Perhaps one hundred years from now, another mode of transportation, probably just now incubating in the scientific laboratories, will take hold. We can only speculate at what such new modes might be.

Selected additional reading

Brannigan, M. (1999). "Cruise Lines Look to the Land to Get Boomers on Board," *Wall Street Journal*, December 6.

De Lisser, E. (1995). "Forecast for Cruise Industry Is Stormy, and Some of the Smaller Fleets May Sink," *Wall Street Journal*, November 24.

Finch, C. (1992). *Highways to Heaven: The Auto Biography of America*. New York: HarperCollins.

Frantz, D. (1999a). "For Cruise Ships' Workers, Much Toil, Little Protection," *New York Times*, December 24.

    (1999b) "Alaskans Choose Sides in Battle Over Cruise Ships," *New York Times*, November 29.

Kay, J. H. (1997). *Asphalt Nation: How the Automobile Took Over America, and How We Can Take It Back*. New York: Crown.

Lubove, S. (1999). "Floating Pork Barrel," *Forbes*, 163(9)(May 3).

Machalaba, D. (1997) "Amtrak Quietly Hauls Cargo on Its Trains, to the Horror of Rivals," *Wall Street Journal*, July 30.

Miller, L., and Stern, G. (1996). "Car-Rental Companies Neglect Core Business, Often Skid into Losses," *Wall Street Journal*," February 15.

Norton, R. (1997). "Train Ride to Nowhere," *Fortune*, February 17.

Raoul, J-C. (1997), "How High-Speed Trains Make Tracks," *Scientific American*, 277(4) (October).

Part III
Being there

4
Hotels

A Head in Every Bed

That's the goal of every lodging enterprise. But as shall soon become evident, achievement of this objective is easier said than done. Many factors come into play: the state of the economy in general, the specific supply/demand features for the industry as a whole, and, of course – as the old real estate saying goes – location, location, and location.

4.1 Rooms at the inn

The airline business is a creation of the twentieth century: It wouldn't exist were it not for the significant technological advances made over the past one hundred years. By contrast, the lodging business has been around for thousands of years, pretty much since the beginning of mankind. The basics of the lodging industry are relatively simple; however, the operational and financial features have, in recent years, become increasingly complex and sophisticated.

The earliest versions of what we have come to know as a hotel or inn go back to the earliest days of recorded history. "Inns" dotted the main Roman roads that led to ancient Britain, and later, in the Middle Ages, hospitality was dispensed by monasteries that provided travelers with separate dormitories. In thirteenth century China, inns were relay houses established by the Mongols to accommodate travelers and provide a postal service. A *ryokan* is simply a traditional Japanese inn.

By 1604, inns must have been pretty important to the communities of that time because an act was passed in England that said, "the ancient, true and proper use of Inns, Alehouses and Victualling Houses was for the Receipt, Relief and Lodging of Wayfaring People traveling from Place to Place and not meant for the entertainment and harbouring of Lewd and Idle People to spend and consume their Money and Time in Lewd and Drunken Manner."[1]

Most early guests shared their accommodations with strangers and often set their own rate of payment. And because most guests arrived singly on foot or by horse or stagecoach there was no need for a large number of rooms. Innkeepers, located primarily along well-traveled routes, were often just homeowners with some extra space and a willingness to provide food and lodging services. Indeed, for most of recorded history, hotels remained small, more like what nowadays would be called an inn or a "bed and breakfast" than a Hilton or Marriott.

Although the word "inn" has been used since the 1400s, the word "hotel," which first appeared in London in the mid-1700s, is derived from the Old French *ostel*. The term came to characterize facilities in Europe and America that could shelter and feed travelers in what could at first be best described as a furnished mansion.

The industry's modern roots, however, go back only to the early 1900s. In 1919, for example, legend has it that on the way to buy a bank, Conrad Hilton bought the Mobley Hotel of Cisco, Texas because that was the only way he could get a place to sleep. The hotel, of course, went on to become the first of a worldwide chain, and the Hilton name became practically synonymous with the word hotel.

In the 1930s and 1940s, the lodging industry gradually evolved into larger nationwide chains largely through buyouts of older, established major city properties. Not much new construction was completed in those decades, scarred as they were by the Great Depression and World War II. More rapid expansion had to await the end of the war, arrival of the middle class baby-boom generation, the sprawl of new suburban communities, technological improvements that opened up air travel to the general public, and construction of the federally funded Interstate Highway System that was born with passage of the Interstate Highway Act of 1956.

Indeed, the new roads were built just in time to feed traffic to new roadside motor hotels, the motels, that had begun to spring up all around the country. And the man most credited with popularizing a family-friendly version of these motels by including in the price of every room the now common but then-revolutionary amenities such as swimming pools, free parking, television sets, and air conditioning was Kemmons Wilson, a Memphis entrepreneur. Wilson built the first Holiday Inn in 1952 and was soon able to expand the concept nationwide via franchising. Shortly thereafter, chains such as Howard Johnson, Hyatt, Marriott, Radisson, and Ramada were similarly formed.

By the 1960s and 1970s, most of the large chains were well established in the United States and their attention turned to overseas markets, where conditions seemed ripe for expansion. The broadening of the airline customer base that developed in response to airline price deregulation and introduction of jet-propelled wide-bodied aircraft such as the Boeing 747 (see Section 2.1) made this possible. For the most part, the lodging industry came out of the great inflation and oil-shortage years of the 1970s in reasonably good shape.

During this time, however, there was also a steady improvement of hotel management systems, which enhanced productivity through introduction of automated reservation systems and computers into virtually every phase of operations. Moreover, it was commonly thought that such computerization would lead readily to vertical integration of airlines and hotels. The idea of the same company capturing all of the traveler's spending – from home to hotel and back again – sounded better in theory than it actually worked in practice.[2]

In the early to mid part of the 1980s, a favorable tax environment featuring accelerated depreciation schedules and easy bank lending policies (boosted by deregulation of the savings and loan industry) stimulated a hotel construction boom that added more rooms than the market could easily absorb. Accelerated depreciation, in particular, increased the attractiveness of hotels as investments that could provide tax shelter against other sources of income and allowed hotels to be operated at a paper loss. Its introduction also underscored the distinctions between the functions of hotel management as opposed to hotel ownership; in other words, the differences between the lodging versus the real estate sides of the business.[3]

Although changes in the Tax Reform Act of 1986, the most extensive since 1954, helped end the room boom, it was at least another seven years before new demand caught up with older supply.[4] The late 1980s were also characterized by a rising number of hotel transactions, by aggressive bidding for so-called trophy properties that related to the Japanese economic bubble of that time, and by the overleveraging of assets to the point where the servicing of debts began to consume more than 10% of industry revenues.[5]

Economic recession and the Persian Gulf War in the early 1990s stunted the lodging industry's growth for a while. But as Figure 4.1 illustrates, by the middle of the 1990s, profits again soared as sharply rising demand finally absorbed the room glut created in the second half of the 1980s and allowed room rates for higher-end major properties to be significantly raised. Yet the apparent prosperity of these times could not relieve the pressures from shareholders for even greater efficiency, which continues through consolidation of hotel chains and brands into just a few large companies. In all, as Table 4.1 indicates, there were almost 29 million hotel beds in the world in 1997. And between 1980 and 1997, the number has been rising at an average annual rate of 3.5%. The industry's milestone events are shown in Figure 4.2.

Table 4.1. *Hotels and similar establishments – accommodation capacity:*
thousands of bed-places and market share, 1980, 1985, 1997

	Bed-places (thousands)			Market share (%)		
	1980	1985	1997	1980	1985	1997
Europe	8,542	8,637	11,375	52.5	47.3	39.3
Americas	6,436	6,933	9,334	39.5	38.0	32.2
E. Asia/Pacific	763	1,694	6,708	4.7	9.3	23.2
Africa	269	525	825	1.7	2.9	2.8
Middle East	141	254	400	0.9	1.4	1.4
South Asia	126	198	310	0.8	1.1	1.1
Total	16,277	18,241	28,952	100.0	100.0	100.0

Source: Tourism Highlights, 1999, WTO.

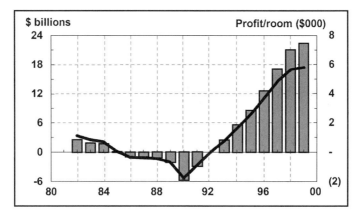

Figure 4.1. Lodging aggregate industry profit, bars (left), and per room, line (right),
1982–99. *Source* data: Smith Travel Research.

4.2 Basics

Structural features

The modern hotel industry is engaged in three distinct activities: owning,
managing, and franchising. The industry can be classified as one in which
chains are oligopolistic in terms of their major properties and largely
monopolistic-competitive for all their smaller brands.[6]

However, the industry may be viewed from many different perspectives
depending on the need of the viewer. For instance, hotels can be segmented
by their target markets (city-center versus roadside motel), by the prices they
are able to charge (luxury, mid-range, budget), or by the types of specialized

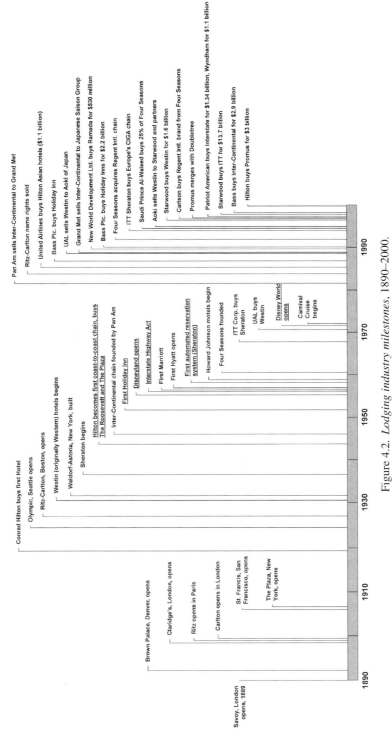

Figure 4.2. *Lodging industry milestones, 1890–2000.*

services and amenities they primarily provide (resort destination, airport, convention, all-suite, casinos). Over time, different segments respond differently to changes in overall economic and local competitive positions. Therefore, even a nationwide surge of construction in one type of property does not necessarily have to have a noticeable affect on the pricing of properties in other segments. The mix of ownership, management, and franchising activities will also determine a company's risk/reward profile and sensitivity to economic changes.

On the whole, though, the hotel industry may be characterized as being especially capital and labor intensive, seasonal, and able to generate large cash flow from depreciation. But unlike airline operations, which tend to have thin margins, hotel margins tend to fall into a wide range of possible outcomes that relate to a combination of local, national, and sometimes international conditions.

Operating features

As of the year 2000, the lodging industry in the United States – accounting for about half the world total – will extend across some 50,000 properties configured into approximately 4 million rooms that generate revenues of nearly $100 billion and pretax profits of around $21 billion. Generally, in the United States and elsewhere, the reasons for travel might typically fall into the following categories even though significant variation from these averages will occur depending on season, region, type of property, and price.

Purpose of trip	Percent of total
Vacation	25
Transient business	30
Conference or group meeting	25
Other, family, or personal	20

No matter what the purpose, however, the first and most important characteristic of the lodging facility is its location. In the case of urban hotels, proximity to the centers of business, shopping, and cultural activities is important. In contrast, for resorts the main feature is that of being located *away* from the normal home and business environments.

Nevertheless, room rates, the prices that the lodging facility can charge the traveler, are significantly determined often as much by location as by any other qualities. Because posted room ("rack") rates are often discounted and because not all rooms may be in service at all times, the industry uses measures such as the *average daily rate* (ADR) or *revenues per available room* (RevPAR). The ADR is derived by dividing total rooms sales by rooms

Table 4.2. *Market mix change comparison, effect on ADR, 500-room hotel (15,000 room-nights per month)*

	Mix A			Mix B		
	Room-nights sold	Weighted avg. rate ($)	Total sales ($)	Room-nights sold	Weighted avg. rate ($)	Total sales ($)
Individual commercial	2,250	100	225,000	2,750	100	275,000
Corporate	4,500	85	382,500	4,500	85	382,500
Tour	3,000	70	210,000	2,500	70	175,000
Conferences & conventions	1,500	75	112,500	1,500	75	112,500
Interline	750	50	37,500	750	50	37,500
Total occupied room-nights	12,000			12,000		
Occupancy	80.0%			80.0%		
Total room sales			967,500			982,500
ADR		80.63			81.88	

Source: Modified from Murthy and Dev (1993).

occupied and is thus a weighted average room rate of all the rooms sold on a particular day. And total inventory is measured in terms *of room-nights* – a property's average available number of rooms times days in the year that theoretically could generate income if the property were to be sold-out every night.

Hotel managements always strive to improve the ADR by changing the mix of guests because even a small upward change in ADR can significantly boost profitability given that fixed and semifixed costs of operations are often 40 to 50% of total costs. Table 4.2 illustrates the impact of a change from Mix A, heavily weighted with tour groups, to Mix B, weighted more toward individual travelers. The $1.25 step-up in ADR would contribute an additional $180,000 (12 months × 12,000 room nights a month × $1.25) of revenue per year, most of which would fall to the bottom line.

However, sometimes a more useful statistic, adopted from airline lingo, is yield per room (YPR). YPR usually provides a more realistic picture of operating performance (when occupancy and ADR are inversely related) than ADR alone because it is calculated by dividing rooms sales by *available* room-nights instead of *occupied* room-nights. It is indeed entirely possible to have a situation involving two adjacent hotels of the same size wherein the one with a lower ADR generates a higher YPR. YPR may also be simply expressed as:

YPR = occupancy rate (%) × average daily rate ($).

The overriding economic principle applied to the setting of per diem room rates is that of price discrimination as discussed in Chapter 1. Hotels will attempt to charge what the market will bear, which is always a function of the customer's ability and willingness to pay: The same room sold at a different time to a different customer will command a different price. In other words, price elasticity is not a constant but is instead a variable in the pricing decision.

Hotels, like airlines, have found a way to technologically address this essential price and room-allocation problem through the use of *yield management* methods that take into account the ongoing seasonal and other shifts in demand for room inventory on a real-time basis. Implicit in these programs are also considerations about the class of available rooms, the probable timing of incoming reservations, and the probable price discounts needed to encourage further sales. In practice, yield management systems are most effective if, as Vallen and Vallen (1996, p.104) note, all or most of the following conditions are present:

- Demand can be clearly segregated into distinct market segments.
- A large percentage of room reservations have a long lead time.
- The property provides a variety of different room types and room rates.
- Demand fluctuates significantly between periods of high and low occupancy.

Although the costs of construction, hotel purchase, and renovation fall into the category of "sunk" costs that (as discussed in previous chapters) should be irrelevant to future pricing strategies, these elements still also occasionally enter into pricing decisions. A reflection of this appears in the industry's conventional rule-of-thumb suggesting an ADR equal to one-thousandth the average construction cost of the room. By this rule, for example, a 200-room hotel built at a cost of $20 million ought to have an ADR of $100 (20 million divided by 200 divided by 1,000).[7]

Moreover, just as in the airline-seat, broadcast-time, or fresh fruit businesses, perishability of product underlies the economic dynamic of room pricing. The revenue that a room might earn is gone forever once the day that it is empty passes. Thus, as the potential use date approaches, there is particular pressure to discount the room price even though this ought to a degree be offset by the need to keep a few rooms available for last-minute bookings which can often be sold at *higher* than average prices that desperate latecomers might be willing to pay.

The end result of the interplay among factors such as room rates, seasonality, degree of local competition, local room taxes, location, national economic conditions, and price discrimination tactics is then finally reflected in the hotel's *occupancy* rate, which is basically a measure of a property's capacity utilization. Since the late 1980s the average occupancy rate for the whole industry has generally ranged between 62 to 65%. This compares to an estimated industrywide breakeven occupancy rate that, according to PricewaterhouseCoopers research, declined (in part as a result of lower debt and equity financing costs) to approximately 55.5% in 1998 as compared to 62.6% in 1992.[8] Figure 4.3 illustrates occupancy and ADR trends for the industry.

In summary, then, on the microeconomic level, hotels operate in very much the same way as do airlines or theme parks. The sunk and initial fixed costs are high, most marginal revenue after breakeven is highly incremental to profits, and typically up to half of the operating cost structure may be variable.

Department data Hotel operations are a composite of many different businesses all rolled into one. Although hotels are defined as places that provide overnight lodging for travelers, they most often do much more than just make a bed, bath, and bureau drawer available to guests. Hotels will typically provide food and beverage services. And operations can be further broken down into categories such as housekeeping, telephone, retail stores, and convention sales, as examples. The degree of emphasis on each area will vary with the nature of the property's market niche. A full-service luxury hotel would provide a wide array of services and require many operating departments. On the other end, a budget motel might not provide anything more than a room and a bed and not have even a basic food and beverage facility on the premises.

No matter what the extent of services, however, operating ratios for each department illuminate a property's financial performance and productivity trends. Over time each type of property will develop standard expected ratios for each department and any significant deviations from the standards will then alert the property's managers to either problems or opportunities for improvements. Is the food costing too much? Is the liquor being stolen? Is the housekeeping department over or understaffed? All of these questions can only begin to be addressed if the department operating ratios are analyzed and compared to normal expected values.

Although it is possible to calculate hundreds of different operating ratios, the most important ratios would involve the rooms and the food and beverage departments. The first breakdown would be to see what percent of total sales are derived from rooms, food and beverage, telephone, retail shopping, etc. The next breakdown would involve the matching of expense to revenue categories, so that each department's operating profit margin and contribution to total operating income can be seen. For a mid-market urban hotel, for example, the rooms department might generate two to three times the operating margin of the food department. Further calculations such as average food and beverage spending per room, cost of maintenance per room and so forth would, of course, also provide useful information for management.

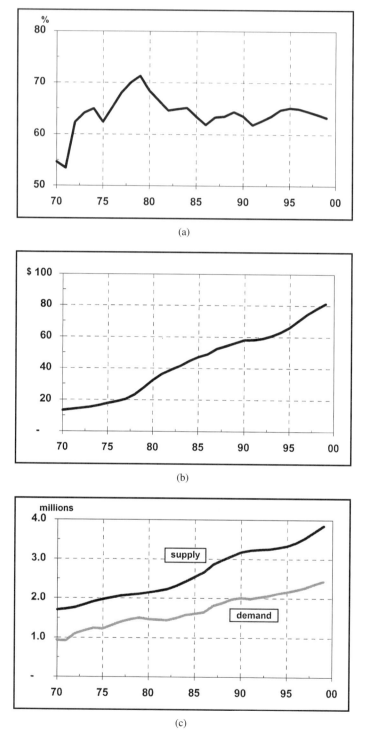

Figure 4.3. (a) Average hotel occupancy rates, (b) average daily hotel room rates, and (c) hotel industry room supply and demand, 1970–99. *Source:* PricewaterhouseCoopers, Smith Travel Research.

Table 4.3. *Hotel department ratio to sales, selected regions, 1996*

	Total world	Asia	Europe	Latin America	North America
Occupancy (%)	67.7	72.9	64.6	62.7	69.2
Average Number rooms	236	304	168	200	284
Average rate ($)	87.42	104.04	78.50	76.61	90.65
Revenue					
Rooms	59.2	57.3	50.9	58.8	66.6
Food & Beverage	33.2	33.4	41.9	28.7	26.8
Telephone	2.6	3.1	2.1	4.2	2.5
Other income	5.1	6.2	5.2	8.3	4.1
Total revenues	100.0	100.0	100.0	100.0	100.0
Departmental expenses					
Rooms	28.6	22.5	33.1	27.7	26.4
Food & Beverage	76.8	73.1	71.9	81.5	80.0
Telephone	69.0	85.1	66.9	94.8	60.9
Other dept. expenses	2.1	1.8	2.2	3.6	1.8
Total dept. expenses	44.8	39.9	49.4	44.4	41.6
Total departmental profit	55.2	60.1	50.6	55.6	58.4
Undistributed operating expenses	25.0	23.3	21.2	30.9	28.2
Gross operating profit	30.2	36.8	29.4	24.7	30.2

Source: Horwath Worldwide Hotel Industry Study, 1997.

But generally, it is the *labor cost percentage* – determined by dividing total department labor costs by total department revenue – that will be among the most important in providing a benchmark overview of operations (with food and beverage usually the highest ratio). Table 4.3 shows the revenue and cost structures in terms of average ratios to sales for hotels operating in the late 1990s. The gross operating profit line at the bottom of this table is of particular significance because it is directly related to the industry's standard measure of profitability: Earnings before interest, taxes, depreciation, and amortization (EBITDA) taken as a percentage of revenue. A hotel running at an EBITDA margin of 35% or above is generally considered by financial analysts to be doing well.

Management contracts Often the owner of a property, perhaps a local builder or business entity, seeks the appreciation potential of a property's real estate and access to its cash flow but has no particular expertise in management of the hotel's operations. In other instances, a hotel chain prefers to spread its scarce capital over more units by taking a small (or no) share of equity in a property. In both instances, a management contract, which is an agreement between the principal hotel owner and a management company, takes advantage of a hotel chain's brand. It is the brand that creates the contract's value and it is the brand that attracts the customers and owners.

Management companies, usually owned by the chains, have the expertise in hotel operations that an owner might not have. And through management contracts a chain can enhance its brand name and capture a greater flow of activity over which to amortize costly investments in design and reservation systems infrastructure. Because of the minimal capital invested, hotel chains will usually find that management contracts are among their most profitable activities.

Management contracts are complex legal and financial documents that may specify a broad range of operations (including the construction phase) over which the management company has control. For the management company, however, the key element is that it is paid whether or not the hotel is profitable. When business conditions are poor, it is the owner that suffers the loss, and when things are going well, it is the owner that reaps the reward. Nevertheless, there are variations on this theme, with incentives built into most contracts so that the management company would benefit to a degree from any pickup in profitability.

Competition among many hotel management companies limits the fees that can be charged in most markets. Typically a management contract fee will be at least 4% of total property revenues or $750 per available room per year. The contracts can be structured in terms of pre-opening and post-opening responsibilities and may also include a mixture of both basic and incentive fees that vary according to the degree to which predetermined performance targets are met. In particular, incentive fees are often based on total income before fixed charges and management fees (IBFCMF), and, in practice, the larger the basic fee, the smaller the incentive fee. For example, as Andrew and Schmidgall (1993, p. 350) note, "an incentive fee may be 15% of IBFCMF when the basic fee is 2% of gross revenue, or 10% of IBFCMF when the basic fee is 4% of gross revenue."

Franchising Hotel companies have increasingly become global brand marketing organizations that look to franchising – the licensing of an exclusive territorial right to a name, a product or a system – as a way to expand and to leverage up their brand equity through an enlarged distribution system. For the hotel chain, a franchising arrangement can enhance profitability because fees earned from franchise operations are relatively large as compared to the amount of capital invested. And, as a local business, the franchisee is also more likely than a large, distant, operator to be responsive to local market needs and conditions (even though this does not necessarily preclude franchising by large companies). However, it is usually the franchisee that, operating as a small-business independent entity, arranges and is liable for construction and ownership of the hospitality property.

In return for various fees, the chain management provides the franchisee with considerable support that would often include site feasibility studies, help in financing, mass purchasing discounts on supplies, advertising, and perhaps most important of all, access to the chain's reservation and yield management systems and frequent traveler programs. From the standpoint of the customer, there should in theory then be no discernible difference in service between the chain's owned and operated properties and those that are franchised.

In practice, though, it is not unusual for franchise operators (especially those of the mom and pop variety) to come into conflict with the chain's management over fees, upkeep requirements, and territorial infringement issues. Franchisors also sometimes have problems with slow-paying, nonconforming franchisees, some of whom may also be skimming (i.e., excluding some sales from gross sales used as a base for calculation of various franchise fees). An even larger risk for franchisors is that franchisees milk the brand (and thus weaken it) by maintaining minimal standards while enjoying RevPAR premiums obtained from the brand's power to attract customers. Because of such conflicts, properties sometimes change allegiances, every few years flying a different chain's flag.

Although fee structures can vary, the typical terms of a franchise agreement would call for a fairly large initial fee that is scaled to the number of rooms in the property, a royalty of 4% of room revenues, an advertising fee of 1.5% of room revenues, a reservation fee of 3.0% of room revenues (or alternatively a fixed dollar amount per reservation), and various other small charges for signs and other services provided to the franchisee.

Time-shares (VOIs) The subject of time-sharing of hotel units (that are more typically condominium units purposely built with kitchen, living room, and other such amenities) could just as easily fit into either of the following sections on marketing or finance; it contains elements of both. As of 1999, more than 2 million Americans had bought time-shares. And according to the American Resort Development Association, a trade group, industry revenues had reached $3.5 billion through sales of a record 318,000 time-share weeks.

Most major chains, particularly those with properties in destination-resort locations have developed programs that permit vacationers to buy the guaranteed right to use a room for a few days a week each year and/or to swap such rights for someone else's right at another location. The rights to use the hotel's facilities through such vacation ownership interests (VOIs) extend for a number of years into the future, often the life of the time-share purchaser. Such rights are generally structured in one of five ways: time-share ownership, interval ownership, leasehold time-sharing, vacation licenses, and club memberships. Of these structures, time-share ownership is by far the most common, entailing transfer of a fee simple estate to the purchaser.[9]

In return for a relatively large upfront payment plus a commitment to pay annual maintenance and other fees, the purchaser of these time-share contracts has what amounts to the equivalent of an equity interest in a lodging at a favorite destination resort. The buyer is guaranteed the space at a nearly fixed cost even if regular room rates in the same property were to double or triple over time and even if it is impossible for non-VOI guests to get a reservation. The buyer also must put up only a fraction of what alternative lodging from, say, renting or buying a vacation house in the same resort area might cost. Up to fifty-two other buyers – one for each week of the year (but typically fifty-one, allowing one week for renovation) – may be contributing to the total buyers' pool.

For the hotel company, this is close to nirvana, although the property owner does run the risk that unanticipated high inflation could eventually impair the value of this kind of contract. Still, initial property development profits will usually be quite high. Sales of the time-share interests will normally cover a significant part (if not all) of the total investment in development of a property, thereby allowing the resort developer/operator to pay down debts, or to collect interest on the floating cash balances.[10] In addition, the time-share manager will normally make a profit on the spread between the wholesale cost of mortgage funds and the price at which such financing is provided to vacation buyers: Buyers will usually put down between 10 and 30% and take a seven-year mortgage on the balance. The operator may also generate income from resort management fees.

Moreover, the property has a guaranteed occupancy rate far into the future, with relatively little risk that the time-share buyer will renege on the commitment. Even if the time-share buyer does renege, the same time-share unit can usually be re-sold, or the lodging can be rented out to non-VOI guests at prevailing regular room rates.

Lastly, the property management reaps promotional and brand-building benefits by having so many relatively prosperous guests experience the joys of the facility through what the time-share buyer perceives as being a personal-equity interest. The benefits to the hotel operator are so great (with operating margins often around 20%) that most of the large hotel chains have, accordingly, designed time-sharing programs.

Marketing matters

Because most hotel markets are very competitive at least for some parts of the year (or sometimes parts of the week) – the shoulder or low seasons, for instance – marketing is a critical tool in filling the rooms and maximizing returns on invested capital. Most major hotel chains spend at least 2 to 4% of total revenues on advertising. However, in addition to the usual advertising and promotional campaigns that companies in most industries conduct, hotels will use to advantage reservation systems, frequent traveler programs, and brand names. The brand names (as further discussed below) suggest to the customer which of four broad categories – luxury (high-end full-service), basic full-service, limited-service, or extended-stay – a particular property presumes to represent.

Table 4.4. *U.S. hotel brand categories, selected examples, 1999*

Category	Representative Brands
Luxury (high-end, full-service)	Four Seasons, Ritz-Carlton, Penisula
Basic full-service	Hilton, Hyatt, Marriott, Sheraton
Limited-service	Hampton Inn, La Quinta, Motel 6
Extended stay	Homewood Suites, Residence Inn

Reservation systems Although there was a time not so long ago when a reservation system was no more than a pencil's marking on a smudged index card, reservation systems have come to function as the main traffic-control and business allocation nerve centers of a hotel's operations. Without the reservation systems, most modern hotels would probably shut down and chaos would reign because neither the hotel desk clerks nor the arriving guests would know who is entitled to accommodation. Current technology embodied in reservation networks allows hotels to handle a volume of traffic that would have been inconceivable in earlier years. And, here again, as in other networks, the *Law of Connectivity* (discussed in Chapter 2) is operative.

A manifestation of this is that reservation systems are also potent marketing tools that can promote a property's unique charms and benefits to faraway travelers who might not otherwise be so informed. The efficiency, courtesy, and general friendliness of the reservation system operators can make a good immediate impression on the prospective guest as perhaps no other promotional medium could. This is important because even small changes in occupancy rates can make a large difference in total profitability (with yield management systems using these data to optimize room rates for specific customer classifications and dates).

Brand names The power of a brand comes from the information that it efficiently conveys to the consumer. Although brands don't always provide the consistency of product and service that they should, in the hotel business a brand name at a minimum suggests the probable pricing range and level of service to be expected, and perhaps functionality and prestige as well. Brands such as the Four Seasons and Ritz-Carlton convey a sense of luxury that the perfunctory, perfectly good budget rooms of Motel 6 do not have and are not designed to give. But both types of brands make marketing statements that attempt to funnel each class of traveler, be it luxury or budget, into the chain of the promoted brand and not another in the same class. Brand names are important intangible assets that, to be effective marketing tools, must be continuously supported. Table 4.4 provides examples of brands in each of four major categories.

The effectiveness of marketing in terms of branding efforts, reservation systems, and pricing structures are then all reflected in the own and cross price elasticities of demand for lodging. Using the same approach as for airlines (Section 2.3), the *own* price elasticity of demand is defined as the percentage change in room demand in market segment X caused by a change in room rates in segment X, all other things being equal. The cross elasticity of demand is defined as the percentage change in room demand in segment X that is caused by a percentage change in room rates in segment Y, all other things being equal. In other words, for two competing hotels, room rate increases (decreases) in one hotel will lead to room demand increases (decreases) in the other hotel.[11]

4.3 Financial and economic aspects

Financing frameworks

Mortgages Whereas it makes sense to use secured debt instruments such as equipment trust certificates for movable collateral such as airplanes and rail cars, it makes more sense to use mortgage-related securities for hotel companies with assets that are of long life and are fixed in location. Of course, hospitality industry companies will tap the conventional equity and debt or commercial lending markets whenever they can. Especially in this industry, however, companies would likely make use of other secured-debt instruments, primarily in the form of mortgage bonds.[12] Although such bonds are nonrecourse and sometimes provide a claim against a specific building, they would more likely have ultimate claims on all the company's property. Collateral trust bonds closely resemble mortgage bonds except that the claim for this type of bond is against securities held by the corporation.

The creation, servicing, and distribution of mortgages and mortgage-backed securities has become a large industry whose interests have traditionally meshed with those of the hotel sector. The driving element, however, has been Wall Street's ability to securitize practically any asset that can over time throw off a reasonably predictable stream of cash. Hotels happen to have many assets – everything from reservation systems to time-share mortgages to bundles of management contracts – that are prospective candidates for such securitization treatments.[13]

REITs Real estate investment trusts or REITS came of age through a 1960s Act of Congress that excused companies from paying any corporate taxes if they passed along 95% of their income to shareholders and had 75% of assets in defined real estate, cash, and government securities. The rules as originally devised and then modified in the Tax Reform Act of 1986 (specifying that REITs could manage their own properties) are spelled out in Internal Revenue Code Section 856 (a). Further changes, reducing the dividend payout requirement from 95% to 90% of taxable income, were made in the REIT Modernization Act of 1999.

Two fundamental types of REITS, the mortgage REIT and the equity REIT, are of importance to hoteliers because they may provide another source of financing that other travel-related companies might not as readily tap.[14] Although it is possible to have a hybrid mortgage and equity REIT, most REITs specialize in the types of properties (apartments, hotels, office buildings, golf courses, etc.), regions, or cities in which they invest.

The mortgage REIT invests in loans secured by real estate, with the mortgages both originated and underwritten by the REIT or purchased in the secondary market. Revenues are derived from interest earned on mortgage loans and income can be affected by fluctuations in interest rates and/or loan defaults.

Equity REITs, in contrast, take an ownership interest in a property as opposed to acting as a lender. Shareholders in such REITs earn dividends or rental income from the buildings and can benefit from rising property values when the properties are sold for a profit. But although a corporation or a trust that qualifies as a REIT generally does not pay federal income tax, REITs are not allowed to pass tax losses to shareholders.[15]

From a financial performance and valuation perspective, REITs are generally judged on what is known as funds from operations (FFO), which is analogous to the EBITDA accounting convention that would be typically used in valuations of airlines, hotels, casinos, theme parks, or media properties. FFO, as adopted by the National Association of Real Estate Investment Trusts, provides a measure of cash from operations and is calculated by adding back real property depreciation expense to net income and adjusting for other extraordinary events.[16] However, as noted by Block (1998, p. 152), FFO is flawed because not all property retains its value every year and because not all REITS capitalize and expense similar items in similar ways. For this reason, the raw FFO data are adjusted for recurring capital expenditures, amortization of tenant improvements, and other items to arrive at an adjusted FFO.[17]

Non-REIT hotel operating companies are known as "C corps" and have the advantage over hotel REITs in that they can reinvest their capital back into the business rather than having to distribute most of their income to shareholders through dividends. However, hotel REITs have two other alternative structures that they can potentially adopt and that mitigate some of the capital-draining limitations of pure hotel REITs. They can either turn themselves into limited partnerships, which do not rely as much on public equity markets for capital, or they can create some "nonqualified" subsidiaries, which, under REIT rules, allow REITs to collect more "nonqualifying income" such as management fees. With such nonqualified units REITs can collect, through management of third-party properties, more than 5% (and up to 25%) of income.

REMICs Real estate mortgage investment conduits, or REMICs, are packages of commercial real estate loans that are assembled and then sold by investment bankers in the secondary financial markets. Such packages are particularly attractive to the major hotel franchise companies and hotel developers who use these funds for acquisitions or to refinance existing obligations.

Normally, only those developers or operators with the strongest balance sheets are candidates for REMIC financings. Collateralized mortgage-backed securities (CMBSs) are also similar to REMICs in purpose and in the way they are assembled and marketed.

Loans and equity In addition, developers of hotel properties will also often seek nonrecourse project financing from life insurance companies, savings and loan organizations, commercial bankers, and credit companies. Such loans would generally fall into three categories:

- short-to-intermediate debt instruments
- long-term debt instruments
- equity structures

Short-to-intermediate loans are used by developers when a project involves high risk, when permanent financing does not cover the entire development cost, or when the developer does not want to share equity. Loan categories of this type include construction loans that are tied to the prime interest rate. Going out further on the debt instrument time horizon are combinations of construction and term loans, in which the developer provides at least 10% of the equity or some other combinations of permanent loans and mortgages.[18] Finally, equity structures might include various limited partnership arrangements or joint ventures between lenders, operators, investors, and developers.

Accounting issues

Although lodging industry operating systems have not required the development of unusual accounting concepts that are outside the realm of Generally Accepted Accounting Principles (GAAP), companies in this industry often lease equipment, and in those situations, the complications of lease accounting, as discussed in Chapter 2, would also be relevant here.

Another hotel accounting feature to be aware of involves asset sales. Most chains will, in the normal course of business, be continuously buying and selling properties and will thus have no need to specifically denote in the accounting statements any of the profits and losses thereby incurred unless such results are individually significant (i.e., material) in total impact. Even so, however, it is still possible that a series of relatively small transactions could have collectively large and distortive affects on reported period income statements.

Probably the most controversial accounting concept in the mergers and consolidations of the 1990s had been in the area of pooling versus purchase accounting. Pooling-of-interests accounting – which is no longer allowed after 2001 – had only been approved if certain strict criteria had been met. In a pooling, two companies combined their assets and liabilities as if they had always operated as a single entity. The advantage was that there is no charge to earnings for what in purchase merger accounting is known as *goodwill amortization*. Such goodwill represents the value of intangible assets such as brand names and reservation systems and operating know-how that a purchaser buys for a price that exceeds the target company's stated book value. In a purchase-accounting type of merger this goodwill must, according to U.S. GAAP, be charged as an expense and written off evenly over no more than forty years (twenty years after calendar 2000). In other countries, the goodwill might be amortized faster. Be it faster or slower, however, if companies had a choice, they would prefer not to have the amortization of goodwill depress their stated earnings results: goodwill charges in large mergers often amount to several hundred million dollars a year.[19]

Economic sensitivities

The hotel industry as a whole is sensitive to changes in general economic conditions. As Miller (1995, p. 56) has noted, the rate of growth in demand for rooms is approximately 75% of the rate of change in Gross National Product, and similar correlations between average room rates and the consumer price index have been observed. However, in terms of timing, the rule-of-thumb is that a downturn in the economy will be reflected in a downturn in occupancy rates, if not also room rates, within six to nine months at the latest. Prevailing monetary and fiscal policies, consumer confidence levels, and a host of other factors – all of which are outside of the control of hoteliers – determine if and when such an economic slowdown will occur. Figure 4.1 has shown that hotel industry profits have been quite volatile and sensitive to overall economic conditions and Figure 4.4 illustrates the close correlation between the annual percent changes in hotel occupancy rates and percent changes in United States GDP.

Yet, regardless of the economy's current performance, one of the most important determinants of profitability appears to be the incremental net supply of new rooms relative to the existing base. Up to the mid-1980s, for example, tax laws encouraged the building of many new rooms, with the result that it was nearly a decade before demand began to catch up with supply. However, once that happened, the industry experienced sharply rising room and occupancy rates and profits (Table 4.5) that extended into the last half of the 1990s. This was reflected in industry pretax profits per room – an important variable in terms of stock market valuation perceptions – rising from zero in 1992 to approximately $5,700 in 1998 (Figure 4.1).

Studies by consulting firm PricewaterhouseCoopers further suggest that changes in demand for lodging respond inversely to changes in airline travel cost indices with a one-year lag and to changes in oil prices with a two-year lag (Figure 4.5).[20] This makes sense intuitively in that lodging demand, which is highly correlated to revenue passenger miles, would be expected to be suppressed to the extent that the higher operating costs of providing transportation services can be passed on to travelers. In this regard it ought to also be noted that about one third of all lodging guests arrive by air.

Another short-run economic factor that might adversely affect margins during upturns would be shortages in the local supply of labor. Although

Table 4.5. *U.S. hotel industry operating performance: Composite of six companies, 1993–98*

	Revenues	Operating income	Operating margin (%)[a]	Assets	Operating cash flow
CAGR (%)[b]	15.8	27.8	10.4	21.3	19.6

[a] Average margin, 1993–98 = 10.0%.
[b] Compound annual growth rate.

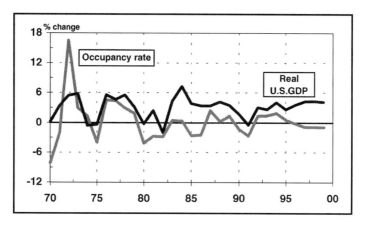

Figure 4.4. Percent change in occupancy rate versus percent change in GDP, 1970–98.

hotels use a mix of union and nonunion workers depending on location and position, overall labor costs would still be at least somewhat correlated to the national minimum wage and be affected by immigration trends. In boom times minimum wage workers may also easily find higher paying jobs in other service industries.

Technological advances have also helped the hotel industry to operate much more efficiently than in the past. The Internet has become especially important in allowing travelers to bypass travel agents and to see in the comfort of their offices and homes instantly available descriptive brochures and room rate and reservation options. Yet, over the long run, technology can also cut in the other direction if, through advanced teleconferencing and e-mail and Internet presentations, people find that they can reduce their expenditures on travel. In these situations the relevant demand elasticities in terms of price and income or other such factors could then be estimated in a manner similar to that illustrated in previous sections.

Hotels, like airlines, probably have fairly limited opportunities to find cost efficiencies of scale outside of the obvious administrative and corporate

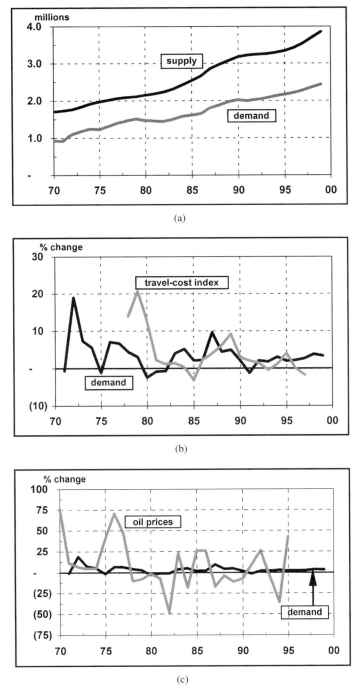

(a)

(b)

(c)

Figure 4.5. (a) Overall room supply and demand, (b) room demand change versus airline travel-cost index changes, lagged one year, and (c) room demand change versus oil price changes, lagged two years, 1970–98. *Source:* PricewaterhouseCoopers.

areas of advertising, reservation systems, frequent traveler programs, property clustering, and computerized billing. For instance, no matter how large a chain or a property grows, it will still take the housekeeping department a fairly constant amount of time to make up a room.[21] Nevertheless, it is likely that there remains enough cost saving available on the administrative side to keep the global merger wheel yet spinning for a long time to come.

4.4 Valuing hotel assets

The valuation of hotel assets is usually a straightforward process in theory if not always in practice. For analytical purposes, the terms hotel or real estate are practically synonymous as the standard financial methods centering on projected cash flows, risk premiums, and discount rates are used regardless of whether a property is referred to as a hotel or as real estate.

In valuing hospitality real estate, *book value*, or *carrying value*, which is the original purchase price less accumulated depreciation, does not usually convey useful information about current market conditions. However, *assessed value*, which is the value assigned to the property for tax purposes and which is defined in terms of market value, may come a little closer to the price for which a property might be sold. Similarly, *insurable value*, the value based on replacement cost, and *liquidation value*, the price an owner is compelled to accept upon quick liquidation, are also misleading.

Real estate appraisal would normally require valuation of a *fee simple title*, which is an estate without limitations or restrictions, or *partial interests*, an estate with some limitations or restrictions. After this, the methodology breaks down into three possible approaches based on cost, comparable sales, or income capitalizations.

The *cost approach* might be useful in providing a rough estimate of what a new building might cost to construct in a specific region. An approximation of reproduction cost could be obtained by multiplying the original cost of a property times a current construction price index that would be a multiple of the construction cost index at the time that the property was built. The cost approach, though, says nothing about valuing income-producing property cash flows.

The asset *transfer price comparison approach* can provide useful price information when a number of similar nearby properties have been recently sold (i.e., transferred to another owner). The comparison works best, for example, with apartments in the same building or single family homes on the same block, and it may sometimes be a guide to valuing hotels situated near each other if the hotels are of similar size and age. Comparable hotel data will often be measured on a transfer price per room or per square foot basis. In addition, the asset's transfer price will be divided by the gross revenues generated by the asset to derive a price to revenues multiple. For instance, a hotel that is transferred for $12 million and generates $6 million of revenues has been sold at a multiple of two times revenues.

Most often, however, hotel real estate would use the *income capitalization approach*. Here, a property's income stream (cash flow excluding maintenance reserves) over a specified period is projected fairly far into the future and an appropriate capitalization rate (multiple) is then applied to this forecasted income stream.

The appropriate capitalization rate (in all cases tied indirectly to interest rate conditions in the economy as a whole) may be derived from a number of sources including capitalization rates for similar recent property transactions. Generally,

market value = (average annual income stream)/(overall capitalization rate),

but this formula greatly oversimplifies the situation. A more sophisticated formula that takes into account the amount of debt financing to total financing would be:

overall capitalization rate $= P_d \times MC + (1 - P_d) \times R_e$,

where P_d is the percentage of debt financing to total financing, MC is the mortgage constant, $1 - P_d$ is the equity financing percentage (because the sum of debt and equity is always 100%), and R_e is the annual required return on the equity portion. The mortgage constant term stands for the capitalization rate for debt, which is the ratio of annual debt service to the original loan principal. It is a function of the interest rate, term of loan, and frequency of loan payments. For instance, on $1 million of debt, an annual mortgage payment of $100,000 that includes the cost of interest and return of principle would result in a mortgage constant of 10%.

A hotel loan for 70% of value, an annual interest rate of 10%, a mortgage constant of 0.10, and a required equity return of 15% would result in the following capitalization rate (CR):

capitalization rate $= (0.7 \times 0.1) + (0.3 \times 0.15) = 11.5\%$.

This capitalization rate may then be used to find the property's capitalized value by dividing an estimate of average annual income by the capitalization rate. The property's income stream over its *economic* life may also be discounted using the capitalization rate as a discount factor.

Discount Factor $= 1/(1 + CR)^n$

where n is the year's income stream being discounted. The sum of the discounted yearly income streams then provides the property's valuation estimate, an example of which (assuming no salvage value after five years) is shown in Table 4.6.

Of course, one important weakness of this approach is that the farther out the income stream projections are made, the more unreliable and unrealistic they may become. An alternative may thus be to instead forecast a property's likely sale price at the end of an investment period (rather than over its

Table 4.6. *Property income streams discounted using overall capitalization rate, an example*

Year	1	2	3	4	5
Income stream	$1 million	$1 million	$1 million	$1 million	$1 million
Discount factor @ 13%	0.8850	0.7831	0.6931	0.6133	0.5428
Discounted income stream	$885,000	$783,100	$693,100	$613,300	$542,800
Total					$3,517,300

economic life) and to then discount to present value the anticipated sale price at the end of the investment period. This amount would then be combined with the sum of the discounted present values of the interim cash flows and would provide an estimate of a property's total present value.

Even so, however, asset valuation procedures will often be unable to directly capture in the discount factors applied to projected cash flows all of the intangible elements that might affect the asset transfer price in the market. Such intangibles might include the following factors:

Prospective local, regional, national, and international economic conditions
Prospective costs of fuel and of travel in general relative to incomes
Visitor demographic and income profiles
Prospective amount of new local competition to be built
Price elasticities (i.e., the prospective ability to raise room and food prices without driving customers away)
Potential for adding rooms or other facilities and attractions such as on-premise health clubs
Potential need for renovation and upgrade
Potential alternative uses of the land
Degree of recognition as a brand name or as a "trophy" property
Management agreement terms and potential encumbrances
Prospects for new local roads or airport facilities or convention centers to be built
Availability of government subsidies or tax breaks
Local political and environmental conditions

A comprehensive valuation process should thus consider all of these elements, which at the most basic level for a hotel, will, as they say, boil down to location, location, and location.

For hotel real estate companies that are publicly held, the sum of the estimated asset valuations divided by the number of shares outstanding will then provide an estimate of value per share. For hotel management companies, valuation is related to the strength of the brand, future unit additions, length of management and franchise agreements, and expansion opportunities. Generally shares will become attractive for purchase or takeover if and when trading at prices significantly under (at least 20%) the estimated asset value per share. Of course, the same approach to public versus private market value comparisons and the use of valuation ratios as described for airlines (Section 2.5) may be also applied here.

4.5 Concluding remarks

It used to be that a hotel operator just had to change the sheets and the towels. Modern hotels have, however, evolved into complex organisms, practically alive with their own daily and seasonal patterns and tied into global information networks. Most hotels today are highly dependent on the technology of reservation systems and yield management methods that are similar to those used by airlines and described in Chapter 2. The major chains have the capital, know-how, broadly distributed properties, and asset bases to widely spread the costs of implementation. For this reason, the industry will continue to consolidate, even though across-the-board cost economies of scale are not likely to be seen (beyond those significant ones derived from Internet marketing, cross-branding of reservations, and centralization of accounting, frequent traveler, and yield management systems).

Growth of this industry will always be tethered to events and conditions beyond direct control. Airlines might raise ticket prices, the cost of oil might rise sharply, local labor availability might be scarce, a competitor comes to town, and so forth. Yet some things such as service quality, property upkeep, advertising and promotion, and room rates fall largely into the controllable category. In the race to stay ahead, hotel managements have no choice but to take advantage of every tactic and tool that they can.

Selected additional reading

Binkley, C. (1999). "Marriott Faces Outcry from 1980s Buyers of Hotel Partnership," *Wall Street Journal*, January 13.

Doherty, J. (2000). "Look Out, Priceline," *Barron's*, March 20.

Garrigan, R. T., and Parsons, J. F. C., eds, (1997). *Real Estate Investment Trusts: Structure, Analysis, and Strategy*. New York: McGraw-Hill.

McDowell, E. (2000). "A Few Weeks to Call Your Own," *New York Times*, January 29.
(1995). "His Goal: No Room at the Inns," *New York Times*, November 23.

McTague, J. (1999). "Plenty of Room for Growth," *Barron's*, September 27.

Orwall, B., Rundle, R. L., and Rose, F. (1997). "Hilton and ITT Took Different Paths to This Confrontation," *Wall Street Journal*, January 29.

Rutherford, D. G., ed. (1995). *Hotel Management and Operations*, 2nd ed. New York: John Wiley & Sons.

Tomlinson, R. (1999). "China Rolls Out the Red Carpet," *Fortune*, 139(10)(May 24).

Part IV
Doing things there

5
Casinos

It's better to be born lucky than to be born rich.

Perhaps nowhere is the preceding sentiment more appropriately expressed than in gaming and wagering, where kings and queens play amidst snake eyes and wild jokers and horses run for the roses. This chapter explores the essential economic features of this fascinating business, for whose services consumers will spend more in the aggregate than for any other forms of entertainment.

5.1 From ancient history

At first

Interest in betting on the uncertain outcome of an event is not a recently acquired human trait. As noted by Berger and Bruning (1979, p. 10), "archaeologists believe that cave men not only beat their wives, they wagered them as well." Evidence of mankind's strong and continuing interest in gambling is found in the following historical examples:

In biblical times, the selection of Saul to govern the Hebrew kingdom was determined by lot.

An ivory gaming board was found in the tomb of Egyptian pharaoh Tutankhamen.

Palamedes, according to Greek mythology, invented dice and taught soldiers how to play with them during the siege of Troy. Ancient Greek worshippers played dice games and bet on horse races.

The Romans invented the lottery, and they wagered on the outcomes of chariot races. The emperor Nero was said to be addicted to such racing.

The earliest playing cards were of Chinese origin and were derived from Korean playing sticks. Cards similar to those of today were used by the French in the fourteenth century and are descended from tarot decks used for fortune telling. France's Louis XV had a deck made of silver, and England's Henry VIII was a notorious gambler.

The sailing of the *Mayflower* to plant a colony in the New World was financed by a lottery. So were some great educational institutions, including Harvard, Yale, and Dartmouth. So was the colonial army that helped create the United States.

Gaming in America

Preliminaries Wagering already had a long and colorful history thousands of years before the United States came into being. But, as Findlay (1986) describes, in the process of its development, the United States added a few exciting chapters of its own – the often ambivalent American public attitudes toward legalization of such activities notwithstanding.

Even in colonial times there appears to have been some pretty fast action: Consider that four years after the *Mayflower* landed, the Virginia Assembly passed a law against gambling, and legislation passed in Boston in 1630 also decreed that "all persons whatsoever that have cards, dice, or tables in their houses shall make away with them before the next court under pain of punishment".[1]

Then there was the country's first lavish casino, referred to as a "rug joint," which opened in New Orleans for round-the-clock operation in 1827. By 1832, a similar place (no doubt frequented by many of the fledgling nation's politicians) had been opened in Washington, DC, on Pennsylvania Avenue.

The year 1850 saw San Francisco, with its gold-rush mentality and 1,000 assorted establishments, become the gambling capital of the West. The cowboy's midwestern equivalent was meanwhile to be found in Dodge City, Kansas. But all kinds of wagering and card playing were also common at that time on Mississippi riverboats, in the terminal port city of New Orleans, and in New York and Chicago. New York, for instance, had an estimated 6,000 gambling locations in the 1850s, and by the 1920s, Miami had become an important hub luring serious bettors.

Although gambling is certainly not unique to the American character, this country has contributed to the development of games such as poker and craps and toward rationalizing the marketing and operating procedures used in modern casinos and lotteries. Indeed, with gross industry revenues

Table 5.1. *Gross handle, revenues, and margins in the U.S., 1982–99*

Year	Total legal gross wager (Handle), $ billions	Gross revenues (Win), $ billions	Gross margin (Retention rate or win rate), %
1999	747.94	58.37	7.8
1998	681.57	55.06	8.1
1997	638.85	51.27	8.0
1996	587.37	50.58	8.6
1995	557.48	44.39	8.0
1994	482.10	39.79	8.3
1993	394.11	34.70	8.8
1992	336.66	30.39	9.0
1991	304.30	26.68	8.8
1990	303.09	26.20	8.6
1989	251.20	23.52	9.4
1988	231.60	21.36	9.2
1987	185.85	18.38	9.9
1986	166.47	16.92	10.2
1985	159.16	15.34	9.6
1984	146.97	13.62	9.3
1983	132.14	11.84	9.0
1982	125.76	10.41	8.3
CAGR:[a] 1982–99	11.1	10.7	

[a] Compound annual growth rate, 1982–96 (%).

Source: Adapted from E. M. Christiansen data originally published in *Gaming Business* (April, May, June, and August 1984), and *Gaming & Wagering Business* (July and August) 1985–1999. See Table 10.3.

exceeding $58 billion (Table 5.1) as of 1999, gaming and wagering activities have become a regular part of life for all income classes and ethnic groups.

The Nevada experience Nevada's history as a center for betting goes back to the mid-1800s. There, as in San Francisco, a boom in precious metals mining attracted many rough-and-ready customers for gambling and affiliated services, including liquor sales and prostitution. Nevertheless, the territory's attitude toward legalization of gaming fluctuated – depending on the perceived degree of corruption and cheating – for over half a century before the state of Nevada finally legalized, in 1931, what could not in practice be stopped.

Curiously, before World War II, gaming activity in Reno was far more developed than in Las Vegas. "Founded" in 1905 by the sale of some Union Pacific railway junction property to private interests, and incorporated in 1911, Las Vegas did not actually begin to come into its own until the 1930s. The catalyst for change was construction of Hoover (alias Boulder) Dam, a major Bureau of Reclamation project located in Boulder City, about thirty miles away. Completion of the dam brought water and electric power to the region and stimulated commercial growth. Also, many itinerant construction workers, who had bought their supplies and had spent their free time gambling in Las Vegas, eventually settled there permanently.

Las Vegas, however, only began to emerge as a world-famous entertainment capital just after the Second World War. The city's proximity to the burgeoning population of Los Angeles and the increasing availability of low-cost air travel contributed significantly to its success. In addition, there was Benjamin "Bugsy" Siegel. As Skolnick (1978, p. 111) indicates,

It had been Siegel's ambition to build a luxurious complex that would offer gambling, recreation, entertainment, and other services catering to the area's increasing tourist trade ... Siegel had persuaded the crime syndicate that he could transform Las Vegas into a legal gambling oasis for organized crime, and he received their backing in 1943. With their support, he started to work on his initial venture – really the first of the major Strip hotels – the Flamingo.[2]

Nevada's decision (in 1946–47) to establish and to fund – through taxes on gross casino winnings – regulation and enforcement agencies that would ensure fair and honest conduct of the games and of casino operations was of further importance.[3] The irony, of course, was that at the start of legalized modern gaming in Nevada, often the only operators with enough expertise to run the games fairly were people previously affiliated with illegal organizations.

As might be expected, the "connections" of some of those operators created law-enforcement problems that surfaced most noticeably in the 1950s, as attempts at state licensing and gaming-control functions came into conflict with formidable mob interests in what was already a lucrative and rapidly growing business. Indeed, it was not until the mid-to-late 1960s that organized crime's grip on the industry's finances began to be loosened as a result of pressure from the Department of Justice and other federal government investigative agencies, and also as a result of large-scale investments by billionaire Howard Hughes.

This process was further accelerated by passage in 1969 of the Corporate Gaming Act, which allowed companies with publicly traded shares to own and operate casinos in the state of Nevada. Ownership by large corporations provided an important means of financing casino-hotel expansions, of attracting middle-class and convention-related customers, and of developing an untainted corps of professional managers. The foundation was thus already long in place for Las Vegas, in particular, to evolve into the world-class destination resort that it became once the first of the large-scale (3,000-room) properties such as the Mirage Hotel were opened beginning in the late 1980s.

Enter New Jersey New Jersey's involvement in casino gaming began much differently than Nevada's. New Jersey's Atlantic City had been a popular ocean resort in the early 1900s. Gradually, however, because of neglect and because of the increasing availability of low-cost air travel, it decayed into an

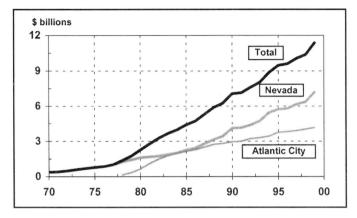

Figure 5.1. Annual casino revenues in Nevada and Atlantic City, 1970–99.

economically depressed slum-by-the-sea. It was always clear, though, that with its proximity to dense population centers in Philadelphia and New York, the town would make an especially attractive location for casinos. And so – with the promise of stimulating urban renewal and providing extra funding for senior citizens' programs – began the efforts of developers to legalize gambling. Voters rejected the first referendum for statewide gambling in 1974, but in 1976 they approved a second one limiting casinos to Atlantic City.

Public reaction to New Jersey's legalization was awesome. Immediately on opening the first Atlantic City casino in 1978, Resorts International was overwhelmed by enormous crowds betting huge stakes. And over the immediately following years the early momentum continued. Despite having only one-tenth as many first-class hotel rooms (5,000 as of 1984) as its Nevada counterpart, Atlantic City had begun to compete effectively with Las Vegas as a major center for entertainment and gaming (Figure 5.1 and Table 5.2). By 1984, for example, table-game and slot revenues in New Jersey had come to within 3% of the Las Vegas total of around $2 billion, and annual visitor arrivals in Atlantic City had reached 28.5 million as compared to 12.8 million in Las Vegas.[4]

Still, there remain considerable differences in the way the casino gaming business operates in Nevada as compared to Atlantic City. In Nevada, hundreds of locations scattered throughout the state are licensed to provide a wide variety of casino gaming services (from simple banks of slot machines to race and sports books), and the sixty largest casinos, according to 1998 *Nevada Gaming Abstract* data, accounted for over 80% of total gross revenues. In contrast, as of the late-1990s, there were only twelve large casino-hotels in operation in Atlantic City, all of them located within five miles of each other. But because of earlier New Jersey regulations, these older casinos are much less varied in the size and in the scope of their offerings than are their Nevada counterparts.[5]

Table 5.2. *Gaming win in Atlantic City and Nevada, 1975–99*

Year	Atlantic City and Nevada casino revenues ($ billion)	Nevada total June fiscal year taxable gaming revenues ($ billion)	Las Vegas (Clark County)		Atlantic City	
			Gross winnings ($ billion)	Visitors (million)	Gross winnings ($ billion)	Visitors (million)
1975	1.066	1.066	0.770	9.2		
1976	1.188	1.188	0.846	9.8		
1977	1.380	1.380	1.015	10.1		
1978	1.805	1.671	1.236	11.2	0.134	7.0
1979	2.306	1.980	1.424	11.7	0.325	9.5
1980	2.917	2.274	1.617	11.9	0.643	13.8
1981	3.563	2.463	1.676	11.8	1.100	19.1
1982	4.093	2.600	1.751	11.6	1.493	23.0
1983	4.454	2.683	1.887	12.3	1.771	26.4
1984	4.943	2.991	2.008	12.8	1.952	28.5
1985	5.367	3.228	2.233	14.2	2.139	29.3
1986	5.647	3.366	2.393	15.2	2.281	29.9
1987	6.205	3.710	2.738	16.2	2.496	31.8
1988	6.809	4.074	3.003	17.2	2.735	33.1
1989	7.119	4.312	3.290	18.1	2.807	32.0
1990	7.864	4.912	3.870	21.0	2.952	31.8
1991	8.403	5.411	4.152	21.3	2.992	30.8
1992	8.913	5.697	4.378	21.9	3.216	30.7
1993	9.319	6.018	4.727	23.5	3.301	30.2
1994	10.069	6.647	5.431	28.2	3.423	31.3
1995	10.901	7.153	5.718	29.0	3.748	33.3
1996	11.340	7.522	5.844	29.6	3.814	34.0
1997	11.479	7.573	5.930	30.5	3.906	34.1
1998	11.907	7.874	6.207	30.6	4.033	34.3
1999	12.663	8.498	6.735	33.8	4.164	33.7
CAGR:[a]						
1980–99	8.0	7.2	7.8	5.6	10.3	4.8

[a]Compound annual growth rate (%).
Source: Las Vegas Convention/Visitors Authority and Atlantic City Casino Association.

In fact, given the constraints of regulation and real estate, Atlantic City's development during the 1990s diverged considerably from that of Las Vegas, where, by the end of the decade, almost half of all casino-hotel revenues were derived from noncasino sources such as rooms, food, and entertainment. While Las Vegas truly became an entertainment capital – a citywide theme park in itself – Atlantic City casinos remained largely as a collection of slot-machine malls attracting primarily day-trip visitors. To at least in part remedy this situation, several large-scale, Las Vegas-style properties will be opened in Atlantic City in the early 2000s.

Indian reservations, riverboats, and other wagering areas The most significant developments of the early 1990s, however, came from the expansion of casino gaming activities onto Indian reservations and riverboats. The federal government's Indian Gaming Regulatory Act of 1988 opened the floodgates by allowing Indian tribes to operate on their reservations, and without restrictions, all forms of gambling previously approved by a state.[6]

Many such state–tribal compacts have, however, been often negotiated under conditions of great controversy because the states – themselves hard-pressed to find sources of tax revenues – have looked more seriously at gaming as a potential new source of income.[7] In 1989, South Dakota used low-stakes casino gaming to revitalize tourism. In 1991, Colorado did the same in the tourist towns of Black Hawk, Central City, and Cripple Creek. Iowa and Illinois also launched their first riverboat casinos in 1991. And by the mid-1990s, several state legislatures, including those of Mississippi (1992), Louisiana (1993), Missouri (1994), and Indiana (1996), had already moved toward legalization of riverboat or other casino-type operations. Although most such riverboats are fairly small by comparison to Las Vegas casino standards, they are collectively large enough to affect the growth of gaming in Nevada and Atlantic City (Table 5.3).

Travel is generally a part of the gaming casino experience, although with so many competing nearby alternatives, the distance traveled does not necessarily have to be far from home. For instance, video lottery terminals (VLTs) – in effect, slot machines tied into a lottery – were widely legalized in the early 1990s. VLTs compete for revenues against established amusement video machines and online ticket lottery systems by essentially turning local restaurants and taverns (and also racetracks) into mini-casinos.

Bingo, too, has developed into an important legalized casino activity that generates gross wagering of around $1.0 billion in the forty-six states where it is played. Indeed, bingo attracts some forty million participants and is the most widespread of all legalized wagering games.

Rapidly growing grosses are also being generated in public poker clubs, which have long been legal in certain populous California counties.

Last, but not least, is gaming on the Internet, which has the potential to eventually become a major source of industry revenues if and when federal and state laws are changed and the security of transactions and the accountability of service vendors can be assured. In this regard, the U.S. Interstate Wire Act (18 U.S.C. §1084) – which prohibits the taking of bets over a network that crosses state or international borders – is a prominent and controversial feature of the current legal landscape even while more than $2 billion of Internet-based, primarily sports-related wagering is already being conducted on offshore Web sites every year.[8]

Table 5.3. Gross handle, revenues, and margins in the U.S. (in $ billions), 1982–99[a]

		Casinos slots Nev/NJ	Table games	State lotteries (regular)	State lotteries (video)	Total legal gambling											
Year	Total					Total horses	Dog racing	Jai alai	Legal book-making total	Card rooms (ex-nevada)	Bingo	Charitable gambling (ex-bingo)	Indian reservation	Non-casino gaming devices	Cruise ships	River-boats	Commercial other
Gross wager (handle)																	
1999	734.18	146.84	201.21	34.99	16.9	2.96	2.05	0.12	2.55	13.07	3.89	6.68	109.34	18.88	8.34	154.41	11.93
1998	668.63	137.52	181.76	35.06	13.9	3.10	2.19	0.15	2.41	11.01	3.97	6.65	102.28	17.09	7.58	135.51	8.45
1997	638.85	133.90	189.25	34.24	11.86	15.34	2.25	0.21	2.57	10.42	3.91	6.03	81.93	16.19	6.53	115.82	8.38
1996	587.37	126.84	178.72	33.84	9.10	14.88	2.43	0.27	2.61	9.93	3.96	5.67	66.00	14.44	6.11	104.42	8.15
1995	557.48	121.30	185.58	32.52	6.36	14.77	2.73	0.30	2.60	9.44	4.13	5.65	57.67	12.86	5.757	88.08	7.74
1994	482.10	113.03	170.83	30.02	4.45	14.16	2.94	0.32	2.66	9.31	4.25	5.05	41.06	8.91	5.10	63.80	6.19
1993	394.11	102.56	150.91	26.94	3.88	13.72	3.24	0.38	2.26	8.35	4.23	4.89	28.96	7.41	4.49	27.12	4.78
1992	336.66	94.56	143.62	25.55		14.06	3.31	0.43	2.11	8.43	4.18	4.70	16.73	3.84	4.28	7.42	3.44
1991	304.30	84.40	149.74	20.99		13.93	3.50	0.49	2.26	8.40	4.23	4.61	5.44	0.36	4.08	1.10	0.77
1990	303.09	76.17	161.64	21.02		14.14	3.47	0.56	2.16	8.38	4.07	4.47	2.64	0.31	3.71		0.38
1989	251.20	65.79	127.77	19.49		13.93	3.21	0.55	1.84	7.56	3.79	4.22	1.00	0.25	1.76		0.02
1988	231.60	57.67	126.30	17.05		13.67	3.26	0.64	1.73	3.45	3.67	3.58	0.35	0.23			
1987	185.83	32.79	112.04	13.14		13.14	3.20	0.71	1.38	3.13	3.98	2.00	0.31				
1986	166.47	28.50	101.44	12.48		12.38	3.02	0.67	1.19	1.12	3.60	1.79	0.29				
1985	159.16	26.18	99.56	10.21		12.24	2.70	0.66	1.13	1.10	3.44	1.68	0.25				
1984	146.97	23.79	92.87	8.13		12.18	2.46	0.67	1.11	1.07	3.15	1.54	—				
1983[a]	132.14	18.80	87.20	5.17		11.65	2.33	0.62	0.85	1.05	3.07	1.40	—				
1982[a]	125.76	14.40	87.00	4.09		11.70	2.21	0.62	0.54	1.00	3.00	1.20	—				
CAGR:[d]																	
1982–99	10.9	14.6	5.1	13.5		−7.8	−0.4	−9.3	9.6	16.3	1.5	10.6					
Gross revenues (win)																	
1999	58.37	8.74	4.24	16.11	1.38	3.48	0.45	0.03	0.12	0.88	0.96	1.69	8.43	2.02	0.59	8.34	0.92
1998	55.06	8.09	3.83	16.33	1.26	3.36	0.48	0.03	0.07	0.74	0.97	1.64	7.89	1.83	0.54	7.29	0.69
1997	51.27	7.61	3.91	15.39	1.10	3.25	0.51	0.05	0.10	0.70	0.96	1.56	6.83	1.74	0.46	6.17	0.63
1996	50.58	7.29	3.78	15.31	0.89	3.18	0.55	0.06	0.09	0.68	0.95	1.47	5.61	1.48	0.43	5.54	0.62
1995	44.39	7.09	3.86	14.62	0.62	3.07	0.61	0.06	0.10	0.76	0.98	1.51	4.04	1.41	0.41	4.65	0.60
1994	39.79	6.61	3.57	13.67	0.46	2.90	0.63	0.07	0.16	0.73	0.99	1.39	3.42	1.08	0.36	3.26	0.49
1993	34.70	6.16	3.23	12.82		2.86	0.70	0.08	0.12	0.66	1.04	1.29	2.59	0.92	0.32	1.46	0.45
1992	30.39	5.83	3.12	11.43		2.93	0.69	0.08	0.10	0.66	1.03	1.24	1.63	0.57	0.31	0.42	0.35
1991	26.68	5.24	3.20	10.23		2.84	0.70	0.10	0.11	0.66	1.05	1.23	0.72	0.16	0.29	0.08	0.06

Upper panel (handle/revenue by year):

Year															
1990	26.20	4.89	3.41	10.29	2.90	0.69	0.11	0.13	0.66	1.02	1.19	0.49	0.13	0.26	0.03
1989	23.52	4.35	3.10	9.63	2.82	0.63	0.11	0.11	0.30	0.91	1.12	0.12	0.12	0.20	0.00
1988	21.36	4.01	3.05	8.42	2.76	0.63	0.12	0.10	0.28	1.06	0.71	0.12	0.10		
1987	18.38	3.59	2.81	6.58	2.68	0.62	0.14	0.09	0.25	0.92	0.62	0.11			
1986	16.92	3.15	2.59	6.33	2.43	0.59	0.13	0.08	0.06	0.92	0.54	0.10			
1985	15.34	2.91	2.54	5.21	2.39	0.53	0.13	0.06	0.05	0.91	0.53	0.09			
1984	13.62	2.65	2.40	4.15	2.36	0.48	0.12	0.05	0.05	0.82	0.54				
1983[a]	11.84	2.36	2.25	3.04	2.26	0.45	0.11	0.04	0.05	0.80	0.46				
1982[a]	10.41	2.00	2.20	2.17	2.25	0.43	0.11	0.03	0.05	0.78	0.40				

CAGR:[d]

1982–99	10.7	9.1	3.9	12.5	2.6	0.3	−8.0	9.4	18.3	1.2	8.9	n.m.	n.m.	n.m.	n.m.

Gross margin (retention rate or win rate)

Year																	
1999	7.95	6.0	2.1	46.0	8.2	117.7	22.1	22.8	4.6	6.7	24.6	25.3	7.7	10.7	7.1	5.4	7.7
1998	8.23	5.9	2.1	46.6	9.0	108.5	22.1	22.8	3.0	6.7	24.5	24.7	7.7	10.7	7.1	5.4	8.2
1997	8.03	5.7	2.1	45.0	9.3	21.2	22.5	22.8	3.7	6.7	24.5	25.9	8.3	10.7	7.1	5.3	7.5
1996	8.61	5.7	2.1	45.2	9.8	21.4	131.0	22.5	3.3	6.9	24.3	25.9	8.5	10.3	7.1	5.3	7.6
1995	7.96	5.8	2.1	45.0	9.7	20.8	21.7	22.4	3.9	7.9	23.7	26.6	8.2	10	7.1	5.3	7.7
1994	8.25	5.8	2.1	45.5		20.5	21.5	22.1	6.0	7.8	23.2	27.5	8.3	12.2	7.1	5.1	8.0
1993	8.80	6.0	2.1	47.6		20.9	21.5	22.3	5.1	7.9	24.5	26.4	9.0	12.4	7.1	5.4	9.3
1992[b]	9.03	6.2	2.2	44.8		20.8	20.9	19.3	4.6	7.8	24.7	26.4	9.8	14.8	7.1	5.6	10.1
1991	8.77	6.2	2.1	48.7		20.4	20.0	20.5	4.7	7.8	24.9	26.7	13.2	43.4	7.1	7.2	8.3
1990	8.65	6.4	2.1	49.0		20.5	20.0	20.4	5.8	7.8	25.0	26.7	18.5	43.2	7.0		8.3
1989	9.36	6.6	2.4	49.4		20.3	19.7	19.5	5.8	4.0	23.9	26.5	12.0	47.3	11.3		8.6
1988	9.22	6.9	2.4	49.4		20.2	19.3	19.4	6.0	8.0	28.7	19.9					
1987	9.89	10.9	2.5	50.1		20.3	19.5	19.5	6.2	8.0	23.1	30.8					
1986	10.17	11.1	2.6	50.8		19.6	19.5	19.5	6.8	5.0	25.6	30.4					
1985	9.64	11.1	2.6	51.0		19.5	19.5	19.5	5.4	5.0	26.5	31.2					
1984	9.26	11.1	2.6	51.0		19.3	19.5	18.3	4.7	5.0	25.9	35.0					
1983[b]	8.96	12.5	2.6	58.9		19.4	19.5	18.0	5.1	4.9	26.0	33.1					
1982[b]	8.28	13.9	2.5	53.1		19.2	19.5	18.0	4.8	5.0	26.0	33.0					

[a] Some figures may not be precise due to rounding.

[b] Prior to 1984, sports books, horse books, and sports cards were combined into "other" category.

[c] The previous 1985 estimate of $582 million in gross revenues for charitable games has been subsequently reduced to $525 million.

[d] Compound annual growth rate.

Source: Adapted from E. M. Christiansen data originally published in *Gaming Business* (April, May, June, and August 1984), and *Gaming & Wagering Business* (July and August) 1985–1999. See Table 5.1.

Table 5.4. *Estimated U.S. casino gaming square*
footage by category, 1997

	Square feet (000s)
Atlantic City	925
Nevada	
Las Vegas	4,300
Laughlin	525
Reno/Sparks	925
Other	300
	6,975
Riverboats	1,600
Indian tribal lands	1,500
	3,100
Total	10,075

Source: Nevada Gaming Abstract, industry estimates.

From all this it would thus appear that the gaming and wagering pie, while continuing to grow at above-average rates in comparison to the overall economy, will continue to be divided into more specialized slices. Moreover, similar patterns are also appearing outside the United States, especially in Canada, Western Europe, and Australia.[9] Major events in the industry's United States history are depicted in Figure 5.2.

5.2 Money talks

The $58 billion sum of gaming and wagering activity in the United States listed in Table 5.1 represents the total revenue (before expenses) that legal gaming operators have retained, or, in other words, won. Conversely, it also represents the net amount that players have lost. Of this total, lotteries (at around $16 billion) and casinos ($13 billion) have been the most important if not fastest growing components (Figure 5.3).[10] By comparison, domestic movie ticket sales in 1999 were only around $7.5 billion and recorded music sales about $13 billion.[11]

Macroeconomic matters

The rate of growth of legalized gambling has been well above that of the aggregate economy for virtually the entire post World War II period. There is, moreover, reason to believe that the growth rate for *illegal* gambling, which probably amounts to at least an additional 15% of the legal total (there is no way to easily measure it) has also probably kept pace. In part, gaming's compound annual growth rate, averaging above 10% during much of the last third of the century, has been a function of simply making the services more

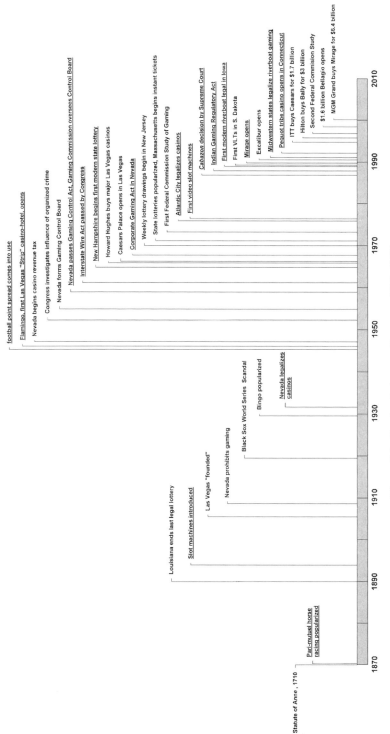

Figure 5.2. Gaming industry milestones, 1870–2000.

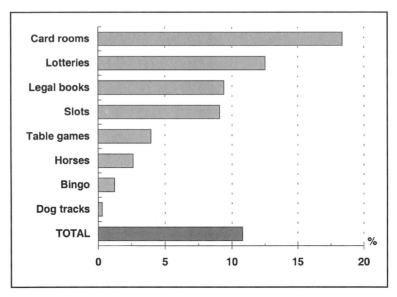

Figure 5.3. Compound annual growth rate comparisons of U.S. gaming revenues by category, 1982–99. *Source data: Gaming and Wagering Business.*

widely available and convenient for players to access. However, none of this could have happened if the public's perceptions of gaming and entertainment-spending preferences had not shifted. In 1960, net public spending (losses to operators of casinos, pari-mutuels, and lotteries) on gaming and wagering accounted for around 0.2% of disposable income, whereas the current share has by now approximately quadrupled (Figure 1.15c).

Still, with game operators often leveraged financially and operationally, the industry's sensitivity to adverse business cycle fluctuations is potentially high. Indeed, judging from spending patterns during the recessions of the early 1980s and 1990s, there is evidence that gaming revenues may be sensitive to both regional and national economic conditions.[12] In an economic downturn, for example, convention-trade travel to Atlantic City and Nevada would normally be curtailed as businesses attempt to pare expenses; as a result, average spending per visitor might be reduced (Figure 5.4).

Many other factors may also decisively affect revenue growth trends in a region. Among the most important are:

Air fares and the cost and availability of gasoline
Recent number of room and square footage additions as a percentage of total industry capacity
Dollar-exchange rates against major Asian and European currencies
Percentage of players coming from outside the region
Projected rates of inflation and factory employment

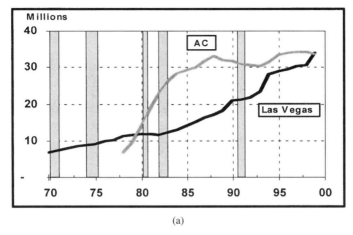

(a)

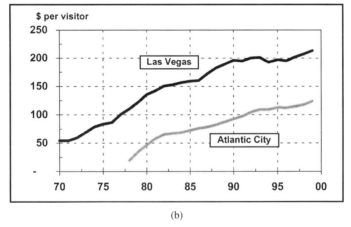

(b)

Figure 5.4. Las Vegas versus Atlantic City, 1970–99; (a) visitors and (b) spending per visitor.

Funding functions

In 1998, municipalities and states collected a total of $19.5 billion from taxes and license fees imposed on gaming and wagering, which, in the United States is regulated by a hodgepodge of state and local laws that reflect the ambivalence of the population toward the conduct of these activities. On the one hand, most jurisdictions have few if any qualms about permitting church or social bingo – a game that, as Cook (1979) notes, has a high cost to the player. Nor do people seem to object to lotteries – a game with even higher costs to the player than bingo. On the other hand, people often rise up in moral indignation against casinos and racetracks, where the operators' percentage is much lower. As Rose (1986) discusses, other anomalies often appear: In communities such as those near Los Angeles, only card games of a precisely defined type are allowed to be played. And in Nevada, the acknowledged sports and race-book and gaming capital of the world, a state lottery is *illegal.*

The logic concerning when and where gaming establishments may advertise has also been peculiar. The Federal Communications Commission, for example, follows a set of antilottery laws passed before the year 1900. However, state-sponsored lotteries, charity events, and Indian-run casinos are exempted from the rules. Until the late 1990s, privately owned casinos thus could advertise only on cable: On broadcast television they had only been allowed to mention their noncasino attractions such as golf courses and restaurants even while competing casinos operated by Indian tribes had been exempted from such restrictions as far back as 1988.[13]

It is not surprising, then, that all of this ambivalence and confusion spills over into the politics of regulation and legalization. Legalization in a state or city is always easier to achieve if, by reason of history and culture, the dominant population groups favor such activities. But what usually precipitates a move toward legal sanction is a need for more social-welfare funding than can be comfortably raised via direct taxation.

Unfortunately, the public may thus sometimes be fooled into thinking that legalization is a costless way to raise net additional revenues. However, several studies – including those of Goodman (1994, 1995), Abt, Smith, and Christiansen (1985), Skolnick (1978, 1979), and Mahon (1980) – indicate that legalization of gaming is not a taxpayers' panacea. Gaming may, for instance, divert revenues needed to support other local retail business establishments. The net revenues raised from its legalization are often relatively small compared to budget gaps, especially if the additional costs of law enforcement and regulation and treatments for new player addictions are also taken into account. Moreover, as Sternlieb and Hughes (1983) and Goodman (1995, p. xi) have suggested, such legalizations tend to spawn huge, politically powerful bureaucracies that may ultimately operate against the public interest and that shift the role of government from being a watchdog of gambling to becoming its leading promoter.

Regulation

Government regulation is more visible in gaming than in any other entertainment-industry segment. It has developed from historical experience with a cash business that has often nourished the coffers of organized crime, deprived government of tax revenues, and plainly cheated ordinary players.

Regulative power usually rests in the state legislatures, which formally legalize gaming activities such as lotteries, tracks, and casinos. Legislators also establish agencies to oversee that all such activities are conducted honestly and competently, and with full accounting of tax revenues to the state. To achieve those ends, regulatory enforcement, investigative, and licensing agencies work in conjunction with local-community interests to promulgate specific standards and rules of conduct.

For example, the Nevada and New Jersey gaming commissions oversee licensing and regulation of casino gaming and slot-machine operations in those states. New Jersey's regulatory bodies are to a great extent patterned on those earlier developed in Nevada, where there is a two-tier structure: The Gaming Control Board works at the staff level on investigation and audit, and the Gaming Commission acts as a quasi-judicial body that deliberates on licensing, revocations, and other related matters.

Agents and investigators representing the Federal Bureau of Investigation (FBI) and the Internal Revenue Service (IRS) have generally played a role ancillary to that of the state commissions. But should any of the state bodies prove ineffectual, it is likely that the federal government would immediately become more actively and visibly involved in industry affairs. The most direct influence would then probably be felt through augmentation of tax-reporting requirements.[14]

The difficulty of designing regulation that balances the needs of the business with what best serves the public's interest can be seen in the case of New Jersey, where, in its zeal to ensure that casinos would be impervious to influence by organized crime, the legislature in that state incorporated particularly detailed instructions in bills to legalize Atlantic City gaming. All employees – initially including restaurant busboys, hotel bellhops, and parking attendants far removed from gaming-transactions areas – had to submit detailed license applications.[15]

As Atlantic City gaming matured, many of these early regulations proved to be unnecessarily stringent, if not actually detrimental to industry growth and profitability. Those standards were then somewhat relaxed as the commission and its enforcement division began to concentrate on licensing of top executives and of people who directly oversee gaming activities and grant credit (dealers, pit bosses, shift managers, and cage personnel). Licensing of slot machines and of companies supplying the industry with goods and services (linen, liquor, food, etc.) also took priority.

Without close scrutiny at the financial-accounting and operational levels, there is a natural tendency for illegal activities to arise. Frauds and tax evasions are still occasionally discovered in lotteries (e.g., irregular printing of tickets), in horse racing (e.g., substitution by "ringers," use of illegal drugs on animals, and fixing of races), and in casinos (e.g., skimming money before reporting to the state). The presence of a strong regulative mandate and ample funding for enforcement and licensing personnel can largely mitigate these problems, providing assurance to the public that games are being fairly conducted and that governments are properly receiving all revenues due.

Regulation is initiated and designed to support the commonweal. Segments of the legalized-gaming industry – even when not directly owned or operated by a state – will thus commonly have a close and lasting relationship with regulatory bodies established and controlled by elected officials. Accordingly, as Skolnick (1978) suggests, there is always the potential for gaming interests to become so politically powerful that they circumvent the spirit if not the actual letter of the law.

Table 5.5. *U.S. gaming company financial operating performance:*
Composite of thirty-seven companies, 1993–98

	Revenues	Operating income	Operating margin (%)[a]	Assets	Operating cash flow
CAGR (%)[b]	9.4	6.4	(2.7)	17.7	8.4

[a] Average margin, 1993–98 = 15.2%
[b] Compound annual growth rate.

Financial performance and valuation

The variety of companies that derive some or all of their income from the operation of legalized gaming and wagering activities is surprisingly broad.[16] In addition to the relatively well-known casino-hotel companies, there are manufacturers of computer components and designers of software used in lottery systems management. There are producers of sophisticated slot and poker machines. Plastics and paper companies make dice and playing cards. And breeding and real estate firms are involved in racing. However, of all these categories, the most readily definable and investable grouping is that of the casino-hotel operators.

Although casino returns on investment (ROI) have varied greatly from company to company, the casino industry has generally prospered in recent decades.[17] Moreover, as shown in Table 5.5, growth rates of revenues, assets, and operating income have mostly remained in balance, thereby enabling the industry to borrow heavily against a relatively small equity base.

Most investors or lenders would thus value a gaming enterprise by analyzing its potential in terms of earnings before taxes, interest, and depreciation and amortization (EBITDA). The multiple that would then be applied to such a projected cash flow figure would be a function of interest rates, local market growth and competitive considerations, the worth of underlying real estate for alternative uses, and general economic conditions.[18]

Similarly, enterprise value could be estimated as follows:

(number of shares × price) + net debt − off-balance-sheet assets.

Wherein net debt is defined as

long-term debt − cash.

Of course, the concepts and methodology – and the existence of normally deep public market discounts to estimated private market values – are similar to those seen in valuations of media properties (see Sections 6.4 and 6.5 of *Entertainment Industry Economics*) or airlines (Section 2.5).

Table 5.6. *Characteristics of casino games*

Games	Edge[a] (%)	Frequency of play (min.)
American roulette	2.7	0.75
French roulette	1.4–2.7	1.5–2
Blackjack	At least 0.6	2–3
Punto banco	1.25	2–3
Craps	1.4–5.6	1.5–2
Baccarat banque	0.9–1.5	2–3

[a]In a rational world it might be expected that the edge would be inversely proportional to the frequency with which the game is played, but this is clearly not so in the actual casino world. In any case, many players are under the illusion that the more often they can play, the more likely they are to win. *Source: Final Report* (1978, Vol. 2, p. 451). London: Royal Commission on Gambling.

5.3 Underlying profit principles and terminology

There are uncountable variations on the thousands of card, dice, and numbers games that have been invented over the millennia. But of these, only a few have been standardized for use in today's legalized-gaming environment. This section presents a framework for understanding how games generate profits on the transactions level.

Principles

It is easy to arrive at an impression that a casino's profits come only out of the collective hides of the losing bettors. But, surprisingly, a governing principle behind the conduct of every profit-making betting activity is to *pay less than true odds* to the winners. Indeed, it is the payment of less than true odds to winners (out of the losers' pool) that provides the casino with its "edge" (Table 5.6), the racetrack with its "take," and the lottery with its "cut." In other words, losers' money is used to compensate winners, but not as adequately as game mathematics would require. Hence, profits are, in a sense, derived from both losers and winners. Pari-mutuel betting, in which various taxes, track fees, and "breakage" charges (see Appendix C) are deducted from the pool of funds contributed by winners and losers, provides another example of this.

With a statistical advantage established, operating profitability is then affected by the number of decisions or completed betting events per unit time. A second governing principle is thus found in the steady pressure to raise or to maintain the rate of decision as high as possible so that statistical advantages are compounded as much as possible over time. If winners are shortchanged of true odds by even a small percentage often enough, then the aggregate amount kept by the game operator (the "house") can be substantial.[19]

A third governing principle in the operation of games of chance is applied when betting limits (the maximum amount permitted to be wagered on each decision) are imposed. Murphy (1976) notes that in a game with 50 : 50 odds (e.g., tossing pennies or betting double or nothing) the usual assumption is that over a long period of time the outcome will be even. This, however, is untrue if one player has limited capital and the other has infinite capital: The expected outcome for the player with limited capital is total loss. The imposition of a betting limit (which, in effect, artificially constrains the player's capital relative to that of the game operator), in and of itself practically guarantees that over an extended period the operator will win all, even without benefit of a house edge.[20] In such cases, it is thus not the edge, but the limit, that defeats the gambler.

In practice, rather than dividing their stake into many smaller units and rebetting, players have the highest probability of winning if they make just one large bet; the house's edge here has minimal opportunity to grind down the player's capital. However, because most people would not enjoy going to a casino or track and making only one bet, people instead tradeoff the probability of winning for entertainment value derived through extended playing time. An excerpt from *Gambling Times* illustrates.[21]

In playing red or black on roulette with one $100 bet, the house edge is 5.26% (there are 18 reds, 18 blacks, and 2 greens – so odds are 20 to 18 against) and a bet may be expected to be won 47.37% of the time – almost an even chance. Now suppose $5 units are bet until $100 are either won or lost. Out of 1,000 trials, on average 873 times there would be a loss of $100, and only 127 times a win of $100. The average amount to bet to obtain a decision would be $1,451 compared to $100 with one large bet.

As for sports betting, an important principle noted by Moore (1996, p. 5) is that "it is the collective public perception that controls the odds." A bookmaker's proposed odds payoff schedule, his "line," thus does not express an opinion on how the two teams will fare. It instead represents the linemaker's expert opinion on what numbers will induce half the public to bet on the underdog and the other half to bet on the favorite.

Terminology and performance standards

A positive expected return to the game operator is realized over many betting events, be they dice rolls, card flips, slot-machine pulls, races run, or lottery tickets sold. The total amount bet is called the *handle*, and the amount that remains for the game organizer after the betting-event result has been determined is the *win*.

In casino table games, cash or cash equivalents, such as credit slips called *markers*, are collected (dropped) into sealed boxes under the tables. The dollar-equivalent aggregates in the boxes have thus become known as the *drop* – a term that also applies to the coins (and/or tokens) fed into slot machines.[22] The *win* rate, expressed as a percentage, is then the total win (over time) divided by the total drop. This percentage is usually referred to as the *hold*.[23] In contrast, at tracks, states charge a fixed percentage of the handle as a "fee" for participation.

Although the operator's positive-expected-return percentage produced by trials over many betting events is generally small – ranging from almost nil at some points in a blackjack game to over 15% for some bets in craps, at the Big Six wheel, in lotteries, in bingo, and at the track – win rates normally range between 10 and 25% of the drop in casinos, 17% or more of the handle in racing, and ∼50% of the handle in lotteries. In effect, then, the win percentage may be viewed as the average proportion of the bankroll of all players taken collectively that would be typically retained by the game operator. Note here, however, that the casino's "edge" (its expected value per unit bet, or, in casino jargon, the house p.c.) in table games is expressed as a percentage of the handle and not as a percentage of the drop (even though these might sometimes be the same).

Moreover, the similarity of conversion of cash at the track into tickets and the converting of cash at the casino into chips does not mean that the handle at tracks and lotteries can be compared to the drop in a casino. In casinos, handle is typically not the drop and may turn out to be a multiple of the drop because (a) it is unusual for all chips (cheques) purchased and counted in the drop to be immediately "invested" in the game and (b) "reinvestment" of chips won or retained in the course of play may increase the handle without correspondingly increasing the drop through additional chip purchases. Such, though, is not the case with pari-mutuel tickets, where there is no fractional retention of the ticket's value. The full face amount of the ticket is bet in each race.

Assume a one-roll-decision dice game in which the casino edge is 2%. The following numerical example should help clarify the terminology. Say there are five bettors, each betting $10 on a throw of the dice. The handle is then $50. Assume further that the players are not using cash, but instead chips issued by the casino and bought at the table for cash. The drop will then also be $50 at the start of the game. Theoretically, for each decision, the casino ought to expect to win 2%, or $1, of the total amount bet. Of course, this may or may not happen over the short run, but it will, on average, occur over the long run (i.e., over many betting decisions).

Now assume for a moment that on the first roll, the players as a group come out even and that they then bet the second roll identically to the first. The handle at that table has now risen to $100, while the drop has remained $50; no player had to buy more chips.[24]

Another hypothetical situation can be examined to illustrate how the hold is over 10% even when the house's edge may be 1%. Suppose that a player beginning with a $100 stake, and buying $100 worth of chips, on each decision happens to experience the long-run average loss specific to that game of 1% per decision. On the first deal of the cards, the casino wins $1, and the player has $99 left over. On the second deal, the casino wins $0.99, and the player has $98.01 remaining. Extrapolating, after eleven decisions the player

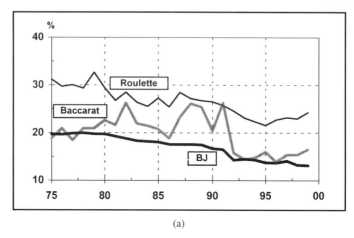

(a)

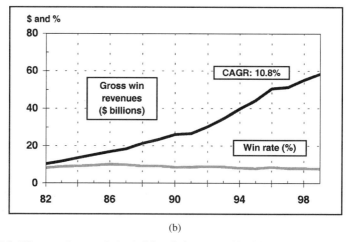

(b)

Figure 5.5. Win rate characteristics in Nevada by game, 1975–99: (a) by game, and
(b) average for all games.

has less than $90, and the casino has more than $10; at this stage, the win as
percentage of the drop (the hold) is over 10% (with the handle over $1,000).

Most games have win rates that over time are characteristic and that can
thus be used as statistical-norm benchmarks against which the performance of
a specific table (or of a casino with many tables) may be measured. Nevada's
characteristic win-rate averages, for example, are shown in Figure 5.5 and
in Table 5.7. From the figure we can see that baccarat is the most volatile
(i.e., has the highest variance) of all games in terms of gross win fluctuations.
Indeed, the variance is so great that casinos occasionally encounter losing
months at their baccarat pits.[25]

Analysis of casino game performances may also be extended well beyond the rudiments just presented. Detailed knowledge of the probability for

Table 5.7. *Hold (% win to drop) for Nevada, 1975–99[a]*

	Major table games				
	Blackjack	Craps	Roulette	Baccarat	Total
Nevada (% total win by source)[b]					
Mean:	20.0	10.4	2.6	5.8	38.7
Hold (% win to drop)					
Mean:	17.0	16.7	26.5	19.9	20.0
Variance:	5.6	3.6	8.5	14.5	6.1

[a]Fiscal years ended June 30 beginning in 1984.
[b]Including slots.
Source: Nevada Gaming Control Board.

each betting-decision result (and of the average number of events per final decision) is required to calculate cost as a percentage of money bet. Such knowledge may then be used to determine the true cost to the casino of player junkets and comps. An interesting rule of thumb mentioned by Kilby (1985), for example, is that a casino has earnings potential of around one average bet per hour. That is, if the average bet is $25, then the casino can expect on average to win that amount in each hour of play.[26]

With slots often accounting for over two thirds of a casino's revenues and floor space, managers are also motivated to compare ROI performances of various machines. A model that can be used for such purposes is described by Johnson (1984, p. 62). As illustrated in the following, it includes variables for coin denomination, hold, average coins played, and cycle time.

Johnson's model uses three equations:

1. denomination × hold × average coins played = win per game.
2. average daily drop ÷ win per game = games played.
3. games played × cycle time ÷ hours operated daily = utilization rate.

A sample calculation is then:

1. $0.05(denomination) × 0.15(percentage hold) × 2.2(average coins played) = $0.0165.
2. To win $25, this machine must be played 1,515 ($25/$0.0165) times.
3. Assuming an average cycle time of 10 seconds, it will take 15,152 seconds (4.21 hours) or a 17.5% utilization rate over 24 hours to reach these earnings.

Although ROI comparisons are made on a win-per-unit basis, the coin-in or handle (i.e., the total number of coins and bills) that a machine attracts is another frequently analyzed aspect because it is an indicator of the relative popularity of a particular game.

5.4 Casino management and accounting policies

Marketing matters

One way to understand the business of a casino (or that of any other wagering establishment) is to visualize it as a retailer, ostensibly of betting
opportunities, but in actuality, of experiences that are stimulating, exciting,
and *entertaining*. That such experiences have an inherent value to the customer is proven time and again by the fact that – although they receive nothing
tangible on-balance in return for the money they spend – the customers tend
to come back for another visit. The marketing challenge is to get customers
into the store through advertising, marketing, and publicity, and to then keep
them shopping for as long as possible under conditions in which "the customer sets the price. . . decides when the show begins and how long it will
last."[27]

Casinos in particular have found it necessary to create marketing images
that most appeal to the core of players they are likeliest to attract. The largest
chains then make further marketing refinements on the basis of statistical
experiments that determine which incentives are the most profitable to implement for each category of player. For example, Mandalay Resort Group
casino-hotels have long and very profitably catered to low- and mid-budget
players who do not require extensive credit-granting facilities or lavish meal
and entertainment services. In contrast, Mirage Resorts (now merged with
MGM Grand) has – without sacrificing the important and vastly broader
upper-middle-income player group – profitably exploited the so-called high-
roller niche, in which practically any whim of the free-spending gamer is
indulged.[28] In addition, some casinos also still attract players by developing
tour and travel discount packages and junkets.[29]

Even with all this, however, market shares for individual companies do not
remain static and it is crucial for managements to accommodate the shifting
demands of players by altering the mix of their games over time. In recent
years, for instance, technological advances in the design of electronic slot
machines (including video poker and blackjack) have made them so popular
that they have come to account, at the expense of table games, for a steadily
rising share of overall industry revenues (Figure 5.6).

But the optimal mix of slots to table games may also, as Greenlees (1988,
p. 12) has noted, vary considerably from one region to another. As has already
been shown in Figure 5.4, the average amounts of money and time spent by
visitors to Las Vegas differ greatly from those to Atlantic City.

Cash and credit

Large casinos will often have millions of dollars in cash and equivalents either
in play or ready for play at the tables and slot machines. To attract and to retain
business, most casinos will also often extend credit and comps (free goods
and services) to their better customers. The short-run management problem,

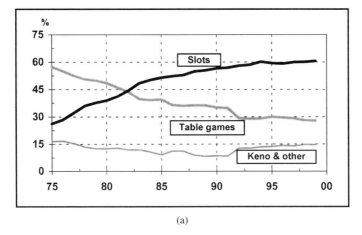

(a)

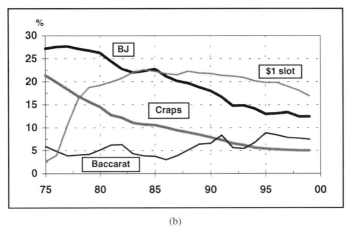

(b)

Figure 5.6. Nevada dollar volume market shares (a) by category, and (b) by game, 1975–99. *Source*: Nevada Gaming Control Board.

then, is to oversee and control the flow of cash, credit, and comps, preventing the abuses by employees and by customers that can naturally be anticipated when there is regular and close contact with sizable amounts of money.

Achievement of such control requires implementation of highly detailed and regimented rules of conduct. But enforcement of the rules must also be accompanied by a strong commitment from upper management to subject any deviations and irregularities to close scrutiny. In practice, this means that operating procedures are broken into many small and well-defined steps: Many people must watch many people as credits and comps are granted and as the cash moves from the pockets of the players into the tables and slots, into the counting rooms, and then finally into a bank vault. The same applies with regard to chips, cash, and credits that are recycled back to tables and cashiers' windows as seed money to conduct the games.

Of all such activities, however, it is in the granting of credit that the casino establishes what is probably the most sensitive and important of relationships with its customers. Credit that is extended and then promptly repaid normally generates very profitable activity because the casino's edge is applied to a bigger volume of play than it would otherwise receive.[30]

But credit also has another, darker side. As Friedman (1974, 1982) has noted, casinos must win their money twice, first having to beat credit players at the tables and then having to collect the amounts they are owed. If a customer receives more credit than can be recycled in full over a reasonable time after play, casino margins will suffer from bad-debt write-offs. Accordingly, strict credit-granting procedures have been developed in both Nevada and New Jersey.[31] Using bank references and other information, managers can, for instance, certify with Central Credit Inc. in Nevada that the customer is in good standing at banks and at other hotel-casinos.

Credit policies usually also reflect casino marketing strategies, the effects of which can generally be seen on the balance sheet through bad-debt allowances as a percentage of accounts receivable. The Showboat hotel-casino in Las Vegas, for example, has a largely cash clientele and therefore virtually no need for bad-debt reserves. Conversely, Caesars Palace has largely positioned itself as a high-roller's mecca, and its allowances have been relatively large, as measured in absolute dollars or as a percentage of receivables. Important deviations from prior reserve-percentage norms often signal changes in marketing policies – or in accounting procedures that may significantly influence reported earnings.

Moreover, rapid growth of receivables net of reserves as compared with the growth of gross win is often an early-warning indicator that current-period performance is perhaps being unsustainably boosted by "borrowing" from performance in future periods. In effect, players are being granted more credit than they can repay over a reasonably short time, and the likelihood is that they are being tapped out (or "burned" out).[32]

Procedural paradigms

Fill slips record the value of the bills, coins, and chips that the cashier's cage issues to the gaming tables, and credit slips record the value of these items returned to the cage. Nevada Gaming Commission Regulations [Number 6.040(5)] specify the method that must be used to transfer cash and equivalents between tables and the cage.[33]

According to the regulations [and following Friedman's (1974) presentation], "all fill slips and credit slips shall be serially numbered in forms prescribed by the board," and the serial numbers must include letters of the alphabet "so that no gaming establishment may ever utilize the same number and series. . . . All series numbers that are received by the establishment must be accounted for. All void slips shall be marked 'VOID' and shall require the signatures of the 2 persons voiding the slip."

In addition, there are several detailed regulations as to how drop boxes are unlocked with two different keys – one issued by the cage and the other by the accounting department at the time the count is scheduled. Once the drop box is opened, regulations specify that the contents of each box or bag be counted and verified by three counting employees and that the count be supported by all credit and fill slips taken from the box.

The count team notes shift win, shift currency drop, shift fill and credits, and shift IOUs to the cage, and it typically sorts a box's contents into (a) currency, (b) chips, (c) fill slips, (d) chip credit slips, and (e) name credit slips. A table shift's records – its *stiff sheets* – will then include the table's opening chip bank (inventory) as a fill slip and the shift's closing chip bank as a chip credit. Calculations by shift can then be made as follows:

currency + chips + name credits + chip credits + closing bank

$\quad$ = table income

opening bank + fills = table fills

table income − table fills = table win.

More specifically, the win or loss at each table in each shift may, as illustrated in AICPA (1984, p. 7), be computed as in the following example:

Cash in the drop box		$6,000
Credit issued and outstanding		3,000
Total *drop*		9,000
Less: Beginning table inventory	$14,000	
Chip transfers		
Fills	5,000	
Credits	(1,000)	
	18,000	
Ending table inventory	(11,000)	7,000
Win		$2,000

Of course, all accounts, including cash, hold IOUs (a customer's check that a casino agrees not to process until some time in the future), and others are verified and balanced according to standard journal-entry procedures. In addition, table-game and slot results are regularly analyzed by shift, using statistical tests to signal possible significant deviations in win and drop figures from previously established averages. In this way, casino managers can detect where there might be any fraud by employees or customers.

Also, when aggregated over longer periods such as a week or a month, these statistics may be analyzed to indicate trends in win per square foot. Such data permit relative-efficiency comparisons to be made to experiences in prior periods and to the performances of other casinos. The analysis is similar to

Table 5.8. *Nevada gaming revenue analysis, fiscal year 1996*

Category	Statewide	Las Vegas Strip
Revenue per square foot[a]		
Pit[b]	$1,909	$3,352
Coin-operated devices[c]	1,043	1,148
Poker and pan	2,422	4,561
Race and sports	566	698
Total casino	$1,218	$1,648
Casino department % of revenues from:		
Pit[b]	33.2%	44.2%
Coin-operated devices[c]	61.4	47.9
Poker and pan	2.7	4.6
Race book	1.4	1.9
Sports pool	1.3	1.5
Total revenue	100.0%	100.0%

[a] Statewide includes 229 locations, Las Vegas Strip 40 locations.
[b] Includes keno and bingo.
[c] Primarily slot machines.
Source: Nevada Gaming Abstract, State Gaming Control Board.

sales-per-square-foot calculations used in the retailing industry. Table 5.8, for example, shows Nevada revenues and average win per square foot data by game category.

5.5 Gambling and economics

The psychological roots of the desire to gamble are complex and not completely understood. In fact, some psychologists (e.g., Halliday and Fuller 1974) view gambling as a neurosis rather than a form of entertainment.

Economists, however, deal with the demand for gaming services through utility-function models. In such models, consumers express their preferences by making purchases according to the utility they expect to derive from the goods or services bought.

To see how this line of thinking evolved, we have to go back over two hundred years. At that time, some mathematicians were concerned about resolving the so-called St. Petersburg paradox, which was presented in the form of a coin-tossing game. In theory, because the expected value (payoff, or return) of the game was infinite, players should have been willing to pay an infinite amount to participate. Yet no one was willing to do so.

Mathematicians Daniel Bernoulli and Gabriel Cramer solved the mystery by rejecting the principle of maximum expected return and by substituting

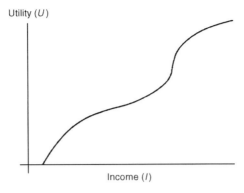

Figure 5.7. An individual's utility function. *Source*: Friedman and Savage (1948).

instead the concept of expected utility. By recognizing the diminishing marginal utility of money (the additional utility derived from additional units decreases as the money value of the prize increases) they could explain the paradox: Participants would determine the amount they were willing to play in a St. Petersburg type of game according to the game's expected utility and *not* its expected monetary returns.

Significant further work on the nature of utility functions was done in the 1930s, when it was demonstrated that unless the function is bounded, new paradoxes can be constructed. It then remained for von Neumann and Morgenstern (1944) to show, in their classic 1940s work on game theory, how the expected-utility hypothesis leads to optimal decisions under conditions of uncertainty.

Friedman and Savage (1948) then later published an important study discussing the application of the expected-utility concept to choices made by individuals. Why, they asked, would many people purchase insurance (pay a premium to avoid risk) and also gamble (undertake risk)? To answer, they postulated (as shown in Figure 5.7) that over some range, the marginal utility of wealth increases, which means that the utility functions of individuals contain both concave (risk-aversion curves graphically represented as outward-bending from the origin) and convex (risk-affinitive) segments. Also, as Yaari (1965) has suggested, players often substitute, for the objective or true probabilities of a game, their own subjective beliefs about those probabilities.

In contrast to the theoreticians just cited, however, other economists have examined the gaming industry through a variety of standard econometric modeling approaches. Eadington (1976), for example, estimated for the Nevada economy the coefficients in a production function of the form $Q = f(K, L, M)$, where Q represents volume of finished product, K is capital equipment, L is labor, and M is quantity of raw materials. From this he was able to draw conclusions concerning economies of scale and the optimal mix and marginal productivities of various games and devices. Still others (e.g., Asch, Malkiel, and Quandt 1984) have, moreover, suggested that certain betting situations and the securities markets are behavioral analogs that can be studied through market-efficiency theories.

In all, the academic literature on gambling and economics has developed rapidly because gaming and wagering activities have so many quantifiable aspects, and because economic analysis can be readily applied to everything from game playing to the determination of optimal casino comp and credit policies.

5.6 Concluding remarks

In total, more is spent on gaming and wagering activities than on movies and recorded music combined. This remarkable situation has, in part, since the early 1950s reflected changes in American life styles as well as advances in lottery, racing, communications, and slot machine technologies.[34] However, the industry's growth potential depends on an unusually broad assortment of social, political, and economic factors. As economists Ignatin and Smith (1976) have noted, the one constant throughout is that gambling possesses both consumption and investment characteristics; it provides direct utility with the hope of financial gain. In other words, people do not gamble only for money; they also gamble because it is entertaining.

Selected additional reading

Alchian, A. A. (1953). "The Meaning of Utility Measurement," *American Economic Review*, March.

Barron, J. (1989). "Has the Growth of Legal Gambling Made Society the Loser in the Long Run?," *New York Times*, May 31.

  (1989). "States Sell Chances for Gold as a Rush Turns to a Stampede," *New York Times*, May 28.

Bass, T. A. (1985). *The Eudaemonic Pie*. Boston: Houghton Mifflin.

Binkley, C. (2000). "The Finest Casino That Could Be Built, That Was the Goal," *Wall Street Journal*, February 2.

Blum, H., and Gerth, J. (1978). "The Mob Gambles on Atlantic City," *New York Times*, February 5.

Brenner, R., and G. A. (1990). *Gambling and Speculation: A Theory, a History, and a Future of Human Decisions*. New York: Cambridge University Press.

Brisman, A. (1999). *American Mensa Guide to Casino Gambling*. New York: Sterling.

Bulkeley, W. M. (1995). "Electronics Is Bringing Gambling Into Homes, Restaurants and Planes," *Wall Street Journal*, August 16.

Bulkeley, W. M., and Stecklow, S. (1996). "Long a Winner, Gtech Faces Resistance Based on Ethical Concerns," *Wall Street Journal*, January 16.

Cabot, A. N. (1999). Internet Gambling Report III. Las Vegas: Trace Publications.

Camerer, C. (1989). "Does the Basketball Market Believe in the Hot Hand?" *American Economic Review*, (December) 79: and comment by Brown, W. O., and Sauer, R. D. (1993). *American Economic Review*, (December) 83.

Charlier, M. (1992). "Casino Gambling Saves Three Colorado Towns but the Price Is High," *Wall Street Journal*, September 23.

Clark, T. L. (1987). *The Dictionary of Gambling and Gaming*. Cold Spring, NY: Lexik House.

Cook, J. (1980). "The Most Abused, Misused Pension Fund in America," *Forbes*, 126(10) (November 10).

Cook, J., and Carmichael, J. (1980). "Casino Gambling: Changing Character or Changing Fronts," *Forbes*, 126(9)(October 27).

Cordtz, D. (1990). "Betting the Country," *Financial World*, 159(4)(February 20).

Demaris, O. (1986). *The Boardwalk Jungle*. New York: Bantam.

Dombrink, J., and Thompson, W. N. (1990). *The Last Resort: Success and Failure in Campaigns for Casinos*. Reno and Las Vegas: University of Nevada Press.

Elkind, P. (1997). "The Big Easy's Bad Bet," *Fortune*, 136(11)(December 8).

(1996). "The Number Crunchers," *Fortune*, 134(9)(November 11).

Emshwiller, J. R. (1992). "California Card Casinos Are Suspected as Fronts for Rising Asian Mafia," *Wall Street Journal*, June 1.

Epstein, R. A. (1967). *The Theory of Gambling and Statistical Logic*. New York: Academic Press.

Hamer, T. P. (1982). "The Casino Industry in Atlantic City: What Has It Done for the Local Economy?," *Business Review*, Federal Reserve Bank of Philadelphia, January/February.

Harris, R. J., Jr. (1984). "Circus Circus Succeeds in Pitching Las Vegas to People on Budgets," *Wall Street Journal*, July 31.

Hirshey, G. (1994). "Gambling: America's Real National Pastime," *New York Times* Magazine, July 17.

Horwitz, T. (1997). "In a Bible Belt State, Video Poker Mutates into an Unholy Mess," *Wall Street Journal*, December 2.

Johnston, D. (1992). *Temples of Chance: How America Inc. Bought Out Murder Inc. to Win Control of the Casino Business*. New York: Doubleday.

Kilby, J., and Fox, J. (1998). *Casino Operations Management*. New York: John Wiley & Sons.

Lancaster, H. (1980). "Casino 'Hosts' Pamper High-Rolling Bettors to Keep Them Rolling," *Wall Street Journal*, September 3.

Lehne, R. (1986). *Casino Policy*. New Brunswick NJ: Rutgers University Press.

Levine, L. (1995). "Requiem for a Thoroughbred?," *Forbes*, 156(14)(December 18).

Liebau, J. (1983). "Tearing Up the Turf," *Barron's*, August 8.

Longstreet, S. (1977). *Win or Lose: A Social History of Gambling in America*. Indianapolis: Bobbs-Merrill.

Messick, H., and Goldblatt, B. (1976). *The Only Game in Town: An Illustrated History of Gambling*. New York: Crowell.

Morehead, A. H., and Mott-Smith, G., eds. (1963). *Hoyle's Rules of Games*. New York: Signet Books, New American Library.

Myerson, A. R. (1996). "A Big Casino Wager That Hasn't Paid Off," *New York Times*, June 2.

O'Brien, T. L. (1998). *Bad Bet: The Inside Story of the Glamour, Glitz, and Danger of America's Gambling Industry*. New York: Times Books.

O'Donnell, J. R., and Rutherford, J. (1991). *Trumped! The Inside Story of the Real Donald Trump*. New York: Simon & Schuster.

Orwall, B. (1996a). "The Federal Regulator of Indian Gambling Is Also Part Advocate," *Wall Street Journal*, July 22.

(1996b). "Gambling Industry Hopes to Hit Jackpot through Consolidation," *Wall Street Journal*, June 10.

(1995). "Casinos Aren't for Kids, Many Gambling Firms in Las Vegas Now Say," *Wall Street Journal*, December 7.

Orwall, B., Rundle, R. L., and Rose, F. (1997). "Hilton and ITT Took Two Different Paths to This Confrontation," *Wall Street Journal*, January 29.

Paher, S., ed. (1976), *Nevada Official Bicentennial Book*. Las Vegas: Nevada Publications.

Painton, P. (1989). "Boardwalk of Broken Dreams," *Time*, 134(13)(September 25).

Passell, P. (1994a). "Foxwoods, a Casino Success Story," *New York Times*, August 8.

(1994b). "The False Promise of Development by Casino," *New York Times*, June 12.

Peterson, I. (1995). "After 20 Years, Atlantic City Starts to Reap Casinos' Benefits," *New York Times*, December 26.

Pileggi, N. (1995). *Casino: Love and Honor in Las Vegas*. New York: Simon and Schuster.

Pollock, M. (1987). *Hostage to Fortune: Atlantic City and Casino Gambling*. Princeton, NJ: Center for Analysis of Public Issues.

Pulley, B. (1998a). "Regulators Find Easy Path to Gambling Industry Jobs," *New York Times*, October 28.

(1998b). "Casino Changes the Fortune of a Hard-Luck Illinois City," *New York Times*, July 21.

(1998c). "Casinos Paying Top Dollar to Coddle Elite Gamblers," *New York Times*, January 12.

Reinhold, R. (1989). "Las Vegas Transformation: From Sin City to Family City," *New York Times*, May 30.

Roemer, W. F., Jr. (1994). *The Enforcer: The Chicago Mob's Man over Las Vegas*. New York: Ivy Books (Ballantine).

(1990). *War of the Godfathers: The Bloody Confrontation between the Chicago and New York Families for Control of Las Vegas*. New York: Donald I. Fine.

Ross, I. (1984). "Corporate Winners in the Lottery Boom," *Fortune*, 110(5)(September 3).

Sack, K. (1995). "Gambling Owners Spend Lavishly to Gain a Voice in Many States," *New York Times*, December 18.

Schwartz, E. I. (1995). "Wanna Bet?," *Wired*, October.

Seligman, D. (1987). "Turmoil Time in the Casino Business," *Fortune*, 115(5)(March 2).

(1975). "A Thinking Man's Guide to Losing at the Track," *Fortune*, XCII(3)(September).

Spanier, D. (1992). *Welcome to the Pleasuredome: Inside Las Vegas*. Reno: University of Nevada Press.

Swartz, S. (1985). "New Jersey Casino Commission Stirs Controversy with Rulings," *Wall Street Journal*, March 11.

Thorp, E. O. (1962). *Beat the Dealer*. New York: Random House (Vintage Books paperback, 1966).

Treaster, J. B. (1982). "Mob Alliance to Share Casino Riches Reported," *New York Times*, September 1.

Useem, J. (2000). "The Big Gamble: Have American Indians Found Their New Buffalo?," *Fortune*, 142(7)(October 2).

Vinson, B. (1986). *Las Vegas behind the Tables*! Grand Rapids, MI: Gollehon.

Wartzman, P. (1995). "Gambling Is Proving to Be a Poor Wager for State of Louisiana," *Wall Street Journal*, September 11.

Wells, K. (1988). "Philip Anderson Has a Feeling He Knows What's in the Cards," *Wall Street Journal*, January 13.

Yoshihashi, P. (1990). "More States Like Odds on Sports Betting Despite Fierce Opposition to Legalization," *Wall Street Journal*, February 1.

6
Amusement/theme parks

Mickey is the mouse that roared.

The American themed amusement park industry – begun in July 1955 by Mickey Mouse, the famous Disney character – has evolved into a multibillion-dollar travel and entertainment segment that draws visitors from around the world and has spawned many imitations. In this chapter, the economic outlines of amusement and theme-park operations are sketched.

6.1 Flower power

Gardens and groves

The roots of this business extend back to medieval church-sponsored fairs and to seventeenth-century France, whose concept of pleasure gardens with fountains and flowers gradually spread throughout Europe. London's Vauxhall Gardens, for example, were established in 1661.[1] By the eighteenth century, as Kyriazi (1976) has noted, entertainment and circus acts, including trapeze and tightrope scenes, ascension balloons, and music were added. In England, meanwhile, affiliations with nearby taverns or inns also became common.

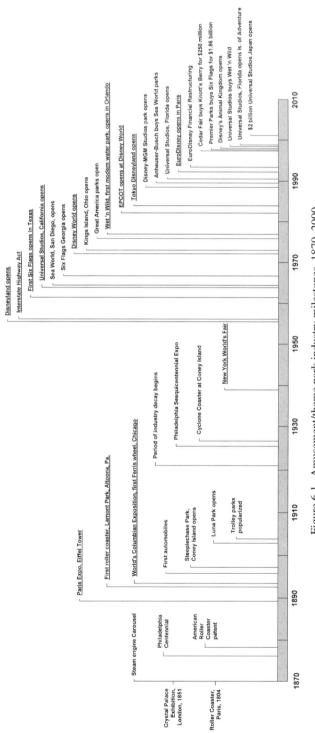

Figure 6.1. Amusement/theme park industry milestones, 1870–2000.

But it was not until the 1873 Vienna World's Fair, held at The Prater, that mechanical rides and fun houses were introduced. As Mangels (1952, p. 4) describes it,

For more than three hundred years, elaborate outdoor amusement centers have existed in several European countries. Known usually as "pleasure gardens" they were remarkably similar to those of today in their general layout and variety of entertainment. Some of the larger parks provided events and devices which thrilled their visitors as keenly as present-day attractions. Queens of the slack wire and daredevils of the flying rings brought gasps of fascinated terror, much as they do beneath the Big Top today . . . free balloon ascensions, and parachute jumps held crowds spellbound as far back as the seventeen-nineties.

In the United States, however, amusement areas did not begin to appear until the late 1800s, when streetcar companies began to build picnic groves to attract weekend riders. But still, as Adams (1991, p. 19) notes, it was the World's Columbian Exposition, held in Chicago in 1893, that "introduced most of the essential elements of American amusement parks." Soon thereafter, food and rides came to be emphasized, and major facilities such as New York's Coney Island sprang into national prominence.[2] Although, by the 1920s, some 1,500 such parks existed in the United States, the Great Depression, the development of movies, television, and automobiles, and the decay of inner cities eventually led to the demise of most.

Modern times

Walt Disney, at first a struggling cartoonist and later a successful filmmaker, liked spending time with his children. Unfortunately, there were few bright, clean parks where all members of the family could have fun. So being an extraordinarily imaginative and entrepreneurial fellow, he envisioned creation of such a park modeled in part after the famous Tivoli Gardens that he had seen in Copenhagen (Thomas, 1976, Chapter 20).[3]

As the legend goes, Disney brought his plans for an amusement park containing themed areas before a rather skeptical and reluctant group of bankers. Yet, with perseverance, bank loans supplemented by borrowing on his life insurance policies, and the sale of concession rights and a 34% equity stake to the young American Broadcasting Company, he nevertheless managed in 1955 to open Disneyland amidst the Anaheim, California, orange groves.[4] The rest, as they say, is history.

Disneyland's immediate success led to numerous expansions. But it was not until the late 1960s that other large public companies began to invest heavily in this business.[5] And the Disney company itself did not until 1971 extend into the swamps of Florida to construct, for an estimated $300 million, the core of Disney World.[6]

As of the late-1990s, theme parks in the United States, which number about thirty majors and a host of smaller ones, generated over $7 billion a year from more than 150 million visitors (Table 6.1).[7] And, as of 1999,

Table 6.1. *Estimated attendance (millions) at major theme park facilities in the United States, 1975–98*[a]

Year	Total	Year	Total
1998	139.1	1985	91.4
1997	139.1	1984	86.9
1996	135.7	1983	93.6
1995	131.3	1982	80
1994	122.5	1981	82.7
1993	124.4	1980	81.7
1992	122.7	1979	80.5
1991	112.5	1978	80.5
1990	114.9	1977	73.2
1989	112.5	1976	68.3
1988	106.4	1975	60.9
1987	104.9	**CAGR:**[b]	
1986	97.6	1980–98	2.1

[a]Fiscal years.
[b]Compound annual growth rate, (%).

it is estimated that on a global basis, the industry generated approximately $14 billion in revenues from attendance of around 550 million people.[8]

In fact, the concept of *location-based entertainment* (LBE) has come to be used as a broader way to more accurately describe technologically sophisticated away-from-home attractions, the largest examples of which are the major theme parks.[9] It is thus not surprising – in view of advances in technology, design, and marketing – that American-style LBE concepts of the late twentieth century are being exported back to Europe and elsewhere around the globe.[10] A compilation of such major theme parks and annual visitor estimates appears in Table 6.2, and a history of developments is displayed in Figure 6.1.

6.2 Financial operating characteristics

Operating a theme park is very much like operating a small city: The streets should be frequently swept clean and occasionally repaved; sewer and sanitation systems should be efficient yet invisible; and police, fire, and health departments should be trained and available at a moment's notice. Those elements alone are difficult for most cities to handle well. But, in addition, a park also issues its own currency in the form of ticket books, and it provides visitor-transportation systems, live-entertainment services, and sometimes extensive shopping, hotel, and car-care facilities.

Furthermore, parks – subject as they are to seasonal and circadian rhythms of attendance and to rapidly changing weather patterns – usually depend on

Table 6.2. *Selected major theme park facilities*

Facility	Year opened	Approximate number of annual visitors, 1999 (millions)
North America		
Disney World, Florida[a]	1971	42.6
Disneyland, California	1955	13.4
Universal Studios, Florida[b]	1990	11.5
Universal Studios Tour, California	1964	5.1
Sea World, Florida	1973	4.7
Busch Gardens, Florida	1959	3.9
Six Flags Great Adventure, New Jersey	1973	3.8
Knotts Berry Farm, California	1940	3.6
Sea World, California, California	1963	3.6
Kings Island, Ohio	1972	3.3
Cedar Point, Ohio	1870	3.3
Six Flags Magic Mountain	1971	3.2
Six Flags/Great America, Illinois	1976	3.1
Canada's Wonderland, Toronto	1981	3.0
Six Flags/Texas	1961	2.8
Six Flags/Georgia	1967	2.6
Hersheypark, Pennsylvania	1907	2.3
Busch Gardens, Virginia	1975	2.3
Kings Dominion, Virginia	1975	2.2
Europe		
Disneyland, Paris	1992	12.5
Tivoli Gardens, Denmark	1843	3.1
De Efteling, Netherlands	1951	3.0
Port Aventura, Spain	1995	3.0
Alton Towers, U.K.	1924	2.8
Europa Park, Germany	1975	3.0
Liseberg Park, Sweden	1923	2.6
Other		
Tokyo Disneyland, Japan	1983	17.5
Lotte World, S. Korea	1989	6.1

[a]Includes Magic Kingdom, Disney-MGM Studios, EPCOT, and Animal Kingdom
[b]Includes Universal Studios and Islands of Adventure
Source: Amusement Business.

Table 6.3. *U.S. theme-park industry operating performance: Composite of four companies, 1993–98*

	Revenues	Operating income	Operating margin (%)[a]	Assets	Operating cash flow
CAGR (%)[b]	6.7	11.9	4.9	15.0	11.1

[a] Average margin, 1993–98 = 20.6%.
[b] Compound annual growth rate.

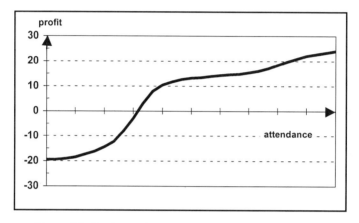

Figure 6.2. Profit as a function of attendance: an illustration.

a largely unskilled seasonal workforce that turns over at inherently high rates. In all, it is not easy to juggle these elements and to further generate a stream of consistently rising profits (Table 6.3). For a specific park, operating-margin performance may thus be uneven and volatile: One year the problem may be high fuel prices; the next it may be abnormally hot summer temperatures, rainy spring weekends, or competition from other events.

No matter what the uncertainties, however, the constant feature is operating leverage, also familiar in the airline and hotel businesses. The costs of labor, electricity, insurance, and so forth remain relatively fixed, and once the breakeven point is reached, every additional admission ticket sold produces a high marginal profit.[11]

Such is the case until the park becomes crowded. At that point, long lines at popular attractions reduce opportunities for impulse spending, crimp the initial good mood of the visitors, and entail additional labor and materials costs. Most parks will find that in analyzing daily results, marginal-profit curves as a function of attendance would probably be similar to the one shown in Figure 6.2.

Table 6.4. *Theme-park operating leverage: an example*

	A	B	C	D
Visitors, avg./day	25,000	30,000	25,000	30,000
Visitor-days (attend.)	2,500,000	3,000,000	2,500,000	3,000,000
Per-cap. Spending ($)	20.00	20.00	24.00	24.00
Total annual revs. ($)	50,000,000	60,000,000	60,000,000	72,000,000
Operating expenses	30,000,000	30,000,000	30,000,000	30,000,000
Operating profits ($)	20,000,000	30,000,000	30,000,000	42,000,000

Table 6.4 furthermore demonstrates how sensitive operating profits are to changes in two key variables: visitor-days (attendance equivalent to the number of separate visitors times the number of days of operation) and average per-capita spending. In this example, it is assumed that because of climatic factors, a park has an effective operating season of 100 days per year, that on an average day there are 25,000 visitors, and that average per-capita spending on admissions, rides, foods, beverages, and trinkets is $20. With a relatively stable operating expense of $30 million, operating earnings, as shown in column A, will be $20 million.

If we assume, however, that the number of visitors increases by 20% to 30,000 per day, while expenses remain largely unchanged, then operating profit will increase by 50% to $30 million (column B). And the same 50% increase in operating profit will naturally appear if attendance holds constant and per-capita spending rises by 20% (column C). But finally, assume that per-capita spending and attendance each rise by 20% (column D). Then operating profit will increase to $42 million – a gain of 110% over that shown in column A.

Of course, in the real world, operating expenses will rise along with attendance, per-capita spending will tend to decrease as attendance rises to near capacity (if only because the crowds are immobilized), and the gains in profit will not be as large as indicated in this simplistic example. But substantial operating leverage, both up and down, will nonetheless still be visible in actual results.

Because the compounding of changes in both attendance and spending has such a great impact on profits, park managers devote much of their time to figuring how each input factor can be increased without adversely affecting any of the others. Toward this end, many fancy mathematical modeling techniques (e.g., linear programming, production-function, and queuing-system estimators) can be used to improve the efficiency of park operations. Norms for average daily attendance conditioned on weather, queuing times, and price elasticities may then be established and tested much as though parks were production-line factories.

Table 6.5. *Financial ratio averages for major theme parks, foreign and domestic, 1997*[a]

	U.S. & Canada	Europe
Mean operating days per year	152.8	170.4
Mean percentage of total revenue		
Admissions	42.4	50.9
Food	22.5	21.0
Merchandise	8.3	7.5
Games	8.0	6.4
Mean operating expenses as a % of total revenues		
Employee wages and benefits	35.4	34.4
Repair and maintenance	6.9	6.6
Advertising	8.0	8.4
EBIT[b]	24.7	24.2
Operating Margin	17.6	16.1

[a] Selected non-Disney parks with >0.5 million admissions.
[b] Earnings before interest and taxes.
Source: International Association of Amusement Parks & Attractions, 1997 Season Survey.

Theme-park operating performance depends on region, weather patterns, number of season days, local demographic and income characteristics, and the amount of capital recently invested. Consequently, it is difficult to establish a representative statistical composite for a typical park. Each facility must develop its own set of standards. Table 6.5 provides some recent industry sample ratios.

6.3 Economic sensitivities

A sense of how this industry's operating performance compares with those of other economic segments is not easily derived. And evidence from the *U.S. Census of Selected Service Industries*, which provides data on employment and payrolls (Table 6.6), suggests that parks have not in the aggregate been able to steadily reduce the inherent labor intensity of operations (i.e., payroll as a percent of receipts).

Unfortunately, there are also difficulties in correlating theme-park admissions trends with important economic time series such as those for GDP or real disposable income. Although an economic recession could be expected to adversely affect admissions growth trends at high-profile themed resort parks, other parks more dependent on day-trip and regional visitors might conceivably do better in such an environment.

As might be anticipated, however, aggregate theme-park admissions do seem to be positively correlated with respect to consumer credit as a percent of personal income, and negatively with respect to the unemployment rate.

Table 6.6. *Service industry census comparisons for amusement parks in the U.S., 1977–97*

	Receipts ($1,000)	Payroll (annual) ($1000)	Employees (paid)	Receipts per Employee ($)	Payroll as % of receipts
1997	6,828,719	1,611,090	106,794	63,943	23.6
1992	5,311,781	1,297,545	80,875	65,679	24.4
1987	3,469,836	818,881	60,414	57,434	23.6
1982	1,823,728	603,654	46,464	39,250	33.1
1977	1,172,419	352,898	37,014	31,675	30.1

Source: U.S. Census of Selected Service Industries.

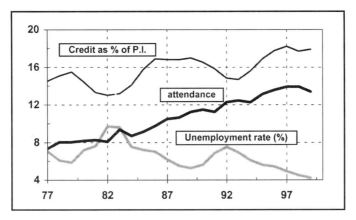

Figure 6.3. Theme park attendance (including Disney's) in the United States in tens of millions versus the unemployment rate (%) and consumer credit as a percentage of personal income, 1977–99.

But the lags, as suggested by Figure 6.3, are not well defined. Some additional variables to consider would, of course, include changes in real admission-ticket and fuel prices, changes in airline fares and foreign exchange rates, and demographic shifts over time. In all, it is likely that the demand for theme-park services is more sensitive to the overall cost of travel relative to incomes than anything else. Worldwide park attendance trends are shown in Figure 6.4.

6.4 Valuing theme-park properties

Real estate – the key asset of any park – normally has the potential to provide long-term returns on investment that, in the end, may surpass the average annual returns obtainable from day-to-day operations. However, for this to

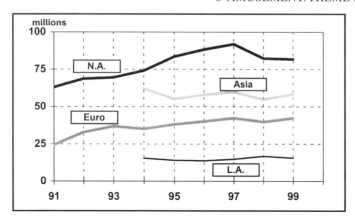

Figure 6.4. Attendance total for top ten parts in North America, Latin America, Asia, and Europe, 1991–99. *Source: Amusement Business* data.

occur, the real estate usually needs to be developed for additional uses (housing, offices, studios, etc.) that are compatible with the park's operations. It also helps, as a hedge against future inflation, if the park happens to lie in the path of ongoing population expansion (e.g., Disneyland, just south of Los Angeles), or if the park, through its own qualities, is able to congeal what would otherwise be haphazard population growth around itself (e.g., Disney World near Orlando).[12]

Given the long-term operating nature of all major parks, the usual established methods for valuing other entertainment properties may also be applied here. As in the broadcasting and cable (or airline and hotel) industries, for example, theme-park asset values are taken as a multiple of projected operating earnings before taxes, interest, and depreciation and amortization (EBITDA). Such multiples would, of course, normally be expected to vary inversely to interest rates. Other factors also affecting the multiple applied to this definition of cash flow would further include:

Age and condition of the park's rides and attractions
Demographic and income trends in the surrounding region
Potential for expanding ride and admissions capacity
Potential for raising prices and/or per capita spending
Prospects for development of nearby transportation facilities
Proximity of other similar attractions

Again, as in other entertainment segments, public market valuations are often considerably below what private market valuations based on a multiple of cash flow might be. Well-situated theme parks with proven operating characteristics are thus often attractive candidates for leveraged buy-outs, in which large institutions will lend a major percentage of the required funding for the buy-out based on the security of the park's cash flow.[13]

6.5 Concluding remarks

In the United States, admissions growth trends have, over long periods, held consistently above the growth trends of real GDP – a fact that has not escaped the attention of investors. The potentially high operating margins and significant free cash flows that are regularly generated by established major park facilities have also been widely recognized.

However, in recent years, the amount of capital investment and technological sophistication required to maintain a leadership position has grown enormously. New motion simulator rides and other computer-controlled "experiences" such as those developed in the framework of "virtual reality" and interactive video games are the new frontiers in the evolution of theme park concepts. It is no wonder, then, that major media companies now view theme-park investments as a natural fit and that theme parks have become important destinations for travelers.

The industry seems to be rather mature in North America, where it has developed into an entertainment form dominated by those few large companies with the marketing expertise and capital to continually upgrade and expand their facilities. Now the industry also seems to be on the verge of substantial growth in other parts of the world. Regardless of location, though, the degree of success will have as much to do with intangible elements – quality of design, efficiency of service, and public fancy – as with anything else.

Selected additional reading

Bannon, L. (1996). "Universal Studios' Plan to Expand in Florida Moves Disney to Battle," *Wall Street Journal*, October 2.

Berck, J. (1994). "When Broadway Meets the Midway, It's Big Business," *New York Times*, August 28.

Braithwaite, D. (1967). *Fairground Architecture: The World of Amusement Parks, Carnivals, & Fairs*. New York: Praeger.

Eisner, M. D. (1998). *Work in Progress*. New York: Random House.

Eliot, M. (1993). *Walt Disney, Hollywood's Dark Prince: A Biography*. New York: Carol Publishing (Birch Lane).

Faison, S. (1999). "Even If You Build Them . . . ," *New York Times*, August 3.

Finch, C. (1975). *The Art of Walt Disney: From Mickey Mouse to the Magic Kingdoms*. New York: Harry N. Abrams.

Flower, J. (1991). *Prince of the Magic Kingdom: Michael Eisner and the Re-Making of Disney*. New York: John Wiley & Sons.

Grover, R. (1997). *The Disney Touch*, rev. ed. Chicago: Irwin.

Gubernick, L. (1999). "How Safe Is That Theme Park?," *Wall Street Journal*, July 23.

Gumbel, P., and Turner, R. (1994). "Fans Like Euro Disney but Its Parent's Goofs Weigh the Park Down," *Wall Street Journal*, March 10.

Hannon, K. (1987). "All Aboard!," *Forbes*, 140(3)(August 10).

Lainsbury, A. (2000). *Once Upon an American Dream: The Story of Euro Disneyland*. Lawrence, KS: University Press of Kansas.

McDowell, E. (1998). "The New Monster of the Midway," *New York Times*, June 21.

Mosley, L. (1987). *Disney's World: A Biography*. Briarcliff Manor, NY: Stein and Day.

Mrowca, M. (1983). "Amusement Park in Ohio Has Its Ups and Downs but Continues to Draw Crowds after 114 Years," *Wall Street Journal*, July 8.

Ono, Y. (1990). "Theme Parks Boom in Japan as Investors and Consumers Rush to Get on the Ride," *Wall Street Journal*, August 8.

Rayl, A. J. S. (1990). "Making Fun: Theme Parks of the Future," *Omni*, 13(2) November.

Ross, I. (1982). "Disney Gambles on Tomorrow," *Fortune*, 106(October 4).

Schickel, R. (1968). *The Disney Version: The Life, Times, Art and Commerce of Walt Disney*. New York: Simon & Schuster.

Schweizer, P., and Schweizer, R. (1998). *Disney: The Mouse Betrayed*. Washington, DC: Regnery Publishing, Inc.

Tagliabue, J. (2000). "Giving Theme Parks a Whirl: Europeans Warm to an American Experience," *New York Times*, September 2.

(1995). "Step Right Up, Monsieur!: Growing Disneyfication of Europe's Theme Parks," *New York Times*, August 23.

Welsh, J. (1999). "Premier Parks Intends to Grow Big by Thinking Small, *Wall Street Journal*, May 12.

7
Tourism

A good holiday is one spent among people whose notions of
time are vaguer than yours. – J. B. Priestly

A broad and generally acceptable definition of tourism suggested by the
National Tourism Policy Study (1978) is that tourism involves people taking
trips to a place or places outside their home communities for any purpose
except daily commuting to and from work.[1] However, no matter what the
precise definition that is applied, the travel industry would certainly be much
smaller if people were not interested in touring – spending leisure time
relaxing, sightseeing, and participating in their favorite resort and vacation
activities.

Although the economics of tourism is a topic closely related to the material presented earlier, it tackles somewhat different issues and analyzes
supply and demand for travel from a perspective that differs from those of
the previous chapters. Here the interest is often expressed in terms of potential for regional economic development or environmental impact or need for
government to implement transportation policies. This chapter provides an
overview of the economics of tourism.

7.1 Don't leave home without it

Money, that is. Indeed, promotion of tourism has always been based on the idea that a region or city could grow economically – provide jobs and business opportunities for its citizens – if tourists spend time and money. For this, a region or city needs something that attracts visitors from other areas. The attraction could be historic old ruins such as the Parthenon in Greece, mystical mountain top scenery such as Macchu Piccu in Peru, the beaches of the Mediterranean coast, the skyscraper canyons of Manhattan, or the gaming tables of Las Vegas and Monte Carlo. But any old steel mill will not do.

Prior to the eighteenth century, travel for purposes of pleasure was rare. But the ancient Greeks apparently did travel to the Olympics. And the ancient world did have some of the earliest and most impressive sightseeing and tourist attractions, including the Great Pyramids in Egypt, the Hanging Gardens of Babylon, and sites of religious significance in Jerusalem. Still, in the times of the Roman Empire or of medieval Europe, most trips to nearby fairs and festivals would not last for more than a day and most of the demand for travel was derived from various trade, educational, and religious needs. As Lundberg (1985, p. 7) notes, "Prior to modern times, travel was pretty much limited to the elite, the nomad, the warrior, and the pilgrim."

The collapse of the Roman Empire in the fourth and fifth centuries led to a steep decline in travel of all kinds and, for most people, travel for pleasure became inconceivable. In this dark period, only the most adventurous would set out on bad roads and risk being assaulted by bandits. Indeed, it was not until the seventeenth and eighteenth centuries that the pace of travel revived, with diplomats, scholars, and the wealthy among the fortunate few able to make what was then coming to be known as the "Grand Tour" of European centers of learning, religion, and trade.

Although travel agents and tour operators began to operate at this time, the modern era of agents dates only from 1841, when an enterprising Thomas Cook began to book trips on the new English railroads of that day. For the upper classes, many of these trips were tied to the emerging popularity of visits to health spas and to seaside bathing resorts. Ultimately, of course, such trips also came to be affordable by the public at large.

However, travel in early America developed somewhat differently than in Europe if only because of the long distances involved. The interior of the continent was first penetrated by travels on foot or on horseback or in small boats. Later, covered wagons crossed the Great Plains and stagecoaches delivered mail in the Old West. But traffic could not expand significantly until the transcontinental railroads of the mid-1800s were built. Only then was it possible to develop large-scale commercial tourist attractions.

Since then – with the modes of transportation available to the public proliferating and the costs of travel relative to incomes declining – tourism has become an important global industry, generating approximately $500 billion of spending at the beginning of the year 2000. In all, global tourist receipts

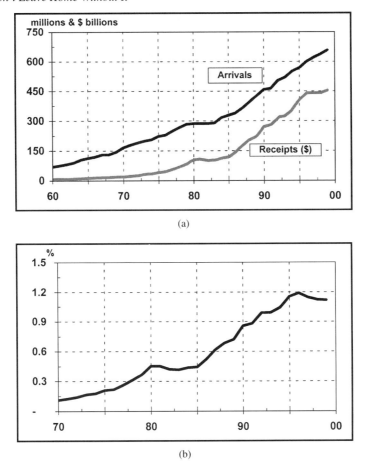

Figure 7.1. (a) International tourist receipts and arrivals, 1960–98. (b) World tourist receipts as a percentage of output, 1970–98. *Source:* WTO and Brown, Renner, and Halweil (1999).

and arrivals, as estimated by the World Tourism Organization (WTO) and shown in Figure 7.1(a), have grown at a compound annual rates of 8.3% and 4.4% respectively between 1980 and 1998. Figure 7.1(b) meanwhile illustrates tourism spending as a percent of gross world output. WTO data on the world's top ten tourist destinations in 1998 are shown in Table 7.1 and tourism receipts and arrivals by region in Table 7.2(a) and (b).

Tourist types Tourists can be classified by their budgets as well as by their purposes for travel and by their psychological propensities. Budget, purpose, and psychology provide three different ways in which developers and marketers can begin to understand a tourist attraction's business potential from the tourist's point of view. But of all of these, characterizations of tourist types

Table 7.1. *World's top ten tourist destinations (arrivals in millions excluding same-day visitors), 1998*

	Arrivals	% of total
France	70.0	11.2
Spain	47.7	7.6
United States	47.1	7.5
Italy	34.8	5.6
United Kingdom	25.5	4.1
China	24.0	3.8
Mexico	19.3	3.1
Poland	18.8	3.0
Canada	18.7	3.0
Austria	17.3	2.8

Source: Tourism Highlights, 1999, WTO.

Table 7.2(a). *Trends of international tourism receipts by region, average annual growth rate, 1989–98*

Region	Increase between 1989 & 1998, US$ billions	Average annual growth rate (%)		
		1989–93	1994–98	1989–98
Africa	5.1	8.8	8.7	8.7
Americas	61.1	10.9	6.2	8.1
East Asia/Pacific	39.5	12.0	3.8	8.9
Europe	110.2	9.2	6.0	7.7
Middle East	5.2	6.1	11.0	8.9
South Asia	2.4	7.9	9.4	9.3
World	223.5	10.0	5.9	8.1

Source: Tourism Highlights, 1999, WTO.

in terms of their budget considerations is the most economically straightforward, leading naturally to marketing aimed at distinct segments defined by income and age. As has already been illustrated in Chapter 2, the estimated changes in demand for each target segment would be reflected in estimated price and income elasticity coefficients.

Although budgets are most fundamental in determination of travel mode and trip distance, purpose cuts across all budget lines and might include everything from working out at health spas, to visiting friends and relatives, to going to football games or attending business conventions. In fact, according to World Tourism Organization data, on a global basis, 40 to 45% of tourists are vacationers, 40% are traveling on business, 8% are visiting friends and

Table 7.2(b). *Trends of international tourist arrivals by region, average annual growth rate, 1989–98*

Region	Increase between 1989 & 1998, in millions	Average annual growth rate (%)		
		1989–93	1994–98	1989–98
Africa	11.1	7.6	6.9	6.8
Americas	33.2	4.5	3.1	3.7
East Asia/Pacific	39.2	10.5	3.1	6.9
Europe	106.2	3.9	3.0	3.8
Middle East	7.1	7.4	5.1	6.9
South Asia	2.0	3.7	7.0	5.9
World	198.8	5.0	3.2	4.3

Source: Tourism Highlights, 1999, WTO.

relatives, and 5% are on government assignments.[2] Intuitively, it would be expected that business and convention-related tourism would be less sensitive to rising prices than would tourism related to vacations and visiting friends and relatives. Furthermore, in contrast to vacationers, business tourists would more likely be constrained by the limits of time. A time elasticity of demand coefficient might thus also be estimated for each tourist segment.

Sociologists and economists have further classified tourists along the lines of their psychological propensities. Indeed, as McIntosh, Goeldner, and Ritchie (1999, p. 235) have suggested, preferences of tourists, especially of the international variety, may be seen as ranging between four extremes:

- Complete relaxation to constant activity
- Traveling close to one's home environment to a totally strange environment
- Complete dependence on group travel to traveling alone
- Order to disorder (i.e., from formal and totally designated to informal and autonomous)

In addition, it is also possible to classify tourists by their psychological dispositions. Cohen (1972, p. 167), for one, suggests that the experience of tourism combines a degree of novelty with a degree of familiarity and the security of old habits with the excitement of change. In his taxonomy, tourists fall into four basic types: (a) organized mass tourists who have virtually every aspect of a trip planned in advance; (b) individual mass tourists, whose trips include a certain amount of individually determined activity away from the group, (c) explorers, who arrange most or all of a trip's details themselves, yet still look for comfortable accommodations and transportation, and (d) drifters, who become almost fully immersed in the foreign culture and care little about physical comforts.

Similarly, Plog (1974) characterizes tourists who are adventuresome and want to be among the first to try new products and services as being *allocentrics* (i.e., focused on varied activities) and those who prefer the familiar in travel destinations as being *psychocentrics*. Most people fall into the middle of a normal distribution between extreme allocentric and psychocentric personalities.

Ecotourism The field of ecotourism began to evolve in the late 1970s, when it became apparent that significant social and environment costs are often incurred in the development and growth of tourism. Although it is difficult to define with precision, ecotourism suggests tourism that has a relatively small affect on local and regional resources and cultures. Moreover, ecotourism is often marketed to environmentally and socially conscious travelers who seek adventurous, back-to-nature elements in their "green travel" experiences.

More specifically, Honey (1999, pp. 22–23) notes that ecotourism necessarily:

- Involves travel to natural destinations
- Minimizes impact
- Builds environmental awareness
- Provides direct financial benefits for conservation
- Provides financial benefits and empowerment for local people
- Respects local culture
- Supports human rights and democratic movements

In all, the field of ecotourism provides a focused view of the costs and benefits of tourism development and growth and another way to classify and to understand the motivations of tourists.[3]

Attraction types Attractions may also be categorized by essential characteristics – mountains, seashore, theme park, casino, museums, shopping – and by ownership and sponsorship factors. Some attractions are nature-made and pretty much available for free, on the order of public goods. Others may be crassly commercialized places or events and be owned and controlled by private companies. And still other situations, perhaps the majority, would involve a mix of private and public support in the form of tax incentives or subsidies. Disney World in Florida and the Bellagio Hotel in Las Vegas would be examples of attractions supported primarily by private interests, whereas Buckingham Palace in London and the Louvre in Paris would be examples of attractions supported primarily by public interests.

Inclusive tours Air-tour (charter) operators emerged principally in Europe in the early 1950s, when scheduled airlines had spare capacity and older planes could be readily refurbished for civilian use. Many of the operators grew large enough to start their own charter (nonscheduled) airlines. Other smaller operators still function essentially as wholesalers that buy (sometimes from scheduled-airlines) blocs of vacant seats at discount and then incorporate destination accommodations and other services as part of inclusive tour (IT) or so-called group inclusive tour (GIT) packages. Such tour operators, who are usually affiliated with travel agencies will generally also block-book hotel rooms at a discount, with the prices depending on season, hotel occupancy, and other such factors. A package might further include car rental, cruise ship, and sports or cultural event elements, which would be otherwise booked separately by what are known as free (or foreign) independent (FIT)-segment travelers.

The IT packager bears the risk of paying for accommodations that may not be used or be used at prices that are too low to fully cover costs. Because of price competition, the probable need to guarantee payment to airlines, and the uncertainty of demand, tour operators may thus in the long run actually end up earning more from interest received on deposits and prepaid holidays and from selling additional services than from direct packaging of tour components.

The primary advantage to the tourist on an IT trip is low-cost fare relative to that commonly found on scheduled flights. However, passengers sacrifice convenience, with departure and arrival times at off-peak hours, crowded conditions, few service amenities, and skimpy meals as parts of the package.

7.2 Economic features

For travelers, the key distinction in the economics of tourism as contrasted with that of travel is that the travel experience in itself becomes an integral part of the tourism experience – an experience that is singular and that cannot be consumed vicariously or at a different time and place. As in touring by cruise ship or sightseeing by motorcoach or bicycle, the travel aspect is not only a means to an end but also an end in itself.

In addition, from an economist's standpoint, tourism has several overriding features that are valid in all situations. For instance, tourism is an invisible export industry because, like the banking and insurance services industries, no tangible products are transported from one place to another. But it is also a highly unstable export because, as Mathieson and Wall (1982, p. 38) note, it is subject to strong seasonal variations as well as to pronounced and unpredictable influences from external forces. The tourist product cannot be stored.

The existence of giant globe-spanning airline and hotel companies notwithstanding, the tourism industry is also still highly fragmented and is closely integrated with other sectors of the economy for the simple reason that tourists require many destination support services. This involves everything from provision of fresh water supplies and sewage disposal systems to shops, restaurants, hotels, and banking and transportation infrastructures. Coordination of such regional tourism *supply* conditions is especially difficult because, as a service activity, tourism requires resources that may be separately or jointly purchased but that are consumed in sequence.[4]

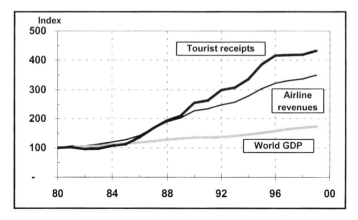

Figure 7.2. World GDP, international airline revenues, and international tourist receipts indexes (1980 = 100), 1980–99. *Source:* WTO and Brown, Renner, and Halweil (2000).

In addition, tourism is price and income elastic. Indeed, as the World Tourist Organization (1994, p. 9) suggests, "if price changes and other factors are disregarded, a comparison solely between international tourist expenditures and world GDP (gross domestic product) can be used as a crude measure of the income elasticity of demand for international travel." Such a comparison, traced in Figure 7.2, "shows that both tourism expenditures and air travel expenditures have increased at twice the rate of world GDP, thus giving a crude income elasticity coefficient of 2.0."

Last, but not least, is price discrimination – another familiar economic feature that is commonly applied in the pricing of tourism-related goods and services. As has already been discussed, price discrimination tactics can be seen in airlines (e.g., first-class versus coach), hotels (e.g., sea view or parking lot view), and in the types of quantity discounts that might be available for different goods and services purchased in different seasons of the year or even at different times of the day.

Multipliers

At first glance, most people would assume that development of tourism can have only positive effects on a local economy. Indeed, justification for the development of tourist attractions is often based on the notion that spending by tourists will stimulate more construction, increase job opportunities and create a larger base of revenues for governments to tax. An increase in tourism may, however, also lead to more pollution of air and water, more traffic congestion and crime, and perhaps even a crowding-out of potentially more lucrative businesses. Thus, in the broadest sense, an increase (or decrease) of tourism will inevitably disturb the existing ecological balance of a region.[5]

The extent to which this happens depends on the degree to which an initial change is amplified through its secondary, repercussionary, effects, much in the same way that, say, an earthquake will produce aftershocks or that a sound made in a small chamber will produce an echo. Economists attempt to measure what the total impact of an initial change of spending for tourism will be on a region's economic output of goods and services by estimating a multiplier of the initial change. This initial change ripples through the economy via effects that are direct, indirect, and induced.

Direct effects are seen in the first round of spending, wherein the change in the local economy's output will be equal to the value of the change in tourist spending. Indirect effects are then seen when, say, the lodging or airline establishment experiences a rise in demand and then needs to increase purchases of food and beverage and laundry services; companies running those services then have to hire more staff and buy more electricity, etc. Finally, all of this activity raises regional income levels, and a portion of this additional income will then be re-spent on local goods and services.

Multipliers can be designed and refined to distinguish the probable impact of spending by different types of tourists. They may also be constructed to show the effects of increased tourism on income, employment (i.e., full time-equivalent jobs created), government revenues, and foreign exchange. Yet such sterile multipliers would not ordinarily take into account the many "quality of life" aspects that are probably important to local residents and that are also central to the new and increasingly influential field of eco-tourism studies. Nor would they indicate the amount of time required for all the various rounds of impact to take effect.

Theoretical models in macroeconomics are usually adopted for estimation of tourist spending multipliers, because a region's economy may be treated as merely a scaled-down version of a nation's economy. To make these models work, the key ingredient is an estimate of the local marginal propensity to spend, which is the percentage of every *additional* dollar of income received that will ultimately be spent on consumption of goods and services. Fortunately, this is a factor that can be approximated from surveys and/or from econometric analysis of local demographic, income, and retail sales data. Following the simple presumption (commonly used in macroeconomic theory) that a part of every unit of income received will be spent (i.e., recirculated), we can express the multiplier, k, as:

$$k = 1/(1 - MPC),$$

where *MPC* is the marginal propensity to consume.

However, this description is far too simplistic to be of any use in the real world; it is only a starting point. For example, as Bull (1995, p. 150) notes, there are always leakages, and the simple model should be modified to take account of the marginal propensity to save, taxation of income, and expenditures on imports. A more sophisticated formulation would thus be as follows:

$$\text{multiplier} = 1/\text{leakages} = 1/[(MTR + MPS) + ((1 - MTR - MPS) \times MPM)]$$

where MTR is the community's marginal tax rate, MPS is the marginal propensity to save as a proportion of gross income, and MPM is the community's marginal propensity to import as a proportion of consumption expenditure. The basic assumption in the calculation of this tourism income multiplier, or ratio, is that all original tourism expenditure turns directly into income.

For example, assume that a community's marginal tax rate and marginal propensity to save are both 20% and the marginal propensity to import is 10%. The community's income multiplier would then be

$$\text{multiplier} = 1/[(0.2 + 0.2) + ((1 - 0.2 - 0.2) \times 0.1)] = 1/0.46 = 2.17.$$

Again, this assumption too may not always hold true because some of the tourism expenditure may leak into transport payments to foreign carriers, payments for food and beverage imports required to service tourists, and a variety of other financial obligations to foreigners. To therefore make the model even more realistic, economists might use what is known as an orthodox, or Keynesian, multiplier model that takes account of most of these import requirements. It modifies the ratio, multiplying it by an import factor, $MPMT$, which is the marginal propensity to import goods and services related to *tourist* needs. In modified form, the multiplier can now be expressed as

$$k = (1 - MPMT) \times 1/\text{leakages}.$$

Generally, the higher is the propensity to consume, the larger the multiplier becomes, and the higher the propensity to import, the smaller the multiplier. But regardless of form, it should be remembered that multipliers provide estimates of the *marginal* (additional) benefits that would be derived from an increase of tourism spending. They *do not* relate total tourism expenditure to total income.[6] Estimated tourist income multipliers in a few selected countries are shown in Table 7.3.

Balance of trade

David Ricardo's classic economic theory of comparative advantage appears to be as applicable in tourism as it is elsewhere in the analysis of international trade. The theory suggests that if one country is more efficient than another in producing goods, gains from trade can be obtained from specialization in the production and export of goods and services in which the country holds a relative comparative advantage. Thus, as Sinclair and Stabler (1997, p. 126) note, countries that have "a large supply of labor and land, as well as plentiful natural resources of wildlife, mountains and beaches, would appear to have a comparative advantage in tourism."[7]

Table 7.3. *Estimated tourist income multipliers for selected countries*

Destination	Personal income multiplier
Turkey	1.96
U.K.	1.73
Egypt	1.23
Bermuda	1.09
Bahamas	0.79
Iceland	0.64

Source: Fletcher (1989).

Many countries, seeking to favorably affect their balance of trade, are accordingly interested in tourism development. But trade balances are influenced by many diverse factors, and forecasts of such balances are fraught with uncertainty. To begin, it is necessary to estimate the receipts from foreign visitors minus payments made abroad by the country's own outbound tourists. In addition, the presence of foreign tourists may require that fairly sizable ancillary international payments for foreign goods and services be made.[8] The degree of a country's success in generating a positive balance of tourist trade may also depend greatly on foreign currency exchange rates and macroeconomic and political conditions.

As for foreign exchange effects on tourism, we should expect that, all other things being equal, countries with relatively strong currencies will experience a decline in tourism demand and that countries with weak currencies should experience an increase. The trends illustrated in Figure 7.3 suggest that the theory works in practice.

Finally, it should also be noted that balance of tourism trade estimates measured in currency terms probably do not fully capture what economists call externalities (uncompensated interdependencies) – the potential positive or negative intangible social effects. If tourism provides work-training opportunities for previously unskilled people, it clearly creates a positive externality. However, if tourism just adds to pollution, crime, and traffic, the externality would evidently be negative for the local residents. A comprehensive cost–benefit analysis of the impact of tourism development (i.e., ecotourism) would require that such externalities be included.[9]

Table 7.4 suggests the approximate tourism contribution to the balance of payments of several important tourist destination countries. It tells us roughly how dependent a country is on tourism earnings by comparison to the sum of what are known as visible receipts (goods) and invisible receipts (services). In 1997, total tourism receipts of US$436 billion compared to total world merchandise exports of US$5,295 billion and to total world commercial services exports of US$1,295. Although the economies of many small countries

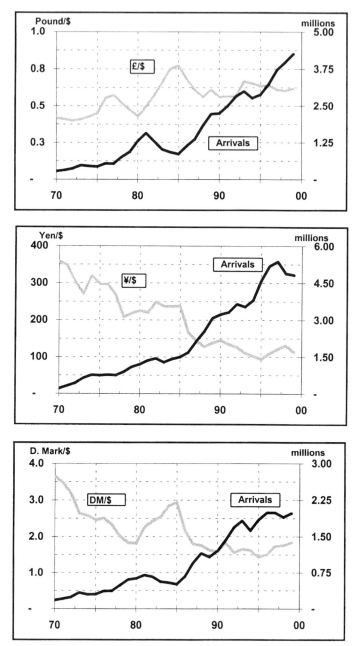

Figure 7.3. International arrivals from abroad at U.S. frontiers versus foreign currency –
U.S. dollar conversion rates for the United Kingdom, Japan, and Germany, 1970–99.

Table 7.4. *Tourism receipts, top six countries (1998) and balance of payments (1997)*

	Tourism receipts ($ billions)	Total receipts, foreign purchases goods & services ($ billions)	Tourism % of total
U.S.	74.2	937.4	7.9
Italy	30.4	310.6	9.8
France	29.7	312.1	9.5
Spain	29.6	131.2	22.6
U.K.	21.3	366.5	5.8
Germany	16.8	591.1	2.8

Source: IMF International Financial Yearbook and WTO Yearbook of Tourism Statistics.

depend greatly on travel and tourism, even for the United States travel and tourism is estimated to be the largest *services* export industry.

Input–output analysis

Tourism's contribution to a nation's economy can also be estimated through analysis of input–output (I/O) tables. The problem, in most instances, is that the Standard Industrial Classification (SIC) system does not facilitate the separate identification of tourism-related activities. For instance, activities such as dining in restaurants would usually include visitors and nonvisitors (i.e., people who are close to their homes). As Okubo and Planting (1998, p. 9) note, "[A] measure of tourism activities would be understated if it included only the output of industries that are typically associated with tourism activities" and "would be grossly overstated if it included all the expenditures on eating and drinking."

To get around these problems, small sample surveys have been used to develop satellite accounts that provide a consistent and systematic way to link tourism demand expenditures to the industries that produce tourism goods and services. The end result is a matrix that would be a much larger version of Table 7.5, which uses money values but could also be calculated in terms of other factors such as employment or land use, for examples. Summing down the columns of a typical I/O table provides estimates of total industry inputs and values added, while summing across the rows provides estimates of final demand and total output. Here, however, the rows and columns have been transposed, with industries (the producing sector) shown across the rows and commodities (the consuming sector) down the columns. From Table 7.5 we can see that in 1992 hotels and lodging places produced $16.6 billion of eating and drinking services as compared to the much larger production of eating and drinking ($220.7 billion) by places that specialize in eating and drinking.

Table 7.5. *Production account of tourism industries, an excerpt, 1992*

	Industry				
Commodity	Hotels and lodging places ($ millions)	Eating and drinking places ($ millions)	Railroads and related services ($ millions)	Taxicabs ($ millions)	Air transportation ($ millions)
Hotels and lodging places	55,913				
Eating and drinking places	16,613	220,685			
Passenger rail			1,226		
Taxicabs				6,614	
Domestic passenger air fares					48,449
International air fares					22,605

Source: Okubo and Planting (1968, p. 14).

Tables of this kind make it possible to estimate the impact that each dollar of increase in tourism expenditure has on other industries, and vice versa. But such estimates implicitly assume that relationships among the various input factors are static and that the marginal input coefficients (using the inputs required per unit of output for each sector) in the matrix are fairly stable. In the real world, input factor relationships are dynamic and capacity limits are frequently reached. When that happens, substantial increases in construction (e.g., new hotels, roads, and airplanes) and in demand for additional services would cause marginal input coefficients to change rapidly.

7.3 Concluding remarks

The definition of tourism is rather flexible, and tourism statistics are thus dependent on how the data are collected and who is doing the collecting. A Webster's dictionary definition limits tourism to the practice of traveling for recreation, whereas some government agencies practically define tourist and traveler as being one and the same. Many people would combine business travel to, say, a convention at Disney World, with a few rounds of golf and tennis. In such instances, any definition is totally blurred.

That said, we know that expenditures for tourism provide important support for travel-related businesses. Income and employment multipliers and balance-of-trade considerations are always at the core of the local decision to invest in tourism facilities, be it a government-financed airport or convention facility improvement or a privately financed hotel-casino or beach resort. Some countries are born with an inherent comparative advantage: when it comes to mountain scenery, for example, any Swiss village will have a comparative advantage to Omaha.

However, implicit in all investment calculations is the assumption that macroeconomic conditions will remain favorable and that tourist attractions in one region can compete effectively with those in others for share of the global tourism market. Up to a point, spending on advertising and promotion and sharp pricing strategies can help in this regard. But it's a ruthlessly competitive world out there and tourist preferences do shift over time.

Selected additional reading

Bishop, M., and Thompson, D. (1992). "Peak-Load Pricing in Aviation: The Case of Charter Air Fares," *Journal of Transport Economics and Policy*, 26(1)(January).

Blaine, T. W. (1993). "Input–Output Analysis: Applications to the Assessment of the Economic Impact of Tourism," in Kahn, Olsen, and Var (1993).

Cater, E., and Lowman, G., eds. (1994). *Ecotourism: A Sustainable Option?* Chichester, UK: John Wiley & Sons.

Cornes, R., and Sandler, T. (1996). *The Theory of Externalities, Public Goods and Club Goods*, 2nd ed., New York and London: Cambridge University Press.

Figgis, P., Neil, J., and Wearing, S. (1999). *Ecotourism Impacts, Potentials and Possibilities*. London: Butterworth-Heinemann.

Frechtling, D. C. (1996). *Practical Tourism Forecasting*. Oxford, UK: Butterworth-Heinemann.

Herman, F. E., and Hawkins, D. E. (1989). *Tourism in Contemporary Society*. Englewood Cliffs, (NJ): Prentice-Hall.

Kass, D. I., and Okubo, S. (2000). "U.S. Travel and Tourism Satellite Accounts for 1996 and 1997," *Survey of Current Business*: Washington, DC: U.S. Department of Commerce, Bureau of Economic Analysis (July).

Oppermann, M., ed. (1997). *Geography and Tourism Marketing*. Binghampton, NY and London: Haworth Press.

Page, S. J. (1999). *Transport and Tourism*. Essex, UK., and New York: Addison-Wesley Longman.

Taplin, J. H. E. (1997). "Generalised Decomposition of Travel-Related Demand Elasticities into Choice and Generation Components," *Journal of Transport Economics and Policy*, 31(2)(May).

Var, T., and Lee, C. K. (1993). "Tourism Forecasting: State-of-the-Art Techniques," in Kahn, Olsen, and Var (1993).

Witt, S. F., and Martin, C. (1992). *Modelling and Forecasting Demand in Tourism*. London: Academic Press.

Part V
Roundup

8
Epilog

To travel hopefully is a better thing than to arrive. – Robert Louis
Stevenson, *An Apology for Idlers*, 1877.

8.1 Common elements

As seen in Chapter 1, leisure time – broadly defined as time not spent at
work – has been expanding very slowly, if at all, in recent years. Indeed,
over the long run, the potential to expand leisure time depends on the rate
of gain in economic productivity, which is in turn affected by the rate of
technological development.

Nevertheless, after deducting life sustaining activities from nonwork time,
we have what is known in the vernacular as free time. But time is never really
free in an economic sense because there are always alternative-opportunity
costs. It is this opportunity-cost aspect, applicable to both leisure and business travel, that enables travel companies to successfully engage price-
discrimination strategies that have positive effects on profits. It is also why,
for all but the shortest trips, travel by air can take share away from other
travel modes even though air tickets may cost significantly more in terms of
monetary cost per trip.

Beyond these generalities are several frequently observed travel industry
characteristics.

- The industries are highly capital intensive

Be it hotels, airlines, cruise ships, theme parks, or casinos, the initial amount of capital investment is large compared to potential future outlays and to ongoing operating and maintenance expenses. Thus, with the possible exception of travel agencies, *travel industry company profitability is normally closely linked and sensitive to the costs of capital* (i.e., interest rates). Also, sunk costs are usually relatively large.

- The industries are highly labor intensive

Travel industries are comprised of segments that largely service the public en masse in functions such as passenger loading, food dispensement, cleaning of rooms, dealing of card games, and so forth. These functions lend themselves to standardization, but not automation, which means that labor intensity will remain high and *profits will always be sensitive to quality and quantity of labor availability and wage rate considerations.*

- Constant returns to scale are dominant

Although cost economies of scale can be achieved in administrative overhead reductions for hotel chains, or quantity discounts in the bulk purchase of, say, airline parts and equipment, *the people-service nature of these businesses suggests that most returns on investment do not improve as the scale of the operation increases.*

- Industry structure tends toward oligopoly but with monopolistic-competitive characteristics

Given the relatively large initial investments required, *most travel industry segments quickly evolve into the monopolistic-competitive and oligopolistic market structures.* As is typical of such structures, there is then need to allocate a proportionately large amount of operating budgets to brand-name maintenance and advertising as a form of product and service differentiation.

- The marginal customer provides a proportionately high profit

With fixed and semivariable costs often accounting for more than half of operating costs, *every incremental customer provides a proportionately high contribution to profit.* This is seen in hotels, airlines, casinos, theme parks, or even in the use of expensive reservation systems.

- Relatively small changes in prices have large effects on profitability

With travel being a mass market business characterized by high operating leverage wherein semivariable and fixed costs of operations are important, *even small price changes, up or down, will usually have a substantial impact on profits, up or down.*

• Price-discrimination strategies are broadly applicable

Because of great differences in customer time-opportunity costs as well as spending budgets, *elasticities of demand vary widely and can be readily exploited in the pursuit of profit maximization.*

8.2 Guidelines for evaluating travel-related securities

The preceding chapters provide a background for analysis of travel industry investments. But many factors not explicitly treated here (Federal Reserve Bank policy, overall economic trends, and investor psychology) also influence investment performance (Figure 8.1).

Happily, it is not necessary to delve into those subjects to extract a few basic investment-decision guidelines.

Cash flows and private market values Companies are usually analyzed in terms of what a private buyer or acquiring public corporation might be willing to pay for the right to obtain access to the cash flow (earnings before deduction of interest, depreciation and amortization, and taxes) of the enterprise. Public market valuations are often in the range of one half to three quarters of private values, which are estimated from going-rate multiples of projected cash flow that have been paid in recent private transactions.

Debt/equity ratios The ability to service debt varies widely among travel companies, but it is always a function of the volatility of projected cash flows. The less volatile the cash flow is, the higher is the debt level relative to equity that can be comfortably accommodated on the balance sheet. Casino-industry companies, for instance, would generally be expected to experience less cash flow volatility than companies in the airline industry. By and large, the major hotel, rail, bus, travel agency, and theme park companies would usually fall somewhere in the middle of the volatility range.

Price/earnings ratios For travel stocks, the price/earnings ratio seems to have lost a great deal of its usefulness as a tool in comparative investment analysis. In hotels, for example, earnings trends can be easily distorted by various frequent writedowns or gains on sales of properties. Furthermore, in the United States (as opposed to Britain and elsewhere), accounting for acquisitions has a major effect on reported earnings because of requirements to write down goodwill. If price/earnings ratios are nevertheless used to compare travel stocks to alternative investments, then adjustments for such differences in the accounting practices must obviously be made.

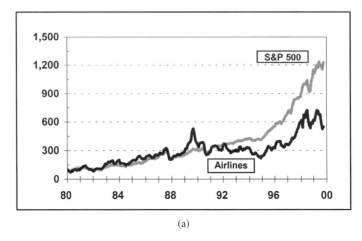

(a)

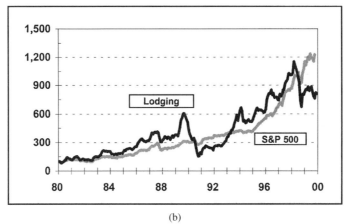

(b)

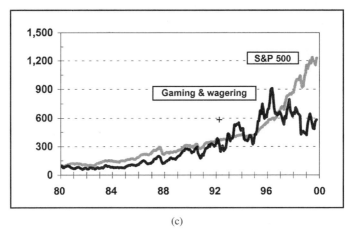

(c)

Figure 8.1. S&P 500 index versus (a) airlines, (b) lodging, and (c) gaming and wagering indexes (+ indicates index modified to include lottery and pari-mutuel stocks), 1980–99.

Price/sales ratios Because price-to-sales ratios do not suffer from the accounting distortions that are frequently present in the calculation of earnings, such ratios have become increasingly popular in the evaluation of common stocks. For travel securities, however, the price/sales ratio (price per share divided by revenues per share) is perhaps most useful as a "reality check" – especially if adjustments that smooth or normalize sales over several periods are made to take into account any evidence that current period sales may be far above or below trend. Sales may be temporarily boosted far above trend, for example, with the opening of large new hotel properties or addition of new airline routes, or they may be temporarily depressed far below trend because of an economic recession. Price-to-sales ratios will be generally correlated to the size of profit margins.

Book value This traditional yardstick for financial analysis normally has little relevance in the evaluation of travel company stock prices because the key earnings power may reside – as in the case of landing slots or gate allocations or brand names – in assets that have already been largely or completely written down or are intangible. Moreover, in the case of real estate assets, the historical cost basis is usually far below what a property might currently be worth. In other words, brand names and other intangible assets may have considerable value, yet not be reflected in the stated book numbers.

8.3 Final remarks

As we have seen from the previous pages, travel is an enormous global business that employs either directly or indirectly at least one out of ten people in the world. Depending on definition, estimates on total world travel and tourism spending begin at the $2 trillion dollar level and rise from there.

The main operating and asset valuation features of travel-related industry segments can be analyzed using standard financial and economic methods. And despite differences in their surface appearances, most travel-industry segments must cope with the same issues and respond in kind to uncontrollable macroeconomic forces that affect the costs of borrowing, labor, and fuel. The prospect of above average-growth for travel industries, however, depends to a large extent on the assumption that global wealth on a per capita basis will continue to rise and to be distributed more widely. The rate at which this happens will be influenced, as always, by politics as much as by gains in productivity.

One hundred years from now a new section in this book will probably be needed to cover the economics of rocket travel and tourism in space. Until that time arrives, though, we can look forward over the nearer term to evolutionary, not revolutionary, changes in the familiar modes of travel.

Appendix A
Sources of information

The most convenient sources of macroeconomic data for use in travel industry studies include the following regular U.S. Department of Commerce publications:

Survey of Current Business, containing personal-consumption expenditure figures for the preceding four years.

U.S. Labor Department, *Monthly Review and Handbook of Labor Statistics*, for articles and data on labor and employment issues.

U.S. Census Selected Services, which contains regional data on revenues, employment, and productivity.

U.S. Statistical Abstract for historical series.

U.S. Industrial Outlook, published every year with forecasts for the next five years.

Information on specific travel business topics is also widely available in the following regularly published non-government–sponsored magazines, newspapers, journals, and Websites:

Advertising Age	*ICAO Web site* (www.ICAO.org)
Airfinance Journal	*Journal of Transportation and Statistics*
Airline Business	*Journal of Transport Economics and*
Amusement Business	*Policy*
ATA Handbook and Web site	www.Lodgingresearch.com
(www.air.transport.org)	*Lodging*
Aviation Daily	*Lodging Hospitality*
Aviation & Aerospace Almanac	www.PlaneBusiness.com
Aviation Weekly	*Travel Agent*
Gaming & Wagering Business	*Tourism & Hospitality Journal*
Hotels	*World Airline News*
Hotel & Motel Management	*World Tourism Organization Yearbook*

Appendix B
Valuation concepts

The valuation approaches discussed in Section 1.6 may be broadly applied to any asset class. However, travel industry analysts will also encounter financial notions of internal rates of return (IRR) and economic value added (EVA). The objective here is not to replicate the detail that would be provided in standard texts on financial theory and practice, but to provide a brief introduction to the basic concepts.

Internal rate of return The time value of money is central to all valuation calculations, which must include the number of periods, n, over which cash flows in or out, present value, pv, future value, fv, and an interest rate, r. Using these elements, project investments are decided on the basis of whether the required rate of return – the return in excess of the project's cost of capital – will be earned and whether such a return is by comparison above those that might be earned by other projects also competing for the same capital at the same time. This required rate of return may also be further specified as the required return to debt capital, k_d, to equity capital, k_e, or to a weighted average of both.

In ranking of alternative investment projects, whether involving a tangible asset such as a new airplane or less tangible assets such as landing rights, an internal rate of return (IRR) analysis is usually helpful, if not always totally decisive. The IRR is defined as the rate of discount, k, that makes the net present value (NPV) equal to zero. Because an increase of the discount rate (i.e., required rate of return) arithmetically decreases the NPV of a project, it is then possible through trial and error to determine the IRR at which a project's NPV declines to zero.[1] Assuming that the project is financed through equity only, then the discovered IRR provides an estimated return on equity (ROE). If the ROE is above the cost of equity capital, k_e, the project should be accepted. If it is equal to the cost of equity capital, an investor might be indifferent to its prospects. And certainly, the project would be rejected if the IRR were below k_e.

This approach will normally lead to decisions that are consistent with a strategy of maximizing NPV, but there are circumstances where this will not always be true. For example, it is possible that no IRR can be determined. Moreover, it is possible that mutually exclusive alternative projects are being considered. Rankings based on NPV alone would provide an immediate decision, whereas rankings based on IRRs suffer from problems of scale and from assumptions concerning the reinvestment rate. For instance, IRR may give the highest rate of return, but it does not indicate the number of dollars of value that might be created. Obviously, a project with an IRR of 40% creating only $100 of NPV should not be chosen over a project with a 25% IRR but that creates $500 of NPV. The IRR method also makes the implicit assumption that a project's cash flows are, over the life of the investment, able to be *reinvested* at the same rate as the IRR. Usually, such an assumption is unrealistic.

Economic value added (EVA) In recent years, EVA analysis (EVA is a registered trademark of Stern, Stewart & Co.) has gained popularity as a management and investment tool that can be applied to the analysis of a wide range of industries. But it has particular relevance here because travel industry businesses are so highly capital intensive.

Essentially, EVA looks at the cost of both debt and equity capital in a business segment or for a business taken as a whole. EVA is then defined as the difference between net operating profit after tax (NOPAT) and the weighted-average dollar cost of capital. In this way, it accounts for a firm's or segment's overall capital cost. Thus,

EVA = NOPAT − $ cost of capital,

where,

$ cost of capital = [% cost of capital/100] × investment,

and

% cost of capital = [debt weight × % after-tax debt cost + equity weight
                                × % cost of equity].

The same equation, just stated a little differently, would also be:

EVA = ROIC − [WACC × invested capital],

where WACC is the weighted average cost of capital, and ROIC is the return on invested capital, which is equivalent to NOPAT/invested capital.

However, as Grant (1997, p. 3) notes, the firm's market value added (MVA) is equal to the present value of the firm's expected future EVA. Therefore,

MVA = [debt + equity value] − total capital.

Companies or business segments that add to economic value (i.e., that earn more than their overall cost of capital) create wealth, and vice versa.

Although EVA methods provide a clear view of a firm's capital-cost and profit relationships in terms of dollars, the method would not necessarily capture nonmonetary, intangible returns that might accrue to a company in the form of brands, prestige, etc. Also, for forecasting purposes, there is nothing that makes predictions of NOPAT as applied in the EVA approach any more reliable or precise than such predictions might be if they were made for any other purposes. An unexpected economic event (e.g., war, recession, or oil shock) would, for example, probably throw EVA project valuation rankings as seriously off course as would happen using more traditional NPV or IRR models. EVA methods therefore do not provide a magic bullet that assures stock market profits, nor do they guarantee that the correct capital allocation choice for a group of prospective project investments will be made.

Appendix C
Major games of chance

In studying the financial economics of gaming, it is essential to have at least a cursory knowledge of how the major games are played. This appendix is designed to provide such knowledge, but it is by no means intended as a complete guide. Many other widely available books contain far greater detail concerning the finer points of play strategy and money management (i.e., the number of units wagered at each betting decision).[1] Tax consequences may also have some relevance.[2]

Blackjack

In blackjack, alternatively known as twenty-one or vingt-et-un, the player's goal is to receive cards totaling more than those of the dealer, but not exceeding 21 – and to do this before the dealer has to show his or her hand. An ace card can be counted as either 1 or 11, other numbers count as their actual values, and picture cards count as 10. Suits do not matter. The payoff to a winning player is equivalent to the amount bet, that is, even money – except in the case of "blackjack" (a "natural" 21 on the first two cards), when the payoff is three units to two.

The player is initially dealt two cards that must be compared against the dealer's two cards, which are positioned in front of the dealer, with one face down and one face up. Although casino rules vary, the dealer generally must "stand" (i.e., cannot draw another card) on the total of 17. Players have an option to request another card (called getting "hit") whenever they want, as long as the cards they already hold total less than 21.

Depending on casino rules, players may also "double down" on certain totals (usually, with a 9, 10, or 11), which means the initial bet can be doubled while drawing one, and only one, more card. Also, if the first two cards are of the same number, a split into two betting hands is permitted, but not always advisable.

The player or dealer exceeding 21 is said to go "bust," and tie hands, in which no money is exchanged, are a "push." (Technically, however, if both player and dealer bust, that kind of tie is won by the dealer, because sequencing requires that players show their hands and relinquish the bets first.)

After seeing that the dealer's face-up card is an ace, a player can also take "insurance," which allows protection against losing in case of a dealer's blackjack (an ace and a 10 card). Insurance is a side bet, at most equal to one-half the amount of the original bet. If the dealer indeed has a natural, the insurance is paid at 2 to 1; otherwise it is lost. The original bet is then settled in the usual way regardless of the decision on the side bet.

Strategies on whether to stand (not request an additional card) or to hit, on how to evaluate a "soft" total (composed with an ace), and on when to double down or to split have been devised by experts in probability theory and computer-simulation techniques. By assigning point values to cards already dealt and by playing proper strategy in response, a "card counter" can obtain information as to the shifting probabilities in the remaining deck. A remaining deck rich in 10-value cards would, for example, make it relatively easier than otherwise for the player to attain a two-card hand close to 21.

The game operator's advantage in blackjack is difficult to compute at any point of play. However, from the top of a deck, blackjack ordinarily provides the house with an edge of a little over 2%.[3] As the game progresses, however, the house edge (which depends importantly on the fact that the dealer turns over his cards *after* the player has gone bust) may disappear, and a skilled card counter can take advantage of such moments by increasing the size of the bet at that time. Blackjack is thus the only casino game that can be beaten by players, and it is this well-advertised fact that has made blackjack the most popular of casino table games.

To win consistently, however, skills in card counting, in play strategy, and in money management must be employed simultaneously in the typical high-speed, pressurized casino environment. But because attainment of such skills requires innate ability in mathematics and extensive study and practice (the patience for which is not apt to be found in most players), the threat to casino profits from self-proclaimed card counters is usually more imagined than real.

Table C.1. *(a) Number of ways to throw a given number with two dice, and (b) point numbers and odds that 7 appears first*

(a)		(b)	
Roll	Ways	Number	Odds
2	1	4	2 to 1
3	2	5	3 to 2
4	3	6	6 to 5
5	4	8	6 to 5
6	5	9	3 to 2
7	6	10	2 to 1
8	5		
9	4		
10	3		
11	2		
12	1		
Total	36		

The presence of card counters has nonetheless tended to unnerve managements, and rather than simply foiling recognized counters by setting low betting limits, casinos have devised a multitude of card-cutting and multideck variations – the effect of which is to slow the rate of play and to probably reduce profitability.

Craps

Craps (Figure C.1) has long been a favorite in American casinos and, along with poker, is a quintessential American game. It evolved from the English game, hazard, and was adopted and refined by American blacks in New Orleans in the early 1800s. Thereafter it spread to immigrant neighborhoods on the East Coast. In contrast to 21, in which probability calculations are especially complicated, the house edge in bank craps as regularly conducted in casinos can be readily computed.

Two cubes (dice) – each die's surfaces marked one through six with embedded dots – are thrown by the player ("shooter") against a backboard on the opposite side of the table. Betting decisions are dependent on the sum of dots on the top surfaces of the dice after they come to rest.

There are 36 possible outcomes (6 times 6), and the probabilities of a number being thrown are measured against those outcomes. With two cubes there are more ways (six) to make a 7 (i.e., $1:6, 2:5, 3:4, 4:3, 5:2, 6:1$) than to make any other number [Table C.1a], and craps uses this as a central theme for decision making.

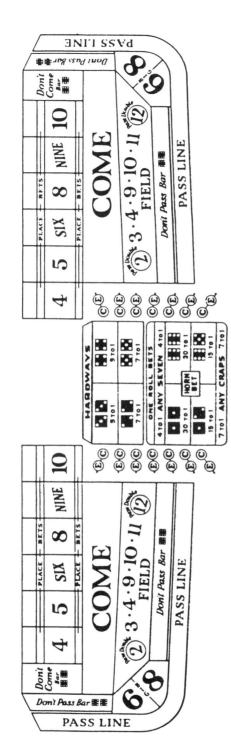

Figure C.1. Craps-table layout. *Source*: Reprinted by permission of the Putnam Publishing Group from *Playboy's Guide to Casino Gambling* by Edwin Silberstang. Copyright 1981 by Edwin Silberstang.

The game focuses on what number the shooter makes on the first roll, the "comeout" throw. A 7 or 11, also known as a natural, provides an even-money win for players betting with the shooter on the "pass line" and a loss for those betting against the shooter on "don't pass." If the outcome is a 2, 3, or 12 (known as craps), the converse is true. However, either the 2 or the 12 is selected by local custom to be used as a "push" or standoff number. Thus, there are no winners or losers if the sum on the top faces of the dice agrees with the designated standoff number indicated by a diagram on the table's felt-cloth layout. Probabilities and game strategies remain the same whichever number is designated for this purpose.

If the comeout throw was neither a natural (7, 11) nor a craps (2, 3, 12), then one of the other possible numbers (4, 5, 6, 8, 9, 10) was thrown. One of those numbers then becomes the "point." Players on the pass line are betting that the point number will appear again before a 7 appears. Don't-line bettors are hoping that 7 appears before the point. Winners are paid even money.

Although there are many additional bets that can be made at any stage in the game, of particular importance is the opportunity to "take the odds" or "lay the odds." From Table C.1(a) it can be seen that there are three ways to make a 4 and six ways to make a 7. Thus, over the long run, 7 is twice as likely to appear as 4, and the correct odds are 2 : 1 in favor of the number 7 [Table C.1(b)]. On some bets (e.g., those involving "taking" or "laying" the odds behind the "line"), casinos will pay off the correct odds, thereby lowering the house edge. As previously noted, however, casinos make their profits by generally *not* paying off correct odds to winners (Table C.2).

So-called front-line bets in craps generate a house edge of 1.41%, calculated by the following method:

Assume a perfect dice shooter on each new comeout roll throws each of the 11 numbers exactly as often as predicted for the long run by probability theory.

To avoid complicated arithmetic with fractions and to derive a lowest common multiple, multiply 36 possible outcomes by 55, which is 1,980.

Then, out of 1,980 throws, a 7 will appear 6/36 of the time (i.e., 330 times). Similarly, a 4 will be made 3/36 of the time (or 165 times), and so forth.

After adding all the winning figures as shown in Table C.3, we can see that there will be 976 winning rolls and 1,004 losing rolls; the house edge is thus the difference of 28 rolls out of 1,980, or 1.41%.

Roulette

Historians disagree on the origin of roulette. Some say it was invented by the French mathematician Blaise Pascal in 1655; others support more arcane theories. In any event, the game has evolved into European and American versions; the European wheel has a single zero whereas the American one has zero and double zero (Figure C.2).

Table C.2. *Craps payout odds*

Bet	Payout odds	Bet	Payout odds
Pass line bet	1 to 1	Don't pass line bet	1 to 1
Come bet	1 to 1	Don't come bet	1 to 1
Pass line odds, come bet odds and buy bets		Don't pass line lay odds: don't come lay odds and lay bets:	
Points of 4 or 10	2 to 1	Points of 4 or 10	1 to 2
Points of 5 or 9	3 to 2	Points of 5 or 9	2 to 3
Points of 6 or 8	6 to 5	Points of 6 or 8	5 to 6
Place bet to win:		Big six or eight:	
Points of 4 or 10	9 to 5	Bets of $6 or multiples thereof	7 to 6
Points of 5 or 9	7 to 5	Bets of less than $6 or odd multiples	1 to 1
Points of 6 or 8	7 to 6		
		Hard ways:	
Field bets:		Hard 6 or 8	9 to 1
3, 4, 9, 10, or 11	1 to 1	Hard 4 or 10	7 to 1
2 or 12	2 to 1		
Proposition bets:			
Any 7	4 to 1		
Any craps	7 to 1		
Two craps or twelve craps	30 to 1		
Three craps or eleven	15 to 1		

Horn high bets: payout based on 2 craps, 3 craps, 12 craps, and 11 payout odds shown above

Mixed in standardized format around the roulette wheel are the numbers 1 through 36 and, in addition, depending on the version, either zero or both zero and double zero. The numbers on the wheel have adjacent background colors that alternate red and black and are arranged so that alternate low and high, odd and even, and red and black numbers are as mathematically balanced as possible. A perfect balance cannot be achieved, because the sum of the numbers 1 through 36 is 666, but the odd numbers sum to 324, and the even numbers sum to 342.

By placing one or more chips on a number, color, or odd or even, the player is betting that a ball spinning near the rim of the wheel will stop on that number, color, or number type. Payoffs on winning odd–even or black–red bets are 1 : 1, but for a specific number the payoff is 35 : 1. With an American double-zero wheel, a total of 38 positions are possible and so the correct odds are 37 : 1. Thus, the casino keeps 2/38 (5.26%) in the American game or 1/37 (2.70%) in the European game.

Table C.3. *Front-line bets in craps*

Number	Times thrown	Winning rolls
Natural 7	330	330
Natural 11	110	110
Craps 2, 3, 12	220	—
Point 4	165	55
Point 10	165	55
Point 5	220	88
Point 9	220	88
Point 6	275	125
Point 8	275	125
Totals	1,980	976

Source: Scarne's Guide to Casino Gambling. Copyright
ⓒ 1978 by John Scarne Games, Inc. Reprinted by
permission of Simon and Schuster, Inc.

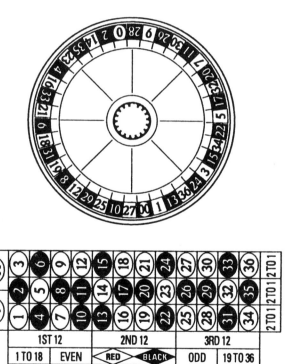

Figure C.2. Roulette wheel and table layout. *Source:* Reprinted by permission of the
Putnam Publishing Group from *Playboy's Guide to Casino Gambling* by Edwin
Silberstang. Copyright 1981 by Edwin Silberstang.

Table C.4. *Roulette bets and odds*

Position	Description	Payout odds
Straight bets		
Straight up	All numbers, zero & double zero	35 to 1
Column bet	Pays off if any of the 12 numbers in the column bet is spun	2 to 1
Dozen	Pays off if 1 through 12, 13 through 24, or 25 through 36 is spun depending on the dozen bet	2 to 1
Red or black	Pays off if the color on the number spun corresponds to color bet	1 to 1
Odd or even	Pays off if number spun corresponds to the bet made	1 to 1
1 to 18 or 19 to 36	Pays off if number spun falls within the range indicated	1 to 1
Combination bets		
Split	Pays off if either of two numbers split is spun	17 to 1
Row	Pays off if any of the three numbers in the row bet is spun	11 to 1
Corner	Pays off if any of the four numbers forming the corner is spun	8 to 1
Five numbers	Pays off if 0, 00, 1, 2, or 3 is spun	6 to 1
Six numbers	Pays off if any of the six numbers in the two rows bet is spun	5 to 1

Other betting variations that are often offered by casinos normally do not significantly affect the casino's percentages. For instance, the *en prison* option reduces the house advantage by half on even-money bets (i.e., color, high–low number, or odd–even). On such bets, when zero or double zero is the outcome of the last spin of the wheel, players may settle for half the original wager or let the original amount ride (imprison the wager). If the choice is to let it ride and the following spin is a winner, the original bet is returned intact. Roulette bets and odds are given in Table C.4.

Baccarat

Baccarat (Figure C.3) and its close cousins, Punto Banco, Chemin de Fer, and Baccarat-en-Banque, are popular high-stakes games in casinos all over the world. All current versions are derived from the Italian *baccara*, first introduced into France circa 1490 and later adopted as a favorite game of the nobility. But it was not until the late 1950s that modern baccarat was taken seriously by Las Vegas casinos.

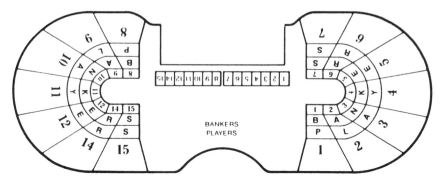

Figure C.3. Baccarat-table layout. *Source:* Reprinted by permission of the Putnam Publishing Group from *Playboy's Guide to Casino Gambling* by Edwin Silberstang. Copyright 1981 by Edwin Silberstang.

The earlier chemin de fer is played the same way as baccarat, except that in chemin, the casino takes no risk because players bet against each other – the house merely acts as a "cutter" for a standard 5% charge taken from the player-banker's winning bet (coup).

In American baccarat, eight standard 52-card decks are shuffled and placed in a "shoe." There may be as many as twelve people seated at the table, and each makes a bet by placing chips for the *Player*, for the *Banker*, or for a tie hand. Winning bets (subject to commissions, as discussed below) are paid even money, and ties usually are paid at 8 to 1.

A bettor and the dealer are each dealt two cards, with picture cards and 10 counting as zero and number cards counting their actual face values. Should the two-card sum be in double digits (i.e., 10 or more), then the right-hand digit is considered the card count. A two-card sum of 14 would thus be counted a 4.

Normally, the gamer's goal is for the side he or she is betting on – either Player or Banker – to have a two-card count of 9. However, if either side has less than 8 or 9 (a "natural") there are fairly standardized rules (Table C.5) that specify when additional cards may be drawn. A count of zero is "baccarat."

Through complicated arithmetic it has been determined, according to Scarne (1978, p. 266), that the chance of the Player's side winning is about 49.33%, and for the Banker's side, 50.67%. The Player's disadvantage, or cost to participate, is thus about 1.34%. However, in order to even out the sides (and save time on making change), the casino retains a 5% "commission" out of the Banker's winnings (it actually recaptures 5% of excess payoff). [Because the Banker's side, on average, wins 50.67% of the hands dealt, the actual charge is 2.53% (0.5067 times 5%).] In so reducing the aforementioned Banker's advantage of 1.34% by 2.53%, the Banker's cost of play after commission then nets to about 1.19% (1.34 − 2.53). Thus, the casino's edge is somewhere between 1.19% and 1.34%.[4] But on bets that Banker and

Table C.5. *Baccarat rules*

Player having		
1–2–3–4–5–10		Draws a card
6–7		Stands[a]
8–9		Natural. Banker cannot draw.

Banker having	Draws when giving	Does not draw when giving
3	1–2–3–4–5–6–7–9–10	8
4	2–3–4–5–6–7	1–8–9–10
5	4–5–6–7	1–2–3–8–9–10
6[a]	6–7	1–2–3–4–5–8–9–10
7	Stands	
8–9	Natural. Player cannot draw.	

Note: Pictures and tens do not count.
[a] If player takes no card, banker stands on 6.

Player have tie hands, casinos usually pay 8 to 1 and have an edge of 14.36%. Consequently, although bets on ties may thus typically account for only 3% of the total money wagered, they represent perhaps 10% of the total won by the house.

Because most of the play, at a rate of about seventy hands an hour, is concentrated on Player or Banker – where the margins are thin – the casino win results for baccarat are generally far more volatile than for any of the other games.

Slots

Slot machines have steadily evolved since Charles Fey first introduced them in San Francisco in 1887 and, for most casinos, they now draw over 40% of revenues and an even larger share of profits.

In recent years, the performance of slots has been greatly enhanced by the development of sophisticated electronic microprocessors. Nonetheless, the basic concept of slot play remains the same as always: to line up certain randomly generated symbols on a window or video screen. In return for so doing, players are rewarded with various levels of monetary prizes determined proportionally by the probability of occurrence.

For example, in a mechanical three-reel model with 20 different symbols per reel, and with each reel spinning independently, the probability of three of the same figures lining up is $1/20 \times 1/20 \times 1/20$, or 0.000125, which is 1 in 8,000. Of course, as in other games, the casino will profit by setting the actual payout to be less than 7,999 to 1. Yet in new microprocessor-controlled machines, "virtual" reels, wherein each reel may represent 256 different numbers, can be created with a much wider range of payouts and probabilities. In New Jersey, by law, slot machines cannot pay out less than 83% of the drop, but there is no such rule in Nevada.

Slot machines today come in many different versions, including "progressives" (which are linked to the coin-drop in other machines), color-action (nonreel) videos, and multi-line–payoff models. But whatever the type, the chief advantages to casinos are the low operating costs and relatively high hold percentages of slots as compared with table games. Indeed, because of the low operating costs, coin-operated machine adaptations of blackjack and poker have also been emphasized by casinos.

Other casino games

Poker

America's all-time favorite private card game, poker, is believed to have evolved from an ancient Persian card game, *As-Nas*. Variations of the game eventually appeared in Europe, and by the early 1800s it had been brought to Louisiana by French settlers. *Poque*, as it was initially known, was refined by active use on the Mississippi riverboats of the 1800s and then spread rapidly through the North after the Civil War.

The principal concept in the game's many variations is to arrange the dealt cards in sequence of value and in suits, and to determine the relative ranking of each player's final hand to establish a winner of the money pool (pot) generated during the course of play. Players bet according to the actual and perceived strengths of the various hands, with bluffing a normal part of strategy.

Despite poker's popularity in private settings, it has not been an important contributor to the earnings of publicly owned casino companies. Most licensed poker-club operators (in California and Nevada), who host the game and ensure its integrity, charge an hourly fee for playing based on the minimum-size bet. Other operators will more generally charge a commission, or so-called rake-off, that equals 5% of the pot.

Low-denomination electronic video-poker machines are, however, expected to represent an increasing proportion of casino coin-operated devices. Management usually sets payout percentages on these machines. Profits are normally similar to those on slots.

Keno

Keno, which is normally a more important profit maker for Nevada casinos than is poker, also benefits from conversion to electronic video units. Keno is played by marking several numbers (spots) out of a total of 80 with a crayon (in the manual version) or with a light pen (in the electronic version). A random-number generator then determines winning spots, and payoffs are made to winners in proportion to how many spots match the preselected choices of the bettor. According to calculations by Scarne (1974, p. 499), the house percentage on a keno ticket varies between approximately 20% and 25% and depends on the number of spots on the ticket.

Big Six Wheel

The Big Six Wheel is fairly popular in Atlantic City and it has been a staple in Nevada for a long time. In older versions, the wheel's rim is divided into 54 spaces, in each of which are representations of the faces of three dice bearing different combinations of the numbers 1 through 6. Bets are placed on a layout containing those numbers. After the wheel is spun and its ratchet peg comes to rest, for every bet that corresponds to a number in the section where the peg stops, there is a winner who is paid even money. If the player bets $1 on the number 2, and the section on the wheel where the peg stops shows dice with faces 1, 2, and 2, the bettor will thus receive $2 (a dollar for each 2) plus return of his original bet. Similarly, if the number is 5, and the stop is at 5-5-5, the payback will be $3 plus the original dollar. The Atlantic City version, however, merely has the numbers 1, 2, 5, 10, 20, and two jokers distributed over the 54 spaces. There are 24 ones, 15 twos, 7 fives, 4 tens, 2 twenties, and 2 jokers. A bet on 1 pays 1 : 1, on 2 pays 2 : 1, and so forth, except for jokers, which pay 45 : 1. The Big Six operator normally has a favorable advantage ranging to over 22%, which makes this game one of the most profitable for casinos. As can be seen from Atlantic City monthly statistics, casino hold percentages often approach 50% on the Big Six.

Bingo

Bingo, an offspring of the Italian lotto game, has been historically prominent in the development of Indian gaming ventures. It emerged after World War I and spread rapidly during the Great Depression years as a back-room attraction at vaudeville shows and carnivals. It remains one of the most popular and widely legalized of wagering activities and is normally very profitable for operators.

The traditional game is played to fill a card's row, column, or diagonal containing numbers between 1 and 75 under the word "bingo." A random-number selector or caller picks the numbers that qualify to fill the card, and the first card so filled is declared prize winner. The house edge for bingo is calculated to be around 22%.

Pai Gow, Fan Tan, Sic Bo

Players from the Orient have a long history of interest in gambling, and this is reflected in marketing studies of Nevada and Atlantic City casinos indicating

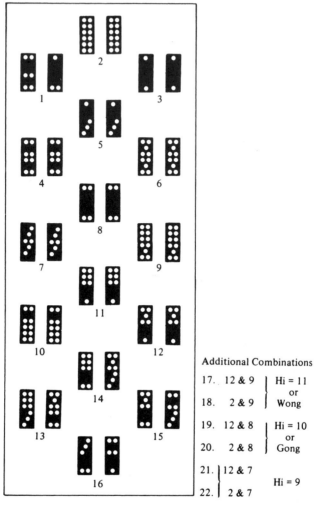

Figure C.4. *Pai Gow*: The chart lists 16 pairs and 4 combinations that compose the top-ranking 20 hands. Hand number 1 is called the king pair; each subsequent pair or hand is one value lower than the hand preceding it. The rank of each lesser hand is determined by the numerical value of the hand after discarding 10s from the total. Examples: Two dominoes 12 and 7 = 19, which becomes a 9 after the 10 is discarded; 8 and 7 = 15, which likewise becomes a 5. The higher number is the winning hand. *Source: Gambling Times*, November 1982.

that such players are among the most avid. To accommodate these good customers, Nevada casinos have introduced three favorite Chinese games, *Pai Gow, Fan Tan*, and *Sic Bo*, the first of which is the most important.

Originated in ancient China, *Pai Gow* (Figure C.4) is played with thirty-two specially designed dominoes that are scrambled and then placed in eight

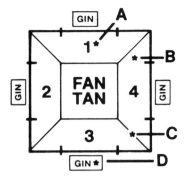

Figure C.5. Table layout for Fan Tan; bets A–D are explained in the text. *Source: Gambling Times*, February 1983.

stacks of four. The dealer and as many as seven players are each dealt one stack of four specially marked dominoes (or cards), with the player to receive the first stack determined by rolling three dice.

The objective is to make two hands of the highest possible value from four dominoes – with both of the player's hands of higher value than the banker's corresponding hands. The player loses if both hands are lower, but if one hand is higher and the other lower, no one wins or loses. The house retains a 5% commission on all winning bets.

Fan Tan (Figure C.5), in contrast, is basically a game of guessing the number of beans in a cup. (A card game has taken the same name, but it is not similar.) A pile of beans is "cut" with a long, thin wand, four at a time, until 4, 3, 2, or 1 is the winning number or section. Figure C.5 illustrates the possibilities: (a) straight up on a number pays 3 to 1; (b) the corner inside the hash mark of a side pays 2 to 1 if the side hits; (c) a split of any two sides pays even money; (d) a gin bet pays even money if the closest side hits and is a standoff if the adjacent sides hit. The house retains 5% of all winning bets as commission.

Sic Bo (Figure C.6) was first brought into the United States by migrant Chinese in the mid-1800s. Three dice are placed in a sealed shaker, and bettors select individual numbers or combinations of numbers that will appear on the dice after shaking. Winning payoffs are made according to the game layout in Figure C.6.

Pan

Pan, short for *panguingue*, is sometimes found in Nevada casinos or is played in commercial clubs. It is a card game related to rummy. The standard 52-card deck is modified by eliminating all eights, nines, and tens. The sevens are in sequence with jacks, and aces rank low, below deuces. Eight decks are generally used, and to each hand, ten cards are dealt, five at a time.

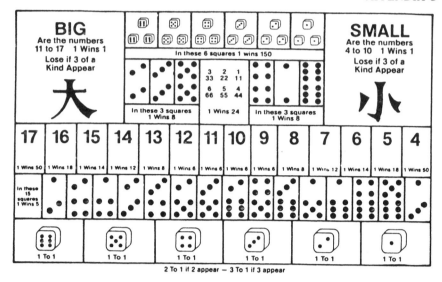

Figure C.6. Sic Bo. *Source: Gambling Times*, January 1983.

By discarding and drawing, a meld or grouping of three cards of the same rank, or a sequence of three in the same suit, is composed. Several rules govern the game, in which the object is to be the first to meld exactly eleven cards.

As in poker or the Chinese games, the house will normally take a percentage of the pot (5%) for conducting the game.

Trente-et-quarante (Rouge et Noir)

This card game is rarely found in U.S. casinos but is quite popular in Europe. In *trente-et-quarante* (literally, thirty-and-forty) (Figure C.7), a dealer and croupier cut and shuffle a six-deck shoe in which cards are dealt face up in two rows: The first and farthest away is the black row, and the nearest is the red row. Dealing continues until the sum of points on the cards exceeds 30 but never 40.

The black row is dealt until the critical value of 40 or less is reached; then the red row is similarly presented. Suits have no value; face cards count 10, aces 1, and others their pip value.

Players can bet on four even-money propositions: red versus black and color versus inverse. The color row whose total is closer to 30 is the winner. When the color of the first card dealt in the black row is the same as the color of the winning row, then color wins; otherwise inverse wins. The bank makes its money when – on an average of once every 47 hands – the total for each row is 31 (called the *refait* or *un après*). The bank then collects half of

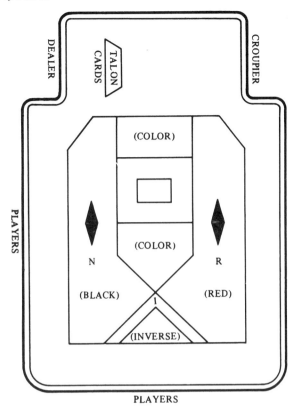

Figure C.7. Table layout for *trente-et-quarante. Source: Gambling Times*, December 1983.

each player's stake, which provides an advantage of 1.25%.[5] All other ties are disregarded, and as in roulette, an *en prison* option may be available.

Mathematical studies of this game have indicated that, as in blackjack, there may be times during the course of play in which the house may have little or no edge. However, it is not clear that effective card-counting strategies exist.

Lotteries

Lotteries have been around a long time and have been used for many purposes. For instance, the concept appeared in classical Greek mythology, and Roman emperors entertained dinner guests with door-prize drawings. But the first recorded money lottery designed to raise funds for government appeared in Italy in 1530. A British defense lottery also was held in 1566. Yet it was the Virginia Company, which colonized Virginia, that provided the prototype for other early American colonial lottery financings. Indeed, founding fathers

Benjamin Franklin and George Washington both sponsored lotteries. And many public-works programs and educational institutions including Harvard, Yale, Columbia, and Princeton were, in part, financed through this means.

Although lottery drawings were very popular in the early 1800s, several large swindles cooled the fervor and, by midcentury, most states had banned sales of lottery tickets. Of course, illegal lottery sales then flourished, and these became especially common in the 1920s and 1930s.

But it was not until 1964, when the state of New Hampshire introduced a sweepstakes game, that lotteries were legally renewed. And by the end of the 1980s, a majority of the states, the District of Columbia, and all Canadian provinces had legalized lotteries as a means of raising funds for welfare and public-works grants.

As a percentage of sales, states typically net about 36–38%: Administrative expenses absorb up to 6%, system operators and designers receive 2%–3%, retail vendors receive a commission of 5%, and winning players receive an average of about 50%. However, payouts of 50% to players appear to be relatively generous only until comparison is made against casino-game payouts, which exceed 85%. Moreover, states may pick up extra income from interest earned on funds escrowed in the time between prize drawings and payments to winners (out of annuities).

Modern lotteries have evolved in several distinct stages. The original New Hampshire-style lotteries employed a sweepstakes concept that had limited appeal because of relatively small payoffs and a long time between ticket purchase and event decision. However, that was remedied in a second stage of development in which many more "instant-winner" scratch-off-type tickets and online three-digit daily number games were introduced, with significant increases in sizes of cash prizes and in numbers of retail outlets handling sales.

By the late 1970s, a third phase of expansion was initiated as greater sophistication of online computer systems made it possible to introduce games of the so-called lotto variety. These games select winners on almost a daily basis and allow for buildup of substantial prize money over several drawings: If the major prize is not won, the money spills over into the pool used for subsequent drawings.

In the state of New York, for example, the player selects 6 out of 54 numbers on two "boards" – panels with boxes labeled 1 to 54. The cost to play two boards is $1, and there are 10 boards on a card. Prizes are paid on a pari-mutuel basis, wherein for each draw (twice a week), 40% of that draw's sales revenue (less 2% prize fund reserve) is allocated as the winning pool for payment of the prizes under the conditions and odds indicated in Table C.6. Of course, many variations on this scheme are possible.

However, as of the mid-1980s, the industry entered a fourth phase featuring the placement of microprocessor-controlled lottery machines – video lottery terminals (VLTs) – that may use bingo, keno, or other similar random-number-generator-based concepts. Such machines are essentially hybrid slot and video game units.

Table C.6. *New York State Lotto-game payout*

First prize: 50% of the winning pool plus any first-prize money carried forward from previous draws. Six winning numbers in one game panel, with odds on a $1 bet (two panels) 1 : 12,913,583.

Second prize: 11.0% of the winning pool for that draw. Any five winning numbers in one game panel. Odds on a $1 bet, 1 : 44,839.

Third prize: 28% of the winning pool for that draw. Any four winning numbers in one game panel. Odds on a $1 bet, 1 : 763.

Fourth prize: 11.0% of the winning pool for that draw. Any three winning numbers plus the supplementary number in one game panel. Odds on a $1 bet, 1 : 597.

Overall odds of winning a prize are 1 : 332 for a $1 bet.

Source: New York State Lottery.

Tracks

Horse races were popular during the reign of England's Henry II (1154–89), and they were regularly scheduled by New York's first English governor in 1665. To this day, horse and dog racing is where direct government participation in legalized betting is greatest.

There are many betting variations now allowed at tracks specializing in thoroughbred racing, harness racing, or greyhound racing. In addition to standard wagering on *win* (bettor collects if the selection bet to win finishes first), *place* (collects on first or second finish), and *show* (collects on first, second, or third finish), more exotic bets such as the quinella, exacta, and daily-double have been designed to heighten public interest.

The variations, however, have not changed the operational economics whereby the state may take up to 20% of pari-mutuel sales, and so-called breakage (actually a rounding of winners' payout to the last nickel or dime) further adds to the state's advantage. The following example, paraphrasing Scarne (1974, p. 51), well illustrates how pari-mutuel betting pools are shared by the state.

Suppose that a race is conducted "where the combined mutuel take of state and track is 15%" and breakage is to a nickel. "Assume that $129,400 was bet on all horses in the win (straight) pool, and the red-hot favorite and eventual winner was backed to the amount of $100,000." The combined state and track deduction of 15% of $129,400 is $19,410, leaving $109,990 in the win pool. The $100,000 wagered on the winner is then deducted from the net $109,990, leaving $9,990 to be divided among holders of winning tickets. "The $100,000 bet on the winning animal is set aside so that it may be returned to the winners."

Dollar odds, meaning earnings on each $1 unit bet on the winner, are then calculated by dividing $9,990 by $100,000 to give "a dollar-odds figure of 9.99 cents." Breakage to the last nickel is then performed, which leaves an additional 4.99 cents on each dollar to the track and the state. That is, the winners give up an additional $4,990, the state and track total becomes $24,400, and the winning wagerers' earnings on each dollar are reduced from 9.99 cents to 5 cents per dollar. As reported in newspapers, the standard $2 win bet in this example would have returned $2.10.

To calculate the return on place bets, "the total amount of money (gross place pool) bet on all the horses to place (run first or second)" is used as the base on which to apply state and track percentages. After subtracting the appropriate percentages from the gross place pool, the amount bet on first and second finish is then deducted to arrive at the net place pool. This is then divided by two because half the pool goes to holders of place tickets on the horse that finished first and the other half to the holders of place tickets on the horse that finished second. The resulting "(half net place pool) is divided by the amount bet to place wagers on the horse whose place payoff is being calculated." Breakage is then deducted.

"The method . . . to compute show mutuels [is] the same as . . . for place mutuels except that three horses who finished first, second, and third share in the show pool."

Depending on the betting variations used and the aggressiveness with which winners reinvest their gains in other races, the player's disadvantage at the track generally ranges upward of 17%. Another disadvantage as compared to sports book betting is that the price of the bet is not fixed but changes right up to the moment before the race begins. Astute sports bettors, however, can often use time to their benefit.

Sports book

Wagering on sports events is probably the most common type of gaming, and it is certainly among the most widespread of illegal activities in the United States. Legal sports betting based on the same principles used by neighborhood bookies is sanctioned and available only in Nevada gaming establishments or at betting shops in England.

Beginning in the late 1930s, the concept most frequently used in both the legal and illegal varieties is that of a *point spread*, which, in theory, mathematically compensates for the different abilities of competing teams. As calculated by expert handicappers, the spread is how many points the winning team's score must exceed the losing team's score in order for wagers on the winning team to be paid. For example, if team A is favored to beat team B by 4 points, and it does so by only 3 points, wagers on the underdog win.

Sports-book operators generally attempt to equalize the total *amounts* bet on both sides of the book and to avoid a "push" (making the exact point spread) by adjusting the spread, or *line*, that is offered to bettors. In football and basketball, for example, wagers (based on a point spread) are normally made at odds of 11 : 10, which means that whether betting favorite or underdog, in effect you wager $11 to win $10. The bookie thus retains a $1 commission known in the vernacular as vigorish or "vig."

In practice, however, this implies a return to the bookmaker of 4.5%, because the bookmaker receives $11 from each side (a total of $22), and, no matter which team wins, retains $1 out of the $22 in total wagered. The bookmaker will obviously attempt to move the point spread (or line) so that an equal number of dollars are wagered on both teams. But if the line has been moved, as it often is, so that the number of dollars on each side are uneven, then the operator might make more or less than the theoretical 4.5% or might actually lose. As Moore (1996, p. 100) shows, the *theoretical keep percentage* equals (true odds minus payoff odds) / true odds. Yet, in fact, for all of Nevada, the sports-book hold percentage in recent years has averaged around 2.8%, compared to an average race-book hold of approximately 15%.

Moreover, as Gollehon (1986) explains, baseball betting differs in that it uses a "money-line" rather than a point-spread system. This is because baseball teams are rated in terms of probability of winning rather than of team point scoring potential. Yet, unlike most other wagering situations, where odds of winning are quoted, in baseball it is the odds *against* winning that are quoted. Thus, in baseball, odds on a favored team may be quoted at 7 to 5, for example, with the first number representing the number of times (out of 12 contests) that a team will typically be expected *not* to win.

The next step is to convert these odds figures into dollar amounts bet. To convert to the bookmaker's $100 betting units requires, for instance, that odds of 7 to 5 be converted to wagers of $140 and $100, respectively. Accordingly, the money-line quoted says −140, with the minus sign in front of the quote to indicate that the team is favored to win. To go with the favored team, a bettor must then put up $1.40 to win each $1.00 and, using the same line, put up $1.00 to win $1.30 on the underdog (which would be quoted as +130). In this case, known as a "dime-line," there is a 10-cent difference between what the favorite takes from the bettor and what the underdog gives.

Theoretically, then, the bookmaker breaks even when the favored team wins and wins when the underdog wins. This works out to about a 2% return to the operator: Of the total of $240 bet on a −140 and +130 line, the operator keeps $10 of the $240 it holds if the underdog wins, which should be half the time if the line is correct. The larger the difference (e.g., there are 20-cent lines), the more profit potential there is for the operator.

Because of the nature of the games and the different ways in which they are bet, football especially attracts far more action [about 40% of all Nevada sports wagering according to Manteris and Talley (1991)] than baseball. However, the spread of sophisticated electronic terminals and computers, which are able to automatically and instantaneously equalize the book by adjusting the spread, will eventually make sports betting technically, if not legally, playable almost anywhere.

Glossary

This abbreviated glossary has been mainly compiled, with permission, from *The McGraw-Hill Dictionary of Economics*, McGraw-Hill, New York, 1974. The *Dictionary of Economic and Statistical Terms*, U.S. Department of Commerce, was supplementary.

Aggregate: The familiar type of summary series shown in most statistical reports. Generally, it is a total, such as the gross national product or retail sales, but sometimes it is an average, such as the index of industrial production or the index of wholesale prices.

Amortization of debt: A gradual reduction of a debt through periodic payments covering the interest and part of the principal. Generally, amortization is used when the credit period is longer than a year. Common examples of amortization of debt are mortgage payments on homes, which extend over a period of twenty years or more.

Asset: A physical property or intangible right, owned by a business or an individual, that has a value. An asset is useful to its owner either because it is a source of future services or because it can be used to secure future benefits. Business assets are usually divided into two categories: current and fixed.

Asset values: The implied price buyers might be willing to pay to obtain control of an asset's profit- and/or cash-generating potential. Asset values fluctuate according to changes in general economic conditions, interest rates, and expected returns.

Block time: In the airline industry, the time on a segment from when the aircraft's engines are switched on at departure to the time they are switched off on arrival.

Bond: A written promise to pay a specified sum of money (principal) at a certain date in the future or periodically over the course of a loan, during which time interest is paid at a fixed rate on specified dates. Bonds are issued by corporations, states, localities (municipal bonds), foreign governments, and the U.S. government, usually for long terms (more than ten years), although any security issued by the U.S. government for more than five years is defined as a bond.

Book value: The value of a corporation according to its accounting records. It is computed by subtracting all debts from assets; the remainder represents total book value. Total book value is also referred to as net assets. If a corporation has assets of $300,000 and debts of $100,000, its total book value is $200,000. In reports of corporations, the book value is usually represented on a per-share basis. This is done by dividing the total book value by the number of shares. In the example given above, if the corporation had 10,000 shares outstanding, its book value would be $20 per share. The book value differs from the par value of the shares and also from the market value.

Breakeven point: The specific volume of sales at which a firm neither makes nor loses money. Above this point, a firm begins to show a profit; below it, it suffers a loss. Breakeven-point analysis is used to compute the approximate profit or loss that will be experienced at various levels of production. In carrying out this analysis, each expense item is classified as either fixed (constant at any reasonable level of output) or variable (increasing as output increases and decreasing as output declines).

Business cycles: Alternate expansion and contraction in overall business activity, evidenced by fluctuations in measures of aggregate economic activity, such as the gross national product, the index of industrial production, and employment and income. A business cycle may be divided into four phases: expansion, during which business activity is successively reaching new high points; leveling out, during which business activity reaches a high point and remains at that level for a short period of time; contraction, during which business volume recedes from the peak level for a sustained period until the bottom is reached; and recovery, during which business activity resumes after the low point has been reached and continues to rise to the previous high mark.

Capitalized value: The terms applied to a technique used to determine the present value of an asset that promises to produce income in the future. To calculate the present value, the total future income expected must be discounted, that is, offset against the cost (as measured by the current interest rate) of carrying the asset until the income has actually been realized. If the asset promises a stream of income, its capitalized value is calculated by adding together the present discounted value of the income in each year. The general formula for this calculation is $I/(1+r)^t$ where I is the annual income, r is the current rate of interest, and t is the number of years involved. In this manner, an investor confronted with a choice of properties can determine which alternative is the most remunerative, though the formula tells nothing about the relative risks involved.

Cash flow: The sum of profits and depreciation allowances. (Instead of profits, many economists use retained earnings, which are profits after taxes and after deductions for dividend payments.) Gross cash flow is composed of total profits plus depreciation; net cash flow is composed of retained earnings plus depreciation. Thus, cash flow represents the total funds that corporations generate internally for investment in modernization and expansion of plants and equipment and for working capital. The growth of depreciation allowances over the years has made them a much more important part of cash flow than retained earnings. To facilitate comparisons of property values, however, entertainment businesses often take cash flow to be profits prior to deductions of interest, depreciation and amortization, and taxes.

Code-sharing: A common airline industry marketing practice where, by mutual agreement between cooperating carriers, at least one of the airline designator codes used on a flight is different from that of the airline operating the flight.

Common stock: The capital stock of a corporation that gives the holder an unlimited interest in the corporation's earnings and assets after prior claims have been met. Common stock represents the holder's equity or ownership in the corporation. Holders of common stock have certain fundamental legal rights, including the following: preemptive rights; the right, in most cases, to vote for the board of directors, who actually manage the company; the right to transfer any or all shares of stock owned; and the right to receive dividends when they are declared by the board of directors.

Competition: The condition prevailing in a market in which rival sellers try to increase their profits at one another's expense. In economic theory, the varieties of competition range from perfect competition, in which numerous firms produce or sell identical goods or services, to oligopoly, in which a few large sellers with substantial influence in the market vie with one another for the available business. Early economists envisioned perfect competition as the most effective assurance that consumers would be provided with goods and services at the lowest possible prices.

Complementary goods: Goods that must be accompanied by another good to be useful (e.g., perfect complements would be a left shoe and a right shoe). Contrariwise, close substitutes would be margarine and butter.

Convertible debenture: A certificate issued by a corporation as evidence of debt that can be converted at the option of the holder into other securities (usually common stock, but sometimes preferred stock) of the same corporation. Each debenture can be converted into a specified number of shares of stock at a stipulated price for a certain period. There are two advantages to convertible debentures for the issuing corporation: (a) The conversion privilege makes the debentures more attractive to investors and tends to reduce interest costs. (b) The debentures facilitate the extinction of debt, because debt declines and equity (stock) increases as holders convert their debentures. The major disadvantage is discrimination against the company's stockholders, whose equity is diluted as the holders of debentures convert them. At all times during the conversion period, there is a price relationship between the debenture and the stock. It is based on the conversion price, the number of shares into which each debenture can be converted, and the value that the market puts on the conversion privilege. For example, a $1,000 debenture that can be converted into 50 shares of common stock at $20 per share will normally trade in the market at a price higher than $1,000 because of the conversion privilege.

Correlation: The statistical technique that relates a dependent economic variable to one or more independent variables over a period of time to determine the closeness of the relationship between the variables. This technique can be used for business forecasting. When more than one independent variable is used, the relationship is called a multiple correlation.

Cost recovery: Accounting method of amortization in which all costs are charged against earned revenue and no profit is recognized until cumulative revenue equals cumulative costs. This method is not acceptable for financial-statement reporting under generally accepted accounting principles.

Current assets: Cash or other items that will normally be turned into cash within one year and assets that will be used up in the operation of a firm within one year. Current assets include cash on hand and in the bank, accounts receivable, materials, supplies, inventories, marketable securities, and prepaid expenses.

Current liabilities: Amounts owed that will ordinarily be paid by a firm within one year. The most common types of current liabilities are accounts payable, wages payable, taxes payable, and interest and dividends payable.

Debenture: A bond that is not protected by a specific lien or mortgage on property. Debentures (debts), which are issued by corporations, are promises to pay a specific amount of money (principal) at a specified date or periodically over the course of the loan, during which time interest is paid at a fixed rate on specified dates. The distinction between a debenture and a note of a corporation is that the debenture, like a bond, is issued under an indenture or deed of trust.

Demand: The desire, ability, and willingness of an individual to purchase a good or service. Desire by itself is not equivalent to demand: The consumer must also have the funds or the ability to obtain funds to convert the desire into demand. The demand of a buyer for a certain good is a schedule of the quantities of that good that the individual would buy at possible alternative prices at a given moment in time. The demand schedule, or the listing of quantities that would be bought at different prices, can be shown graphically by means of the demand curve. The term *demand* refers to the entire schedule of possibilities, not only to one point on the schedule. It is an instantaneous concept, expressing the relationship of price and the quantity that is desired to be bought, all other factors being constant.

Depreciation: A reduction in the value of fixed assets. The most important causes of depreciation are wear and tear (loss of value caused by the use of an asset), the effects of the elements (i.e., decay or corrosion), and gradual obsolescence, which makes it unprofitable to continue using some assets until they have been fully exhausted. The annual amount of depreciation of an asset depends on its original purchase price, its estimated useful life, and its estimated salvage value. A number of different methods of figuring the amount of depreciation have been developed. Using the simple straight-line method, which considers depreciation a function of time, the annual depreciation cost is calculated by dividing the cost of the asset (original minus salvage cost) equally over its entire life.

Discounted-cash-flow method: A method of measuring the return on capital invested. The value of a project is expressed as an interest rate at which the project's total future earnings, discounted from the time that they accrue to the present, equal the original investment. It is more precise than most of the other methods used to measure return on capital invested because it recognizes the effect of the time value of money. It can be used to determine whether a given project is acceptable or unacceptable by comparing each project's rate of return with the company's standard.

Discount rate: Interest rate charged member banks by the Federal Reserve for the opportunity to borrow added reserves. Also used in DCF methods.

Discretionary spending: A measure, developed by the National Industrial Conference Board, that reflects the extent of consumer spending as the result of a decision relatively free of prior commitment, pressure of necessity, or force of habit. It includes all personal expenditures not accounted for specifically or in equivalent form in imputed income, fixed commitments, or essential outlays. The series measures the growth and ability of American consumers to exercise some degree of discretion over the direction and manner of their spending and saving.

Drop: A term used in the gaming industry to indicate the total monetary-equivalent value of cash, IOUs ("markers"), and other items that are physically deposited or dropped into a cash box of a gaming table or slot machine.

Econometrics: The branch of economics that expresses economic theories in mathematical terms in order to verify them by statistical methods. It is concerned with empirical measurements of economic relations that are expressible in mathematical form. Econometrics seeks to measure the impact of one economic variable on another to enable the prediction of future events or provide advice on economic-policy choices to produce desired results. Economic theory can supply qualitative information concerning an economic problem, but it is the task of econometrics to provide the quantitative content for these qualitative statements.

Economic growth: An increase in a nation's or an area's capacity to produce goods and services coupled with an increase in production of these goods and services. Usually, economic growth is measured by the annual rate of increase in a nation's gross national product (GNP) as adjusted for price changes.

Economic model: A mathematical statement of economic theory. Use of an economic model is a method of analysis that presents an oversimplified picture of the real world.

Economics: The social study of production, distribution, and consumption of wealth.

Ecotourism: Though there is no wide agreement on a strict definition, the term often suggests tourism that does not disturb the ecological balance of a region's resources of land, labor, transportation, and other assets. Also known as "green tourism."

Elastic demand: The percentage change induced in one factor of demand divided by a given percentage change in the factor that caused the change. For example, if the price of a commodity is raised, purchasers tend to reduce their buying rate. The relationship between price and purchasing rate, which is known as the elasticity of demand, expresses the percentage change in the buying rate divided by the percentage change in price.

Elasticity: The relative response of one variable to a small percentage change in another variable.

Equilibrium: The state of an economic system in which all forces for change are balanced, so that the net tendency to change is zero. An economic system is considered to be in equilibrium when all the significant variables show no change over a period of time.

Equity: Amount of capital invested in an enterprise. It represents a participative share of ownership, and in an accounting sense it is calculated by subtracting the liabilities (obligations) of an enterprise from its assets.

Excess reserves: The surplus of cash and deposits owned by commercial member banks of the Federal Reserve System over what they are legally required to hold at Reserve Banks or in their own vaults. The excess-reserve position of a bank is an indication of its ability to invest in government bonds or to make loans to customers. Therefore, if the Federal Reserve System is trying to stimulate business in periods of economic sluggishness, it buys government bonds from private sellers, thus increasing bank reserves, and vice versa.

FIT: Denotes the free or foreign independent traveler market segment. *See also* IT, below.

Foreign exchange: All monetary instruments that give residents of one country a financial claim on another country. The use of foreign exchange is a country's principal means of settling its transactions with other countries.

Franchise: A brand for goods and services that provides a distinct identity and that can be globally extended through franchise agreements that provide local owners with quantity purchase discounts, advertising and real estate support, etc. Airlines have distinct franchises in the routes that they fly (e.g., those of British Air, American, United, etc.). Hotel chains, car rental companies, travel agencies, and restaurant chains use franchise agreements to extend the brand (e.g., McDonald's, Hilton, Marriott, Avis, Carlson, etc.).

Free reserves: The margin by which excess reserves exceed borrowings at Federal Reserve Banks. They are a better indicator of the banking system's ability to expand loans and investments than excess reserves. Manipulation of the net free-reserve position of member banks is an indication of the monetary policy that the Federal Reserve wishes to pursue.

Gross Domestic Product (GDP): The measure of the value of all goods and services produced in a country no matter whether that output belongs to natives or foreigners. It is different from GNP, which measures output belonging to U.S. citizens and corporations wherever that output is created. In actuality, in the U.S., the differences between the values of the two series have been slight. *See* Gross National Product.

Gross National Product (GNP): The most comprehensive measure of a nation's total output of goods and services. In the United States, the GNP represents the dollar value at current prices of all goods and services produced for sale plus the estimated value of certain imputed outputs, that is, goods and services that are neither bought nor sold. The rental value of owner-occupied dwellings and the value of farm products consumed on the farm are the most important imputed outputs included; the services of housewives are among the most important nonmarket values included. The GNP includes only final goods and services; for example, a pair of shoes that costs the man-ufacturer $2.50, the retailer $4.50, and the consumer $6.00 adds to the GNP only $6.00, the amount of the final sale, not $13.00, the sum of all the trans-actions. The GNP can be calculated by adding either all expenditures on currently produced goods and services or all incomes earned in producing these goods and services.

Gross win: The casino equivalent of revenues or sales in other businesses. It is from the gross win that operating expenses must be deducted.

Handle: A term used in the gaming industry to indicate the total dollar amount bet on the outcome of an event.

Hold: A term used in the gaming industry to indicate how much of the drop is retained (won) by the game operator through the course of play. Hold can be expressed as a percentage of the drop, in which case it is known as the hold percentage, often in a shorthand way called "win."

Income effect: A term used in demand analysis to indicate the increase or decrease in the amount of a good that is purchased because of a price-induced change in the purchasing power of a fixed income. When the price of a commodity declines, the income effect enables a person to buy more of this or other commodities with a given income. The opposite occurs when the price rises. By using indifference curves, it is possible to separate the income effect from the so-called substitution effect, in which the demand for a price-reduced good rises as it is substituted for other goods whose prices have remained constant.

Indifference curve: A graphic curve that represents the various combina-tions of two goods that will yield the consumer the same total satisfaction. For example, a household may receive the same satisfaction from consum-ing four pounds of steak or one pound of chicken. By assuming that the two commodities can be substituted for each other, it is possible to draw an indifference schedule that contains all of the possible combinations of the commodities that will yield the same satisfaction. When the schedule is plot-ted on a graph, with one commodity along the vertical axis and another along the horizontal axis, the curve that connects the points is called an indifference curve.

Inelastic demand (inelasticity): A term used to describe a proportionally smaller change in the purchase rate of a good than the proportional change in price that caused the change in amount bought. When the demand for a product is inelastic, a relatively large price change is necessary to cause a relatively small increase in purchase. To calculate the elasticity of demand, the percentage change in buying rate (the quantity bought per period of time) is divided by the percentage change in price.

Inflation: A persistent upward movement in the general price level. It results in a decline in purchasing power.

Interest: The price paid for the use of money over a period of time. Individuals, businesses, and governments buy the use of money. Businesses pay interest for the use of money to purchase capital goods because they can increase production and productivity through the introduction of new plants and new machines.

Inventory: Supply of various goods kept on hand by a firm to meet needs promptly as they arise and thus assure uninterrupted operation of the business. In manufacturing, for example, inventory includes not only finished products awaiting shipment to selling outlets, but also raw materials and countless other items required for the production and distribution of the product.

IT: Denotes the inclusive tour (i.e., packaged travel segment). Sometimes also known as GIT for group inclusive tour and contrasts to FIT (*see above*).

Labor force: According to the concept of the U.S. Department of Labor and the U.S. Bureau of the Census, the noninstitutionalized population, sixteen years of age or older, who either are employed or are looking for work.

Lead–lag relationship: The timing of changes in one statistical series in relation to changes in another series. The term is frequently used in sales forecasting, which makes use of the timing pattern between a company's sales and a particular economic indicator.

Liabilities: The debts or amounts of money owed by an individual, partnership, or corporation to others. Considered from another point of view, liabilities are the claims or rights, expressed in monetary terms, of an individual's or a corporation's creditors. In accounting, liabilities are classified as either short-term or long-term liabilities or as secured or unsecured liabilities. Short-term liabilities are those that will be satisfied, or paid, within one year.

Load factor: Term used by airlines, for a single sector flight, to indicate the passengers carried as a percentage of the seats available for sale. On a network of routes, the load factor is obtained by taking total passenger-miles as a percentage of total seat-miles available.

Macroeconomics: Modern economic analysis concerned with data in aggregate as opposed to individual form. It concerns itself with an overall view of economic life, considering the total size, shape, and functioning of economic experience rather than the workings of individual parts. More specifically, macroeconomics involves the analysis of the general price level rather than the prices of individual commodities, national output or income rather than the income of the individual firm, and total employment rather than employment in an individual firm.

Marginal cost: The additional cost that a producer incurs by making one additional unit of output. If, for example, total costs were $13,000 when a firm was producing two machine tools per day and $18,000 when it was producing three machine tools per day, the marginal cost of producing one machine tool was $5,000. The marginal cost may be the same or higher or lower in moving from three to four machine tools. The concept of marginal cost plays a key role in determining the quantity of goods that a firm chooses to produce. The purely competitive firm, which faces a given price set in the market, increases its output until marginal cost equals price. That point is the firm's best-profit output point. The imperfectly competitive firm equates marginal cost to marginal revenue (additional revenue) to obtain the highest profits. For most firms, marginal costs decline for a while and then begin to rise. The pattern of the marginal-cost graph depends on the nature of the firm's production function and the prices of the goods that it buys.

Marginal propensities: The marginal propensity indicates the proportion out of every dollar of additional income that consumers, on the average, are willing to save, invest, spend. import, etc. Marginal propensities are central to macroeconomic theories and models such as those of economist John Maynard Keynes in the 1930s.

Marginal revenue: The additional revenue that a seller receives from putting one more unit of output on the market.

Margins: *See* Profit margin.

Market share: The ratio of a company's sales, in units or dollars, to total industry sales, in units or dollars, on either an actual basis or a potential basis for a specific time period.

Microeconomics: Modern economic analysis concerned with data in individual form as opposed to aggregate form. It is concerned with the study of the individual firm rather than aggregates of firms, the individual consuming unit rather than the total population, and the individual commodity rather than total output. Microeconomics deals with the division of total output among industries, products, and firms and the allocation of resources among competing uses. It is concerned with the relative prices of particular goods and the problem of income distribution.

Model: In econometrics, an equation or set of equations depicting the causal relationships that are believed to generate observed data. Also, the expression of a theory by means of mathematical symbols or diagrams.

Modern portfolio theory: A theory that enables investment managers to classify, estimate, and control the sources of investment risk and return.

Monopoly: A market structure with only one seller of a commodity. In pure monopoly, the single seller exercises absolute control over the market price because there is no competitive supply of goods on the market. The seller can choose the most profitable price and does so by raising the price and restricting the ouput below what would be achieved if there were competition.

Monopsony: A market structure with a single buyer of a commodity. Pure monopsony, or buyer's monopoly, is characterized by the ability of the single buyer to set the buying price. In the case of a monopsonist who maximizes profits, both the buying price and the quantity bought are lower than they would be in a competitive situation.

National income: The total compensation of the elements used in production (land, labor, capital, and entrepreneurship) that comes from the current production of goods and services by the national economy. It is the income earned (but not necessarily received) by all persons in the country in a specified period.

Nonborrowed reserves: A reserve aggregate consisting of total bank reserves (deposits of the Federal Reserve and vault cash) minus borrowings by member banks from the Federal Reserve.

Oligopoly: A type of market structure in which a small number of firms supplies the major portion of an industry's output. The best-known example in the U.S. economy is the automobile industry, in which three firms account for 65% of the output of passenger cars. Although oligopolies are most likely to develop in industries whose production methods require large capital investments, they also cover such diverse items as cigarettes, light bulbs, chewing gum, detergents, and razor blades. In economic theory, the term *oligopoly* means a mixture of competition and monopoly. The benefit or harm to the economy at large by oligopolies remains in dispute.

Operating cash flow: In the media and travel industries, earnings before depreciation and amortization, interest, other income, and taxes.

Operating income: Earnings before interest, other income, and taxes.

Opportunity costs: The value of the productive resources used in producing one good, such as an automobile, instead of another good, such as a machine tool. With relatively fixed supplies of labor and capital at any given time, the economy cannot produce all it wants of everything.

Paretian optimum: A situation that exists when no one (say person *A*) in a society can move into a position that *A* prefers without causing someone else (person *B*) to move into a position that *B* prefers less. In other words, a situation is not a paretian or social optimum if it is possible, by changing the way in which commodities are produced or exchanged, to make one person better off without making another person (or persons) worse off. *See* Second-best theory.

Partnership: A type of business organization in which two or more persons agree on the amounts of their contribution (capital and effort) and on the distribution of profits, if any. Partnerships are common in retail trade, accounting, and law.

Passenger-miles (kilometers): The number of passengers on a flight multiplied by the stage distance as measured in miles or kilometers.

Personal-consumption expenditures: Expenditures that reflect the market value of goods and services purchased by individuals and nonprofit institutions or acquired by them as income in kind. The rental value of owner-occupied dwellings is included, but not the purchases of dwellings. Purchases are recorded at cost to consumers, including excise or sales taxes, and in full at the time of purchase whether made with cash or on credit.

Personal income: According to the concept of the U.S. Department of Commerce, the amount of current income received by persons from all sources, including transfer payments from government and business, but excluding transfer payments from other sources. Personal income also includes the net incomes of unincorporated businesses and nonprofit institutions and nonmonetary income, such as the estimated value of food consumed on farms and the estimated rental value of homes occupied by their owners.

PFC: In airlines, passenger facility charges (i.e., charges to passengers for use of airport facilities). PFC revenues are used to pay for runways, terminals, and other related assets.

Price/earnings ratio: The current market price per share of a company's stock expressed as a multiple of the company's per-share earnings.

Production function: The various combinations of land, labor, materials, and equipment that are needed to produce a given quantity of output. The production function expresses the maximum possible output that can be produced with any specified quantities of the various necessary inputs. Every production function assumes a given level of technology; once technological innovations have been introduced, the production function changes.

Productivity: The goods and services produced per unit of labor or capital or both; for example, the output of automobiles per person-hour. The ratio of output to all labor and capital is a total productivity measure; the ratio of output to either labor or capital is a partial measure. Anything that raises output in relation to labor and capital leads to an increase in productivity.

Profit margin: Net profit from operations divided by net sales and expressed as a percentage. This percentage measures the efficiency of a company or an industry. Nevertheless, profit margins vary widely among industries and among companies within a given industry. *See* Returns.

Profits: The amount left over after a business enterprise has paid all its bills.

Prospectus: Any communication, either written or broadcast by radio or television, that offers a security for sale. The prospectus contains the most important parts of the registration statement, which must give all information relevant to the issue.

Public good: A good for which the costs of production are independent of the number of people who consume it. National defense is an example where one person's consumption does not diminish the quantity available to others. TV programs are almost pure public goods because the program, no matter how it is recorded, remains unchanged regardless of how many people view it. In contrast, pure *private goods*, once consumed by an individual, are no longer available for someone else. For private goods, say a slice of bread, the costs of production *are* related to the number of people who consume it.

Rack Rate: The maximum published rate applicable to a hotel's room-type segment.

Regression line: A statistical term that indicates a relationship between two or more variables. The regression line was first used by Sir Francis Galton to indicate certain relationships in his theory of heredity, but it is now employed to describe many functional relationships. A regression, or least-squares, line is derived from a mathematical equation relating one economic variable to another. The use of regression lines is important in determining the effect of one variable on another.

Required reserves: The percentages of their deposits that U.S. commercial banks are required to set aside as reserves at their regional Federal Reserve Bank or as cash in their vaults. Reserve requirements vary according to the category of the bank.

Returns: The earnings or profit compensations received for owning assets or equity positions. Also, returns on sales are equivalent to profit margins.

Risk: The exposure of an investor to the possibility of gain or loss of money. Profit is the investor's reward for assuming the risk of economic uncertainty, such as changes in consumer tastes or changes in technology. The financial risk is based on natural, human, and economic uncertainties.

Second-best theory: A theory that analyzes alternative suboptimal positions to determine the second best when some constraint prevents an economy from reaching a paretian optimum. *See* Paretian optimum.

Secular trend: A statistical term denoting the regular, long-term movement of a series of economic data. The secular trend of most economic series is positive, or upward, indicating growth, the angle of the trend depending on how fast or how slow the growth rate is.

Sherman Antitrust Act: A U.S. federal statute, enacted in 1890, that forbids all contracts in restraint of trade and all attempts at monopolization. The main purposes of the act were to prevent the exercise and growth of monopoly and to restore free enterprise and price competition.

Spectral analysis: In statistics and econometrics, a technique for isolating and estimating the duration and amplitudes of the cyclical components of time series. It results in separating the random from the systematic components of time series.

Spoilage: In airlines, the term refers to seats for which demand exists but which, for various reasons, nevertheless actually depart empty.

Supply: The ability and willingness of a firm to sell a good or service. The firm's supply of a good or service is a schedule of the quantities of that good or service that the firm would offer for sale at alternative prices at a given moment in time. The supply schedule, or the listing of quantities that would be sold at different prices, can be shown graphically by means of a supply curve. The term *supply* refers to the entire schedule of possibilities, not to one point on the schedule. It is an instantaneous concept expressing the relationship of price and the quantity that would be willingly sold, all other factors being constant.

Tax credit: A legal provision permitting U.S. taxpayers to deduct specified sums from their tax liabilities.

Tax deduction: A legal provision permitting U.S. taxpayers to deduct specified expenditures from their taxable income.

Time series: A set of ordered observations of a particular economic variable, such as prices, production, investment, and consumption, taken at different points in time. Most economic series consist of monthly, quarterly, or annual observations. Monthly and quarterly economic series are used in short-term business forecasting.

Underwriter: Any person, group, or firm that assumes a risk in return for a fee, usually called a premium or commission.

Unemployment rate: The number of jobless persons expressed as a percentage of the total labor force. The U.S. counts as unemployed anyone sixteen years of age or over who is out of work and would like a job (even if that person is doing little about finding one).

Utility: The ability of a good or a service to satisfy human wants. It is the property possessed by a particular good or service that affords an individual pleasure or prevents pain during the time of its consumption or the period of anticipation of its consumption. The degree of utility of a good varies constantly. Thus, utility is not proportional to the quantity or type of the good or service consumed.

Warrant: An option that gives the holder the privilege of purchasing a certain amount of stock at a specified price for a stipulated period. There are two types of warrants: *stock-purchase warrants* and *subscription warrants*. Stock-purchase warrants (also called option warrants) are sometimes issued with or attached to bonds, preferred stock, and, infrequently, common stock. They entitle the holder to buy common stock in the same corporation at a certain price. Some of these warrants limit the right to buy to a specified period; others are perpetual. Stock-purchase warrants are sometimes attached to the underlying issue and cannot be detached; their value is a part of the bond or preferred stock. Others are detachable, sometimes after a waiting period, and frequently have inherent value that depends on the current price of the common stock.

Wet lease: Refers to aircraft leasing that requires the lessor to provide the lessee with aircraft, crew, and sometimes also maintenance and insurance. Altogether, known as ACMI.

Win: *See* Gross win.

Working capital, net: The excess of current assets over current liabilities. These excess current assets are available to carry on business operations. As demand increases in prosperous times, a large volume of working capital is needed to expand production.

Workweek: The number of weekly hours per factory worker for which pay has been received, including paid holidays, vacations, and sick leaves. In the United States, workweek figures cover full-time and part-time production and related workers who receive payment for any part of the pay period ending nearest the fifteenth of the month. Because of increasing amounts of paid holidays, vacations, and sick leave, the paid workweek exceeds the number of hours actually worked per week. The average-workweek series compiled from payroll data by the U.S. Bureau of Labor Statistics differs from the series of weekly hours actually worked that is compiled from household surveys by the U.S. Bureau of the Census. It also differs from the standard or scheduled workweek, because of such factors as absenteeism, part-time work, and stoppages

Yield: 1. The percentage that is derived from dividing the annual return from any investment by the amount of the investment, for example, a stock's annual per share dividend payment rate divided by its per share price. 2. In airlines, the average revenue per passenger-mile, obtained by dividing total passenger revenue by the total passenger-miles. 3. In hotels, the yield per room, calculated by dividing room sales by available room-nights instead of occupied room-nights. 4. In cruise ships, similarly, revenues per available berths.

References

Abt, V., Smith, J. F., and Christiansen, E. M. (1985). *The Business of Risk: Commercial Gambling in Mainstream America*. Lawrence: University of Kansas Press.

Adams, J. A. (1991). *The American Amusement Park Industry: A History of Technology and Thrills*. Boston: Twayne Publishers (G. K. Hall & Co.).

AICPA (1984). *Audits of Casinos*, New York: American Institute of Certified Public Accountants.

Andrew, W. P., and Schmidgall, R. S. (1993). *Financial Management for the Hospitality Industry*. East Lansing, MI: Educational Institute of the American Hotel & Motel Association.

Antoniou, A. (1991). "Economies of Scale in the Airline Industry: The Evidence Revisited," *Logistics and Transportation Review*, 27(2)(June).

Asch, P., Malkiel, B. G., and Quandt, R. E. (1984). "Market Efficiency in Racetrack Betting," *Journal of Business* 57(2)(April):165–75.

BAA (1978). *Long Term Airport Traffic Forecasting*. London: British Airports Authority.

Baggaley, P. A. (1999). "Analyzing an Airline's Credit Quality," in *Handbook of Airline Finance*. Washington, DC: *Aviation Week* (McGraw-Hill).

Barnhart, R. T. (1983), "Can Trente-et-Quarante Be Beaten?" *Gambling Times* 3(8) (December).

Barrett, N. S. (1974). *The Theory of Microeconomics Policy*. Lexington, MA: Heath.

Becker, G. S. (1965). "A Theory of the Allocation of Time," *Economic Journal* LXXV(299)(September):493–517.

Belobaba, P. D. (1998a). "Airline Differential Pricing for Effective Yield Management," in *Handbook of Airline Marketing*. Washington, DC: *Aviation Week* (McGraw-Hill).

(1998b). "The Evolution of Airline Yield Management: Fare Class to Origin–Destination Seat Inventory Control," in *Handbook of Airline Marketing*. Washington, DC: Aviation Week (McGraw-Hill).

Berger, A. J., and Bruning, N. (1979). *Lady Luck's Companion*. New York: Harper & Row.

Bishop, M., and Thompson, D. (1992). "Peak-Load Pricing in Aviation: The Case of Charter Air Fares," *Journal of Transport Economics and Policy*, 26(1)(January).

Binkley, C. (2000) "Casino Chain Mines Data on Its Gamblers and Strikes Day Dirt," *Wall Street Journal*, May 4.

Block, R. L. (1998). *Investing in REITS*. Princeton (NJ): Bloomberg Press.

Boyar, K. D. (1997). *Principles of Transportation Economics*. Reading, MA: Addison-Wesley.

Braunlich, C., Cabot, A., Thompson, W., and Tottenham, A. (1999). *International Casino Law*, 3rd ed. Reno, NV: Institute for the Study of Gambling and Commercial Gaming, University of Nevada.

Brown, J., and Church, A. (1987). "Theme Parks in Europe," *Travel & Tourism Analyst*, London: *The Economist*, February.

Brown, L. R., Renner, M., and Halweil, B. (1999). *Vital Signs*, 1999. New York: Worldwatch Institute and W. W. Norton.

Bull, A. (1995). *The Economics of Travel and Tourism*, 2nd ed. Melbourne: Longman Australia.

Burton, J. S., and Toth, J. R. (1974). "Forecasting Long-Term Interest Rates," *Financial Analysts Journal*, 30(5)(September/October):73–87.

Butler, G. F., and Keller, M. R., eds. (1999). *Handbook of Airline Finance*. Washington, DC: Aviation Week (McGraw-Hill).

(1998). *Handbook of Airline Marketing*. Washington, DC: Aviation Week (McGraw-Hill).

Button, K. J. (1993). *Transport Economics*, 2nd ed. Cheltenham, U.K. and Northampton, MA: E. Elgar.

Cabot, A. N., ed. (1995). *Nevada Gaming Law*, 2nd ed. Las Vegas: Lionel Sawyer & Collins.

Christiansen, E. M. (1998). "1997 U.S. Gross Annual Wager," *Gaming & Wagering Business*, July and August issues.

(1989). "1988 U.S. Gross Annual Wager," *Gaming & Wagering Business*, 10(7)(July) and 10(8)(August).

Cobb, C., Halstead, T., and Rowe, J. (1995). "If the GDP Is Up, Why Is America Down?" *The Atlantic Monthly*, 276(4)(October).

Cohen, E. (1972). "Toward a Sociology of International Tourism," *Social Research*, 39(1)(Spring).

Cook, J. (1979). "Bingo!" *Forbes*, 124(3)(August 6):37–45.

Cukier, K. N. (2000). "The Big Gamble," *Red Herring*, (April).

Damodaran, A. (1996). *Investment Valuation*. New York: John Wiley & Sons.

Dargay, J. M. (1993). "Demand Elasticities: A Comment," *Journal of Transport Economics and Policy*, 27(1)(January).

Davis, M. D. (1973). *Game Theory: A Nontechnical Approach*. New York: Basic Books.

De Grazia, S. (1962). *Of Time, Work and Leisure*. New York: Twentieth Century Fund.

DeSerpa, A. C. (1971). "A Theory of the Economics of Time," *Economic Journal* (December):828–46.

Dickinson, B., and Vladimir, A. (1997). *Selling the Sea: An Inside Look at the Cruise Industry*. New York: John Wiley & Sons.

Doganis, R. (1991). *Flying Off Course: The Economics of International Airlines*. London and New York: Routledge.

Eade, R. H. (1996). "Casino Cage Operations," in *The Gaming Industry: Introduction and Perspectives*. Las Vegas: University of Nevada; New York: John Wiley & Sons.

Eadington, W. R., ed. (1976). *Gambling and Society*. Springfield, IL.: Thomas.

Elkind, P. (1999). "The Hype Is Big, Really Big, At Priceline," *Fortune*, 140(5)(September 6).

Fennell, D. A. (1999). *Ecotourism: An Introduction*. London and New York: Routledge.

Fey, M. (1989). *Slot Machines*. Reno, NV: Liberty Belle Books.

Final Report (1978). London: Royal Commission on Gambling, (July), Vol. 2.

Financial Accounting Standards Board (1983). *Accounting Standards: Original Pronouncements*. Stamford, CT: FASB.

Findlay, J. M. (1986). *People of Chance: Gambling in American Society from Jamestown to Las Vegas*. New York and Oxford: Oxford University Press.

Fishbein, M. (1967). "Attitude and the Prediction of Behavior," in *Readings in Attitude Theory and Measurement*, Fishbein, M., ed. New York: John Wiley.

Fletcher, J. (1989). "Input–Output Analysis and Tourism Impact Studies," *Annals of Tourism Research*, 16(4); also in Khan, Olsen, and Var (1993).

Frantz, D. (1999). "Cruise Lines Reap Profit from Favors in Law," *New York Times*, February 19.

Friedman, B. (1974, 1982). *Casino Management*, rev. and enlarged edition. Secaucus, NJ: Lyle Stuart.

Friedman, M., and Savage, L. J. (1948). "The Utility Analysis of Choices Involving Risk," *Journal of Political Economy*, 56(4)(August):279–304.

Fujii, E., Im, E., and Mak, J. (1992). "The Economics of Direct Flights," *Journal of Transport Economics and Policy*, 26(2)(May).

Garvett, D. S., and Avery, A. (1998). "Frequent Traveler Programs: Moving Targets," in *Handbook of Airline Marketing*. Washington, DC: Aviation Week (McGraw-Hill).

Garvett, D. S., and Hilton, K. J. (1999). "What Drives Airline Profits? A First Look," in *Handbook of Airline Finance*. Washington, DC: Aviation Week (McGraw-Hill).

Gawlicki, S. M. (2000). "The Financing Tool of Choice," *Investment Dealers' Digest*, January 31.

Gee, C. Y., Makens, J. C., and Choy, D. J. L. (1997). *The Travel Industry*, 3rd ed. New York: Van Nostrand Reinhold.

Ghez, G. R., and Becker, G. S. (1975). *The Allocation of Time and Goods Over the Life Cycle*. New York: National Bureau of Economic Research.

Gibbs, N. (1989). "How America Has Run Out of Time," *Time*, 133(17)(April 24).

Glaister, S. (1981). *Fundamentals of Transport Economics*. Oxford, UK: Basil Blackwell.

Gollehon, J. (1986). *All about Sports Betting*. Grand Rapids, MI: Gollehon.

Goodman, R. (1995). *The Luck Business: The Devastating Consequences and Broken Promises of America's Gambling Explosion*. New York: The Free Press (Simon & Schuster).

 (1994). *Legalized Gambling as a Strategy for Economic Development*. Northampton, MA: Broadside Books.

Goodwin, P. B. (1992). "A Review of New Demand Elasticities with Special Reference to Short and Long Run Effects of Price Changes," *Journal of Transport Economics and Policy*, 23.

Grant, J. L. (1997). *Foundations of Economic Value Added*. New Hope, PA: Frank J. Fabozzi.

Greenhouse, L. (1999). "Justices Strike Down Ban on Casino Gambling Ads," *New York Times*, June 15.

Greenlees, E. M. (1988). *Casino Accounting and Financial Management*. Reno and Las Vegas: University of Nevada Press.

Halliday, J., and Fuller, P., eds. (1974). *The Psychology of Gambling*. New York: Harper & Row.

Hanlon, P. (1996). *Global Airlines: Competition in a Transnational Industry*. Oxford, UK: Butterworth–Heinemann.

Hanson, B. (2000). "Price Elasticity of Lodging Demand," PricewaterhouseCoopers, January 20.

Harden, B., and Swardson, A. (1996). "America's Gamble," *Washington Post*, March 3–6.

Harris, L. (1995). *The Harris Poll* 1995, # 68. New York: Louis Harris & Associates, Inc.

Hedges, J. N., and Taylor, D. E. (1980). "Recent Trends in Worktime: Hours Edge Downward," *Monthly Labor Review* (U.S. Department of Labor), 103(3)(March).

Henderson, J. M., and Quandt, R. E. (1971). *Microeconomic Theory: A Mathematical Approach*, 2nd ed. New York: McGraw-Hill.

Homan, A. C. (1999). "Changes in Airline Operating Expenses: Effect on Demand and Airline Profits," in *Handbook of Airline Finance*. Washington, DC: *Aviation Week* (McGraw-Hill).

Honey, M. (1999). *Ecotourism and Sustainable Development: Who Owns Paradise?* Washington, DC: Island Press.

Huizinga, J. (1955). *Homo Ludens: A Study of the Play-Element in Culture*. Boston: Beacon Press.

Ignatin, G., and Smith, R. (1976). "The Economics of Gambling," in *Gambling and Society*, W. R. Eadington, ed., pp. 69–91. Springfield, IL: Thomas.

Ingersoll, B. (1999). "Airports, Airlines Rev Up for Duel Over Funding Plans," *Wall Street Journal*, August 31.

Jackson, C. (1984). *Hounds of the Road: A History of the Greyhound Bus Company*. Bowling Green OH: Bowling Green Popular Press.

Jacobs, J. A., and Gerson, K. (1998). "Who Are the Overworked Americans?" *Review of Social Economy*, vol. LVI (4)(Winter).

Johnson, R. (1984). "Applying the Utilization Theory to Slot Decisions," *Gaming Business*, April.

Juster, F. T., and Stafford, F. P. (1991). "The Allocation of Time: Empirical Findings, Behavioral Models, and Problems of Measurement," *Journal of Economic Literature*, June, vol. 29.

Kanafani, A. (1983). *Transportation Demand Analysis*. New York: McGraw-Hill.

Khan, M. A., Olsen, M. D., and Var, T., eds. (1993). *VNR's Encyclopedia of Hospitality and Tourism*. New York: Van Nostrand Reinhold.

Kilby, J. (1985). "Estimating Revenue through Bet Criteria," *Gaming and Wagering Business*, 6(3)(March).

Klein, H. J. (1982). "Gaming's Growing Slice of the American Leisure Pie," *Gaming Business*, 3(9).

Kraus, R. (1978). *Recreation and Leisure in Modern Society*, 2nd ed. Santa Monica, CA: Goodyear Publishing.

Krippendorf, J. (1987). *(Ferienmenschen) The Holiday Makers: Understanding the Impact of Leisure and Travel*. London: Heinemann.

Kusler, J. A. (1991). "Ecotourism and Resource Conservation: Introduction to Issues," in *Ecotourism and Resource Conservation: A Collection of Papers*, Kusler, J. A., ed., Volume 1. Madison, WI: Omnipress.

Kyriazi, G. (1976). *The Great American Amusement Parks: A Pictorial History*. Secaucus, NJ: Citadel Press.

Levy, H., and Sarnat, M. (1972). *Investment and Portfolio Analysis*. New York: Wiley.

Lindberg, K. (1991). *Policies for Maximizing Nature Tourism's Ecological and Economic Benefits*. Washington, DC: World Resources Institute.

Linder, S. B. (1970). *The Harried Leisure Class*. New York: Columbia University Press.

Lintott, T. M. R. (1999). "Securitization of Aircraft Assets," in *Handbook of Airline Finance*. Washington, DC: *Aviation Week* (McGraw-Hill).

Lundberg, D. E. (1985). *The Tourist Business*, 5th ed. New York: Van Nostrand Reinhold.

Lyon, R. (1987). "Theme Parks in the USA," *Travel & Tourism Analyst*, London: The Economist Publications, January.

Machalaba, D. (1999). "Can Fast Trains and Local Beer Save Amtrak?," *Wall Street Journal*, January 27.

Mahon, G. (1980). *The Company That Bought the Boardwalk*. New York: Random House.

Mangels, W. F. (1952). *The Outdoor Amusement Industry: From Earliest Times to the Present*. New York: Vantage Press.

Manteris, A., and Talley, R. (1991). *SuperBookie: Inside Las Vegas Sports Gambling*. Chicago: Contemporary Books.

Mathieson, A., and Wall, G. (1982). *Tourism: Economic, Physical and Social Impacts*. London and New York: Longman.

McIntosh, R. W., Goeldner, C. R., and Ritchie, J. R. B. (1999). *Tourism: Principles, Practices, Philosophies*, 8th ed. New York: John Wiley & Sons.

McLaren, D. (1998). *Rethinking Tourism and Ecotravel*. West Hartford, CT: Kumarian Press.

Meyer, J. R., and Oster, C. V., Jr. (1987). *Deregulation and the Future of Intercity Passenger Travel*. Cambridge, MA: MIT Press.

Miller, L. C. (1995). "Underwriting the Investment," in Raleigh and Roginsky (1995).

Moore, J. (1996). *The Complete Book of Sports Betting*. New York: Carol Publishing (Lyle Stuart).

Morrell, P. S. (1997). *Airline Finance*. Aldershot, UK and Brookfield, VT: Ashgate.

Murphy, J. M. (1976). "Why You Can't Win," *Journal of Portfolio Management* (fall).

Murthy, B., and Dev, C. S. (1993). "Average Daily Rate," in Kahn, Olsen, and Var (1993).

Nasaw, D. (1993). *Going Out: The Rise and Fall of Public Amusements*. New York: HarperCollins (Basic Books).

National Gambling Impact Study Commission Report (1999). Washington, DC: U.S. Government Printing Office and www.ngisc.gov.

National Tourism Policy Study (1978). Washington, DC: U.S. Government Printing Office.

Neulinger, J. (1981). *To Leisure: An Introduction*. Boston: Allyn and Bacon.

Okubo, S., and Planting, M. A. (1998). "U.S. Travel and Tourism Satellite Accounts for 1992," *Survey of Current Business*. Washington, DC: U.S. Department of Commerce, Bureau of Economic Analysis (July).

Oum, T. H., Waters, W. G., and Yong, J. S. (1992), "Concepts of Price Elasticities of Transport Demand and Recent Empirical Evidence, *Journal of Transport Economics and Policy*, 26.

Owen, J. D. (1988). "Work-Time Reduction in the U.S. and Western Europe," *Monthly Labor Review*, 111(12)(December).

(1976). "Workweeks and Leisure: An Analysis of Trends, 1948–75," *Monthly Labor Review* (U.S. Department of Labor), 99(8)(August).

(1970). *The Price of Leisure*. Montreal: McGill–Queen's University Press.

Pearson, G., and Strahler, J. (1995). "Airline Scheduling," in *Handbook of Airline Economics*. Washington, DC: *Aviation Week* (McGraw-Hill).

Petzinger, T., Jr. (1995). *Hard Landing: The Epic Contest for Power and Profits That Plunged the Airlines into Chaos*. New York: Times Books.

Plog, S. C. (1974). "Why Destination Areas Rise and Fall in Popularity," *The Cornell Hotel and Restaurant Administrative Quarterly*, 14(4)(February).

Provost, G. (1994). *High Stakes: Inside the New Las Vegas*. New York: Dutton (Truman Talley).

Puzo, M. (1976). *Inside Las Vegas*. New York: Grosset & Dunlap.

Raleigh, L. E., and Roginsky, R. J., eds. (1995). *Hotel Investments: Issues & Perspectives*. East Lansing, MI: Educational Institute of the American Hotel & Motel Association.

Ritter, S. (1999). "Supreme Court to Review Ban on Casino Ads," *Wall Street Journal*, January 18.

Roberts, K., and Rupert, P. (1995). "The Myth of the Overworked American," *Economic Commentary*. Cleveland: Federal Reserve Bank of Cleveland, January 15.

Roberts, P. (1995). "The Art of Goofing Off," *Psychology Today*, 28(4)(July/August).

Robinson, J. P. (1989). "Time's Up," *American Demographics*, 11(7)(July).

Robinson, J. P., and Godbey, G. (1997). *Time for Life: The Surprising Ways Americans Use Their Time*. University Park, PA: Penn State Press.

Rones, P.L., Ilg, R. E., and Gardner, J. M. (1997). "Trends in Hours of Work Since the Mid-1970s," *Monthly Labor Review*, BLS, U.S. Department of Labor, April.

Rose, I. N. (1986). *Gambling and the Law*. Los Angeles: Gambling Times.

Ryan, C. (1991). *Recreational Tourism: A Social Science Perspective*. London and New York: Routledge.

Rybczynski, W. (1991). "Waiting for the Weekend," *The Atlantic Monthly*, 268(2)(August), and *Waiting for the Weekend* (New York: Viking).

Scarne, J. (1978). *Scarne's Complete Guide to Gambling*. New York: Simon & Schuster.

(1974). *Scarne's New Complete Guide to Gambling*. New York: Simon & Schuster.

Schafer, A., and Victor, D. (1997). "The Past and Future of Global Mobility," *Scientific American*, 277(4)(October).

Schisgall, O. (1985). *The Greyhound Story: From Hibbing to Everywhere*. Chicago: Ferguson J. G. (Doubleday).

Schor, J. B. (1991). *The Overworked American: The Unexpected Decline of Leisure*. New York: Basic Books.

Sharp, C. H. (1981). *The Economics of Time*. Oxford, UK: Martin Robertson.

Siemers, E., and Harris, E. (1999). "Airlines Begin to Click With Internet-Booking Services," *Wall Streeet Journal*, August 2.

Silberstang, E. (1980). *Playboy's Guide to Casino Gambling*. New York: Playboy Press.

Sinclair, M. T., and Stabler, M. (1997), *The Economics of Tourism*. London: Routledge.

Skolnick, J. H. (1979). "The Social Risks of Casino Gambling," *Psychology Today*, 13(2)(July).

(1978). *House of Cards*. Boston: Little, Brown.

Smith, G. V., and Parr, R. L. (1994). *Valuation of Intellectual Property and Intangible Assets*, 2nd ed. New York: John Wiley.

Smith, S. J. (1986). "The Growing Diversity of Work Schedules," *Monthly Labor Review*, U.S. Department of Commerce, BLS, November, vol. 109, no. 11.

Smith, S. L. J. (1995). *Tourism Analysis: A Handbook*, 2nd ed. Essex, UK:Longman.

Spring, J. (1993). "Seven Days of Play," *American Demographics*, 15(3), March.

Stefanelli, J. M., and Nazarechuk, A. (1996). "Hotel/Casino Food and Beverage Operations," in *The Gaming Industry: Introduction and Perspectives*. New York: John Wiley & Sons.

Sternlieb, G., and Hughes, J. W. (1983). *The Atlantic City Gamble*. New York: Twentieth Century Fund; Cambridge, MA: Harvard University Press.

Stewart, G. B., III. (1991). *The Quest for Value*. New York: HarperCollins.

Stone, T. A., Lynes, T., and Fisher, R. I. (1999). "The Securitization of Aircraft Lease Receivables," in *Handbook of Airline Finance*. Washington, DC: *Aviation Week* (McGraw-Hill).

Stonier, J. E. (1998). "Marketing from a Manuafacturer's Perspective: Issues in Quantifying the Economic Benefits of New Aircraft, and Making the Correct Financing Decision," in *Handbook of Airline Marketing*. Washington, DC: *Aviation Week* (McGraw-Hill).

Straszheim, M. R. (1969). *The International Airline Industry*. Washington, DC: The Brookings Institution.

Thomas, B. (1976). *Walt Disney: An American Original*. New York: Simon & Schuster (Pocket Books, 1980).

Thorp, E. O. (1984). *The Mathematics of Gambling*. Secaucus, N.J.: Lyle Stuart.

Trost, C. (1986). "All Work and No Play? New Study Shows How Americans View Jobs," *Wall Street Journal*, December 30.

U.S. Congress (1999). National Gambling Impact Study Commission Report.

U.S. General Accounting Office (1998). *Intercity Passenger Rail Financial Performance of Amtrak's Routes*. Washington, DC: Bureau of Transportation Statistics (May).

(1997). *Amtrak's Financial Viability Continues to Be Threatened*. Washington, DC: Bureau of Transportation Statistics (March).

Vallen, G. K., and Vallen, J. J. (1996). *Check-In Check Out*. Chicago: Irwin.

Van Horne, J. C. (1968). *Financial Management and Policy*. Englewood Cliffs, NJ: Prentice-Hall.

Vanocur, B. (1999). "None Dare Call It Earnings: REIT Industry Again Looks at FFO, and Arguments Ensue," *Barron's*, June 7.

Veblen, T. (1899). *The Theory of the Leisure Class*. New York: Macmillan (paperback, New American Library, 1953).

von Neumann, J., and Morgenstern, O. (1944). *Theory of Games and Economic Behavior*. New York: Wiley.

Werner, F. M. (1999). "Leverage and Airline Financial Management," in *Handbook of Airline Finance*. Washington, DC: Aviation Week (McGraw-Hill).

White, L. J. (1979). "Economies of Scale and the Question of Natural Monopoly in the Airline Industry," *Journal of Air Law and Commerce*, 44.

Williamson, O. E. (1968). "Economies as an Antitrust Defense," *American Economic Review*, 58(1)(March).

(1966). "Peak Load Pricing and Optimal Capacity under Indivisible Constraints," *American Economic Review* (September).

Witt, S. F., and Moutinho, L. (1994). *Tourism Marketing and Management Handbook*, 2nd ed. Hertfordshire, UK: Prentice-Hall International.

Witt, S. F., and Witt, C. A. (1992). *Modeling and Forecasting Demand in Tourism*. London and San Diego: Academic Press.

World Tourist Organization (1994). *Aviation and Tourism Policies: Balancing the Benefits*. London and New York: Routledge.

Yaari, M. E. (1965). "Convexity in the Theory of Choice Under Risk," *Quarterly Journal of Economics*, May.

Zeisel, J. S. (1958). "The Workweek in American Industry 1850–1956," in *Mass Leisure*, Larrabee, E., and Meyerson, R., eds. Glencoe, IL: The Free Press.

Notes

Chapter 1

1. As De Grazia (1962, p. 13) notes, it is obvious that "time on one's hands is not enough to make leisure," and free time accompanied by fear and anxiety is not leisure.

2. As Smith (1986, p. 8) has further noted, surveys indicate that for full-time, day-shift plant workers, the average workweek decreased by 0.8 hour between 1973 and 1985 but that, over the same period, "the schedule of full-time office workers in the private sector rose by 0.2 hour, with the result that the workweek of these two large groups converged markedly."

Also, Hedges and Taylor (1980) show that hours for full-time service workers declined faster than for white-collar and blue-collar employees between 1968 and 1979. And the Bureau of Labor Statistics estimated that the percentage of nonagricultural salaried jobs in which the workweek exceeded 49 hours rose to 18.5% in 1993 as compared to 14.2% in 1973. See also Supplementary Table S1.1.

3. The Harris nationwide cross-section sample survey of 1,501 adults found that the estimated hours available for leisure have been steadily decreasing from 26.2 hours per week in 1973 to 16.6 hours per week in 1987. Harris argues that an apparent combination of economic necessities and choices by women who want to work has increased the number of families in which both husbands and wives hold jobs. Also see Gibbs (1989).

Table S1.1. *Average hours and earnings for production or nonsupervisory workers, selected industry categories, 1965–99*

Year	Total private[a]			Manufacturing			Services		
	Weekly hours	Hourly earnings	Weekly earnings	Weekly hours	Hourly earnings	Weekly earnings	Weekly hours	Hourly earnings	Weekly earnings
1965	38.8	$2.46	$95.45	41.2	$2.61	$107.53	35.9	$2.05	$73.60
1970	37.1	3.23	119.83	39.8	3.35	133.33	34.4	2.81	96.66
1975	36.1	4.53	163.53	39.5	4.83	190.79	33.5	4.02	134.67
1976	36.1	4.86	175.45	40.1	5.22	209.32	33.3	4.31	143.52
1977	36.0	5.25	189.00	40.3	5.68	228.90	33.0	4.65	153.45
1978	35.8	5.69	203.70	40.4	6.17	249.27	32.8	4.99	163.67
1979	35.7	6.16	219.91	40.2	6.70	269.34	32.7	5.36	175.27
1980	35.3	6.66	235.10	39.7	7.27	288.62	32.6	5.85	190.71
1981	35.2	7.25	255.20	39.8	7.99	318.00	32.6	6.41	208.97
1982	34.8	7.68	267.26	38.9	8.49	330.26	32.6	6.92	225.59
1983	35.0	8.02	280.70	40.1	8.83	354.08	32.7	7.31	239.04
1984	35.2	8.32	292.86	40.7	9.19	374.03	32.6	7.59	247.43
1985	34.9	8.57	299.09	40.5	9.54	386.37	32.5	7.90	256.75
1986	34.8	8.76	304.85	40.7	9.73	396.01	32.5	8.18	265.85
1987	34.8	8.98	312.50	41.0	9.91	406.31	32.5	8.49	275.93
1988	34.7	9.28	322.02	41.1	10.19	418.81	32.6	8.88	289.49
1989	34.6	9.66	334.24	41.0	10.48	429.68	32.6	9.38	305.79
1990	34.5	10.01	345.35	40.8	10.83	441.86	32.5	9.83	319.48
1991	34.3	10.32	353.95	40.7	11.18	455.03	32.4	10.23	331.45
1992	34.4	10.57	363.61	41.0	11.46	469.86	32.5	10.54	342.55
1993	34.5	10.83	373.64	41.4	11.74	486.04	32.5	10.78	350.35
1994	34.7	11.12	385.86	42.0	12.07	506.94	32.5	11.04	358.80
1995	34.5	11.43	394.34	41.6	12.37	514.59	32.4	11.39	369.04
1996	34.4	11.82	406.61	41.6	12.77	531.23	32.4	11.79	382.00
1997	34.6	12.28	424.89	42.0	13.17	553.14	32.6	12.28	400.33
1998	34.6	12.78	442.19	41.7	13.49	562.53	32.6	12.84	418.58
1999	34.5	13.24	456.78	41.7	13.91	580.05	32.6	13.36	435.54

[a]Data relate to production workers in mining and manufacturing, construction workers in construction, and nonsupervisory workers in transportation and public utilities, wholesale and retail trade, finance, insurance, real estate, and services.
Source: Employment and Earnings. U.S. Department of Labor, Bureau of Labor Statistics.

4. In more detail, Schor's data indicate that the annual hours of paid employment of labor force participants in 1969 and 1987 changed as follows:

	1969	1987	Change
All participants	1,786	1,949	163
Men	2,054	2,152	98
Women	1,406	1,711	305

These estimated changes in hours worked appear strikingly high. It seems that although the analysis has probably been correct in catching the direction of change, it may not have correctly estimated its magnitude. Schor's book is so politically imbued with an anticapitalist theme that the methodology and the objectivity of its findings are accordingly suspect. See also Robinson and Godbey (1997) and *The Economist*, December 23, 1995, p. 12.

5. Robinson (1989, p. 35) found, for example, that "people aged 51 to 64 have gained the most free time since 1965, mainly because they are working less. Among people in this age group, the proportion of men opting for early retirement increased considerably between 1965 and 1985." Also, Robinson and Godbey (1997) suggest that Americans, in the aggregate, have more time for leisure because of broad trends toward younger retirements and smaller families. Except for parents of very young children, or those with more than four children under age eighteen, everyone else, they say, has gained at least one hour per week since 1965.

6. Roberts and Rupert (1995) state that the presumption of declining leisure is a fallacy. "Previous studies purporting to have uncovered such a fact have not adequately disentangled time spent in home production-activities ... from time spent enjoying leisure activities. [W]hile hours of market work and home work have remained fairly constant for men since the mid-1970s, market hours have been rising and home production hours have been declining for women.... Possible reasons include an increase in market versus nonmarket productivity or labor-saving technological advancements in the home."

7. Rones, Ilg, and Gardner (1997) concluded that, between 1976 and 1993, "after removing the effect of the shifting age distribution, average weekly hours for men showed virtually no change (edging up from 41.0 to 41.2 hours), and the average workweek for women increased by only a single hour [but] ... a growing proportion of workers are putting in very long workweeks ... This increase is pervasive across occupations, and the long workweek itself seems to be associated with high earnings and certain types of occupations."

8. Divergence of results in studying hours of work may be caused by differences in how government data are used. For example, such data generally are based on hours paid, rather than hours worked. This means that a worker on paid vacation would be counted as working, even though he or she is not. Also, hours per job, rather than hours per worker are used.

9. Rybczynski (1991) provides a detailed history of the evolution of the weekend. And Spring (1993) provides a study of the popularity of spare-time activities classified by day of the week. Television viewing, consuming one third of free time on weekdays and one fourth on weekends, leads the list by far on every day of the week.

10. Also, studies comparing time allocation in different countries can be found in Juster and Stafford (1991), where, for example, it can be seen that both men and women allocate more time for leisure in the United States than in Japan or Sweden. Data from government reports of various countries (as shown in the *Wall Street Journal* of October 2, 1992) suggest that the average working hours per year as of the early 1990s were as follows:

Japan	2,120
Britain	1,950
U.S.	1,940
France	1,680
Germany	1,590

11. The apparently reduced rate of improvement between 1973 and 1990 may have been caused by unexpected sharp cost increases for energy and capital (interest rates), by high corporate debt levels, or perhaps by the burgeoning "underground" (off-the-books) economy not directly captured in (and therefore distorting) the NIPA numbers. However, applications of new technologies, in turn, are believed to have boosted productivity growth in the 1990s.

12. There are many fine texts providing full description of these tools; see, for example, Henderson and Quandt (1971).

13. In most mathematical presentations, the independent variable or "cause" of change is presented along the horizontal x axis and the dependent variable on the vertical y axis. Economists, however, have generally found it more convenient to depict prices (the independent variable) and quantities by switching the axes. Thus, prices are usually seen on the vertical axis and quantities on the horizontal one.

14. In Linder (1970), standard indifference-curve/budget-line analysis is used to show how the supply of labor is a function of income and substitution effects. The standard consumers' utility function is $V = f(Q, T_c)$, where Q is the number of units of consumption goods, and T_c is the number of hours devoted to consumption purposes. Two constraints are $Q = pT_w$, and $T = T_w + T_c$, where p is a productivity index measuring the number of consumption goods earned per hour of work (T_w), and T is the total number of hours available per time period.

To maximize utility, V now takes the Lagrange multiplier function

$$L = f(Q, T_c) + \lambda[Q - p(T - T_c)]$$

which is then differentiated with respect to Q, T_c, and multiplier λ.

15. See Trost (1986) and *Monthly Labor Review*, U.S. Department of Commerce, Bureau of Labor Statistics, November 1986, No. 11.

16. Owen's (1970) exhaustive study of these issues leads to a model supporting the hypothesis of a backward-bending labor-supply curve and suggesting that demand for leisure activity has positive income and negative price elasticities consistent with economic theory.

17. Utility can often be visualized in the form of a mathematical curve or function. For instance, the utility a person derives from purchase of good x might vary with the square root of the amount of x (i.e., $U(x)$ = square root of x). Also see Section 10.5 and Levy and Sarnat (1972).

18. A dependency ratio is the number of people who are net consumers (children and senior citizens) divided by the number of net producers; see, for example, Burton and Toth (1974).

19. Regulation is often deemed politically necessary to offset alleged imperfections in the market economy. At times, for example, there have thus been movements to contain monopoly power, to control excessive competition, to provide public goods, and to regulate externalities.

20. The complete PCE tables include much greater detail than is shown here. The total transportation category includes user-operated (cars), purchased local, and purchased intercity transportation.

21. The estimate of 4.6% to 5.3% for 1992 appears in Okubo and Planting (1998, p. 9). It was also found that value added in travel and tourism represented 1.9% to 2.2% of GDP, with hotels and lodging generating the highest value added.

22. However, the entertainment services series as a percentage of total recreation spending has demonstrated considerable volatility since 1929. This series hit a peak of nearly 50% in the early 1940s, when there were relatively few consumer durables available. Then, for a dozen or so years ending in the late 1970s, the percentage had been confined to a fairly narrow band of 33 to 36%.

23. GNP measures output belonging to U.S. citizens and corporations wherever that output is created, whereas GDP measures the value of all goods and services produced in a country no matter whether that output belongs to natives or foreigners. In actuality, in the U.S., the differences between the values of the two series have been slight.

However, critics of National Income Accounting, for example, Cobb, Halstead, and Row (1995), argue that GDP measurements allow activities in the household and volunteer sectors to go entirely unreckoned. As a result, GDP measurements mask the breakdown of the social structure and are grossly misleading. "GDP does not distinguish between costs and benefits, between productive and destructive activities, or between sustainable and unsustainable ones. The nation's central measure of well-being works like a calculating machine that adds but cannot subtract . . . The GDP treats leisure time and time with family the way it treats air and water: as having no value at all" (pp. 64–67).

24. The Herfindahl-Hirschman Index (HHI) – used by the Department of Justice in determining whether proposed mergers ought to be permitted – is calculated as the sum of the squared market shares of each competitor in the relevant product and geographic markets:

$$\text{HHI} = \sum_{i=1}^{n} S_i^2$$

where S is the market share of the ith firm in the industry and n equals the number of firms in the industry. Generally, near monopolies would have an HHI approaching 10,000, modest concentration would fall between 1,000 and 1,800, and low concentration would be under 1,000.

In regard to airlines, Hanlon (1996, p. 62) notes that, "[E]ven where increasing concentration is simply the result of efficient firms becoming more dominant, once they achieve this greater dominance they will enjoy a greater degree of monopoly market power, which they may then use to raise prices. "Williamson (1968) had earlier shown how the balance between market power and efficiency depends on the price elasticity of demand for the particular goods or services, with the degree of monopoly market power of a firm represented by its price-cost margin, which is (price minus marginal cost)/price. Firms with no monopoly power (i.e., operating under textbook definitions of perfect competition) would have a ratio of zero.

Chapter 2

1. OPEC, the Organization of Petroleum Exporting Countries, was established in 1960 for the purpose of stabilizing oil prices. In the 1970s, however, in response to political pressures and the need of the member countries for more income, OPEC was able to significantly raise the price of oil in two large steps.

2. Many bilateral agreements follow along the lines of the U.S. and British agreement that was a compromise signed in Bermuda in 1946. Both countries then undertook to model other future agreements on the Bermuda pattern. As Doganis (1991, p. 29) notes, a significant clause of the Bermuda agreement was that "while both governments maintained their ultimate right to approve or disapprove the tariffs proposed by the airlines, they agreed that where possible such tariffs should be arrived at using the procedures of the International Air Transport Association." The other significant clause involved so-called fifth freedom rights. In bilateral negotiations, the freedoms are as follows:

First Freedom: The right to fly over another country without landing.

Second Freedom: The right to make a landing for technical reasons (e.g., refueling) in another country without picking up or setting down revenue traffic.

Third Freedom: The right to carry revenue traffic from your own country (A) to the country (B) of your treaty partner.

Fourth Freedom: The right to carry traffic from country B back to your own country A.

Fifth Freedom: The right of an airline from country A to carry revenue traffic between country B and other countries such as C or D.

Sixth Freedom: The right of an airline, registered in country A, to carry traffic to a gateway – a point in A – and then abroad to a third country C. The traffic has neither its origin nor ultimate destination in country A.

Seventh Freedom: The right of an airline, registered in country A, to operate entirely outside of country A, in carrying traffic between two other countries.

Eighth Freedom: The right of an airline, registered in country A, to carry traffic between any two points of country B (often referred to as cabotage).

In the Bermuda-style agreement, fifth freedom rights are relatively unrestricted, allowing airlines to set the frequency and capacity on routes between two countries without regulatory interference as long as the other airline doesn't complain. Freedoms of the sixth to eighth degrees are rarely accepted.

3. The spirit of deregulation along with support for growth of international travel was manifest in the Helsinki accord of 1975 and the International Air Transportation Competition Act of 1979 (passed by Congress in early 1980). The Helsinki accord established principles of operation that simplified and harmonized the administration of international travel, especially across national frontiers. The Air Transportation Act, however, was also designed to strengthen the competitive position of U.S. international air carriers, provide more freedom for carriers to set rates and establish routes, eliminate operational and marketing regulations with respect to capacity and flight frequency, integrate domestic and international operations, increase the number of U.S. gateway cities, provide foreign lines with increased access to U.S. cities, eliminate discrimination against U.S. carriers, and promote and develop civil aeronautics. See also Gee, Makens, and Choy (1997, p. 311).

4. After 1995, all scheduled carriers operating aircraft with ten or more seats were required to comply with FAA Part 121 certification procedures.

5. These unions are the largest for each labor group, but there are others. For example, American Airlines employees are represented by none of these unions.

6. Doganis (1991, p. 23).

7. However, it is difficult to determine the precise profit contribution from carriage of freight and mail because, in most instances of scheduled services, the operating costs of the flight and the fixed costs of the terminal, service equipment, and so forth are combined with costs related to serving passengers. Calculation of cargo-carriage contributions to profits would thus require somewhat arbitrary allocation of costs among the different categories.

8. Another related term is *spill*, which is the difference between nominal demand from passengers who want to fly on a segment and the load (i.e., passengers who actually fly the segment).

9. Up to a point, the carrier with a larger than average capacity share in a given market will gain a greater than proportional share of the revenue in that market. Conversely, carriers with a smaller than average capacity share will earn a smaller than proportional share of the total revenue in that market. This notion is known as the S-curve effect, where the S-curve is a plot of revenue share, the independent variable, against market share, the dependent variable. This is discussed in greater detail in Butler and Keller (1999, p. 32 and p. 39) in an article by Skinner, Dichter, et al.

10. The advertising intensity ratio is discussed further in Hanlon (1996),

11. In response to many complaints about this, the CAB in 1984 ordered that vendors must offer primary terminal displays that rank flights based on fares and service factors rather than on carrier identities and that connecting flights must be listed according to objective criteria. Nevertheless, the reservation systems remained inherently biased in favor of online connections over interline connections. However, as noted, current DOT rules do not permit such bias but do allow agents to install their own screen "preferences." The four global reservation distribution systems in use as of the late 1990s were SABRE, Amadeus, Galileo, and Worldspan.

12. According to Garvett and Hilton (1999, p. 181), it appears that an airline's profitability is most closely related to yield management effectiveness, ownership structure (i.e., government versus private) and/or tenure of airline, and unit revenue. Stage length (i.e., an airport-to-airport segment) and customer satisfaction were also factors. They note that yield and load factors are not necessarily correlated with profits. Profits require both high load factors and high yields at the same time (i.e., high revenue per available seat-kilometer). Homan (1999, p. 508) suggests "that for every 1 percent decrease in yield, quantity demanded (by RPMs) increases by about 0.7 percent. Additionally, for every 1 percent increase in real GDP, demand increases by over 0.9 percent." See also Belobaba (1998a and b).

13. In 1995, airlines began to cap commissions for round-trip domestic flights costing more than $500 at $50 and for one-way flights at $25. In 1997, commission rates dropped to 8%, from 10% for domestic and international travel originating in the U.S. and Canada. And in 1998 a $100 cap on round-trip international flights was first imposed. For flights booked on the Internet, commissions are $10 a ticket.

Note, also, that in order to operate agents must have what are known as airline Reporting Corporation (ARC) appointments, without which they cannot sell any tickets. These appointments require everything from the employment of a manager with at least two years of ARC-appointed agency experience to the need for a safe in which to store blank ticket stock. Airlines keep close track of tickets sold and monies owed by agents, and they require prompt remittances. Agents, in contrast, must usually wait longer than a week or two to be paid by their travel customers. Airlines see agents in the domestic market as being good at issuing tickets but not being good at marketing.

14. New services such as those provided by Priceline.com enable travelers to name the price they are willing to pay for a ticket, and to thus presumably reap significant discounts. Airlines are willing to cooperate because they can sell otherwise empty seats at close to departure time without subverting their normal higher-price structure. See also Siemers and Harris (1999) and Elkind (1999).

15. For instance, a 1977 National Transportation Survey, showed that the percent of trips made by air in 1977 was 52.8% for travelers with household income above $50,000 and only 25.3% for those with household income of $15,000 to $25,000. See also Meyer and Oster (1987, p. 185).

16. These studies include those by the British Airports Authority (BAA, 1978). See also Doganis (1991, p. 222).

17. See also Fujii, Im, and Mak, (1992) and Antoniou (1991).

18. The *Law of Connectivity* is also called Metcalfe's Law, named after Robert Metcalfe, one of the Internet and Ethernet engineering pioneers. The law is usually applied to electronic networks such as the Internet. It becomes operative once the number of nodes surpasses a critical mass. Otherwise, the network fails.

19. However, at overcrowed hubs, for example, the ratio of block-hours to air-hours rises. As Pearson and Strahler (1995, p. 426) note, every 0.01-point increase in the annual ratio collectively costs the nine largest U.S. airlines $150 million in additional operating expenses. This datum is found in U.S. DOT Form 41.

20. An example in transportation would be the cross-elasticity of demand for airline service versus rail service between New York and Washington, D.C. Given that the travel time from center city to center city is probably on the average about the same using either rail or air, any noticeable change in the price of rail or air service would likely have a measurable effect on demand for the competing service.

21. As Dargay (1993, p. 87) notes, demand elasticities vary widely and are often influenced by the type of model and data used, the functional specification, degree of aggregation, and several other factors. But there is also the possibility of "nonsymmetric" or "irreversible" price effects or "hysteresis" in the demand relationships. In other words, "consumers may not respond similarly to rising and falling prices, as it is traditionally assumed, but instead react in a more complex fashion dependent not only on the direction and magnitude of the price change, but also on previous price history. If this were the case, the elasticity itself would be dependent on the evolution of prices so that empirical estimates would be sensitive to the time period used for the analysis."

22. As Boyar (1997, p. 288) notes, several methods have been proposed for dealing with problems of allocating nonunique fixed costs. "One way of eliminating the arbitrariness of the residual fixed cost allocation is to accept some inefficiency and to use a second best pricing scheme . . . Second best cost allocation, also called *Ramsey pricing*, recovers fixed costs by marking up the variable costs of different user groups by different amounts determined by the elasticities of demand. Under Ramsey pricing all user groups pay something toward the fixed costs of the system, but those who have the lowest elasticity of demand are given the highest markups over marginal cost. That is, those groups with fewest alternatives will have prices raised over marginal cost by the largest amount."

23. For example, according to Eurocontrol, which tries to coordinate European air-traffic control, if capacity stays constant, every 1% rise in traffic produces a 5% increase in delays. See *The Economist*, February 5, 2000.

24. In thinking about the peak-load pricing problem Glaister (1981, p. 68) suggests that "in the absence of queues, the service is obtained by those who value it most *relative to* other things. If cheap fares are provided at times of severe peaks then the cost to society of building the capacity to cope with these peaks may be very much higher than the values placed on the service even by those who value it most. . . . Long run marginal cost pricing (i.e., peak pricing) together with a suitable system of compensation could make everybody at least as well off as under constant pricing." As Ingcrsoll (1999) suggests, passenger facility charges (PFCs) are often politically contentious. See also Williamson (1966) and Bishop and Thompson (1992).

25. Boyar (1997, p. 84).

26. Werner (1999, p. 189) notes "that there are three commonly used measures of the amount, or 'degree', of leverage in a company. All three are economic elasticities, the percentage change in one variable in response to the percentage change in another. They may be calculated from an income statement organized to identify fixed and variable costs." The degree of operating leverage (DOL) indicates the percentage change in EBIT (earnings before interest and taxes) for a given percentage change in revenues. The degree of financial leverage (DFL) is the percentage change in EPS (earnings per share) for a given percentage change in EBIT. And the degree of total leverage (DTL) is the percentage change in EPS for a given percentage change in revenues.

27. Baggaley (1999, p. 319) observes that the median interest coverage in 1997 for passenger airlines rated investment grade by Standard & Poor's was 4.6x, but for those rated in the BB category, it was 3.8x, and for those in the B of CCC categories, the median was 2.4x.

28. Insurers, banks, and other financial institutions may invest in equipment trust obligations or certificates adequately secured and evidencing an interest in transportation equipment, wholly or in part within the United States, if the obligations or certificates carry the right to receive determined portions of rental, purchase, or other fixed obligatory payments to be made for the use or purchase of the transportation equipment.

29. Morrell (1997, p. 187) notes that the first international securitization of aircraft was offered by Guinness Peat Aviation (GPA) in 1992. Fourteen aircraft valued at $380 million were leased. Equity investors in this would get a 10–12% return in annual dividends plus a share in any residual value from the aircraft at maturity. Until GPA ran into financial difficulties it was, along with International Lease Finance Corporation (ILFC), one of the two dominant firms in the aircraft leasing business. More recently, General Electric Capital Asset Services (GECAS) has become one of the major firms, and ILFC was acquired by American insurance giant AIG in 1990. See also Stone, Lynes, and Fisher (1999), Lintott (1999), and Gawlicki (2000).

30. Although the criteria for classifying leases appear in theory to be unambiguous, in practice, there can be differing interpretations. Over the years, the FASB has thus attempted through the issuance of several additional statements to clarify certain aspects of FASB Statement 13.

Note also that another type of operating lease is known in the industry as the *wet lease*. This is the leasing of an aircraft complete with crew and all other technical support. It is similar to the chartering of aircraft except that the lesee would have the necessary operating licenses and permits and would operate the wet-lease flights with its own flight designation. When aircraft, crew, maintenance, and insurance are included, the lease is also referred to by the acronym ACMI.

31. The lease versus purchase decision is discussed in more mathematical detail in Stonier (1998).

32. Morrell (1997, p. 49) also notes that U.K. rules for accounting for leases define a financial/capital lease – also known as full pay-out lease – requiring placement on the balance sheet as: "a lease that transfers substantially all the risks and rewards of ownership of an asset to the lessee. It should be presumed that such a transfer of risks and rewards occurs if at the inception of a lease the present value of the minimum lease payments amounts to substantially all (normally 90% or more) of the fair value of the leased asset." In addition, "a more difficult problem occurs with extendible operating leases, which usually have a lease term that covers the economic life of the aircraft, but give the lessee airline the opportunity to break the lease at no penalty . . . at various intervals over the term. British Airways have a number of aircraft leased in this way, and originally left them off balance sheet."

33. Technically, this is done on the income statement by increasing passenger services expenses by the incremental costs (including food, fuel, taxes, etc.) of carrying the award passengers at a future date while the same amount is recorded on the balance sheet as an accrued liability. Then, when the award passenger is carried, the incremental cost is deducted from expenses and the liability on the balance sheet is extinguished. Using this method, the operating profit in each year is not distorted by the award. Note that since 1999, the methods follow Securities and Exchange Commission Staff Accounting Bulletin 101, which requires that revenues from sale of mileage credits is deferred and recognized when transportation is provided. Such frequent flyer/traveler award programs began in the early 1980s and were originally patterned on the "green stamps" that food retailers used in the 1950s and 1960s to encourage customer loyalty. See also Garvett and Avery (1998) and *Business Week*, March 5, 2000.

34. Calculation of the level of deferred revenue depends on assumptions concerning the proportion of points to be redeemed and the mix of awards to be taken up and also on the yield assigned to the mileage or points attributed to the expected take up of free travel awards. As noted in the IATA Accounting Guide, the redemption rate is affected by the threshold of points required before a member can redeem a reward, the time until award expiration, and the award redemption experience of the airline. Many airlines estimate the likelihood of redemption using algorithms based on historical patterns.

35. In recent years, the value of gates, routes (especially long-haul), and landing slots (such as those at London's Heathrow) has increased enormously as airlines have tried to increase the frequency and reach of their services. Control of a large percentage of gates and slots at an airport can give the airline a predominant, almost monopolistic, position that would normally translate into greater pricing power and therefore higher valuation. In the early 1990s, for instance, United bought Pan Am's Heathrow landing rights for $400 million and American bought TWA's for $445 million. At around the same time, Delta bought Pan Am's Atlantic routes for $1.3 billion. And in the mid-1980s, United bought Pan Am's Asia routes for $750 million.

36. Normally, anything less than a 20% discount to estimated value does not provide enough leeway for the uncertainty of a transaction occurring and for the possibility that costs of mounting an acquisition campaign could be quite high. Availability of pooling versus purchase accounting and additional tax-related issues will also often have a bearing on the size of trading discount.

37. Again, as noted at the beginning of Section 2.4,

$$WACC = \text{debt}/(\text{debt} + \text{equity}) \times r_d + \text{equity}/(\text{debt} + \text{equity}) \times r_e,$$

where r_d is the cost of debt expressed as an interest rate; and r_e is the cost of equity, as estimated using risk premiums and risk adjustment factors (known as betas).

38. The first two rules are intuitively obvious. As for the third, Petzinger (p. 189) goes on to explain that marginal pricing is a worthy strategy for the last seat sold but not for selling the first because by selling everything so cheap, total revenue is not maximized and the value of the product in the mind of the consumer is debased.

Chapter 3

1. It also didn't hurt that popular television series of the seventies included *The Love Boat* (1977–86) and *Fantasy Island* (1978–84).

2. The first Royal Caribbean ship, *Song of Norway*, went into service in 1970.

3. *Voyager* had a contract price of approximately $500 million not including capitalized interest, change orders or owner's extras.

4. The choice of a country depends on many factors including the place where the vessel is financed, the operating costs, and the routes the vessel sails. The United States and Britain, for example, have strict regulations concerning the use of unionized labor. So-called flag-of-convenience countries include Panama and Liberia, which are the most popular, and also Bermuda, the Bahamas, and the Netherlands Antilles. The higher operating costs with U.S. registration are in part caused by the U.S. requirement that all ships registered in the U.S. use only licensed American officers and that three quarters of the unlicensed crew be U.S. citizens. See Dickinson and Vladimir (1997, p. 66) for more details. Note also that the Passenger Shipping Act of 1896 precluded foreign-flagged vessels from operating between U.S. ports when there is no U.S. flag competitor.

5. Sections 883 and 884 of the IRS code are relevant. Section 883 says that certain foreign corporations are not subject to U.S. income or branch profits tax on U.S. source income derived from or incidental to the international operation of a ship or ships or on income from the leasing of such ships. See, for example, Royal Caribbean's 1998 10-K report to the SEC. The tax issue was also covered in "Cruising for Fun and Profit" by the CBS show *60 Minutes* on October 24, 1999. Note also, that on February 8, 2000, the United States Treasury Department issued proposed regulations to Section 883. The proposals exclude from gross income for purposes of federal taxation the income derived by foreign corporations from the international operation of ships as long as a publicly traded corporation's stock is not closely held (i.e., more than 50% is held by persons who each own less than 5% of the shares).

6. Actual occupancy levels for the industry, equivalent to load factors in airlines, are compiled by the Cruise Line International Association (CLIA) based on information from the member lines. CLIA takes the number of potential passengers based on 100% occupancy times the number of bed-days as the denominator and actual number of passengers times the number of bed-days as the numerator.

7. Also, as Dickinson and Vladimir (1997) suggest, prolonged overcapacity leading to price volatility and commoditization of services probably most adversely affects the visiting friends and relatives (VFR) segment of the travel market.

8. Of course, cruise lines also have high and low seasons for bookings. January through March, known as the "wave season", accounts for as much as 30% of a full year's bookings.

9. However, unlike hotels, if more than two people stay in the room (some cabins can accommodate three or four passengers), the occupancy is considered to be over 100%.

10. Larger ships can also spread the high fixed cost of on-shore infrastructure facilities over a larger revenue base and also a multitude of brands.

11. Although the comparisons here are largely to airlines and hotels, the industry prefers to view a cruise as a vacation alternative, with land-based resorts as the primary competition.

12. Other important competitors in the U.S. are Alamo and Dollar, and in Europe, Europcar.

13. A key factor here is the quantity discount received by car rental companies in their fleet purchases from manufacturers. Given that several of the automobile manufacturers have from time to time held partial equity interests in rental companies, the discounts on fleet purchases may amount to more than 30% of retail car prices.

14. See Meyer and Oster (1987, p. 165).

15. Although the ICC was charged with a mandate to promote the bus industry while protecting the public interest, as almost always happens in regulated sectors, the ICC ended up better protecting the industry's interests.

16. Motivation for greater regulation was also kindled by the financial failure of a large Indiana bus company.

17. See also Jackson (1984) and Schisgall (1985).

18.   According to U.S. Government Accounting Office (1998 and 1997) reports, in the fiscal years ended 1995, 1996, and 1997, Amtrak revenues and losses (in \$ millions) were \$1,497, \$1,555, and \$1,674 for revenues, and -\$808, -\$764, and \$-762 for losses, respectively. Congress gave Amtrak a mandate to break even by the end of 2002. If it doesn't, Amtrak faces substantial restructuring or liquidation. See Machalaba (1999).

19.   Subsidies are also required to maintain rail services in Europe and elsewhere. However, the relatively short routes and high population densities as well as high gasoline prices in Europe make rail a viable alternative there.

20.   Additional information is available from the American Public Transportation Association website www.apta.com.

Chapter 4

1.   From an *Encyclopedia Britannica* article on hotels.

2.   United Airlines proved this through its purchase of the Westin chain in the early 1980s and its sale of Westin a few years later.

3.   In hotels, for example, once fixed costs are covered, a large part of every incremental dollar of revenue contributes to profits and the variance of earnings and cash flow (EBITDA) tracks fairly closely. However, in the real estate business, depreciation and interest expenses are prominent characteristics with much greater variance between earnings and EBITDA usually evident.

4.   The Tax Reform Act of 1986 ended the Investment Tax Credit, which since 1976 had allowed builders to deduct 6 1/2% of the capital cost of a project against taxes, and it also changed partnership rules. In addition, depreciation schedules were increased to 31.5 years from 18 years and earned income could no longer be sheltered by passive investment losses. Moreover, use of so-called non recourse bullet-loan financing – popular in the 1980s and featuring five to ten years of payments with a large payoff required at the end of the loan period – later led to a large number of hotel foreclosures when, in the midst of the weak-demand environment of the early 1990s, many payoffs came due.

5.   By comparison, as of the end of the 1990s, debt service consumed only around 4% of industry revenues.

6.   Of course, in a local situation a hotel or motel may be the only one in town or for miles around. In that case, the particular property would be a monopoly.

7.   The Hubbart Room Rate Formula, described in Vallen and Vallen (1996, p. 231), provided a widely used standardized approach for setting average room rates until the industry began using newer computer software that enabled more precise tracking of demand estimates in the application of yield management techniques. The Hubbart formula essentially estimated what the average room rate should be to be able to cover all expenses and a return on equity for the investor. The formula, however, provided no detail related to room size and class of quality variations.

8.   Selected segment breakeven occupancy rates in 1998 were found to be as follows:

Upscale	63.0%
Midscale (without food & beverage)	49.0%
Economy	41.0%
Upper-tier extended-stay	60.0%

9. In the time-share structure, the purchaser becomes a tenant in common with other purchasers of the same unit and owns 1/52 of the unit. Interval ownership is similar in concept except that common tenants agree to an interval in which there is an exclusive "right to use" for a specified period. The interval ownership typically reverts back to tenancy in common after between twenty and forty years. In leasehold structures, the purchaser leases the premises for a specified period of time but prepays the lease. Although vacation license structures also contain a similar "right to use" during designated times or in specific periods, the time-share buyer in these arrangements does not have an ownership interest in real property. Neither do purchasers of club membership arrangements, which are usually of shorter term (ten years) than the others.

10. For example, if each unit is sold for $20,000 for each of fifty-two weekly periods a year and there are 100 units, the developer's gross sales potential is $104 million.

11. For example, estimates by PricewaterhouseCoopers suggest that at upscale hotels a 1% rise in price (i.e., in real ADR) results in a 0.4% decline in room demand and a 0.6% decline in occupancy percentage points for each $1 increase in real ADR. The cross elasticity for the economy sector against midscale hotels without food and beverage indicates even greater sensitivity, with a 1% increase in economy prices raising midscale demand by 0.8% and with each $1 change in economy real ADRs raising midscale occupancy percentage points by 1.4%. See Hanson (2000).

12. Mortgage bonds can be classified as being either open or closed. If they are closed, no more bonds may be issued against the mortgage. However, there may not be any limit as to the amount of bonds that may be secured, and if so, the issue is open.

13. Securitization converts identifiable and predictable cash flows into securities that may be easier to trade than are other forms of debt because different packages (tranches) of such securities can be designed to appeal to investors desiring different combinations of rights and risks. Also, the risk can be spread over a number of borrowers and the costs of administration may be lower.

14. A third type of REIT, known as a paired-share REIT, was limited to four companies that had been grandfathered into this particular structure when REITs were formed. For a long time, the paired-share structure allowed a REIT company and an operating company to function side-by-side, minimizing tax payments as compared to normal C corporations. Such tax advantages, for example, allowed Starwood Lodging to outbid Hilton in the 1998 takeover battle for ITT's Sheraton chain. In response, Congress clamped down, and paired-share REITs are no longer factors in the market. Even Starwood changed over to a regular corporate structure in 1998.

15. New equity REITs may also be formed with existing properties and/or real estate partnerships through an Umbrella Partnership Real Estate Investment Trust (UPREIT). This entity differs from a traditional REIT because a limited partnership structure is utilized, with the REIT functioning as general partner. The arrangement allows existing partnerships (or property holders) to contribute their property in exchange for a limited partnership interest in the new REIT operating partnership. After a period of time (usually one year) limited partners who contributed property can exchange some or all of their interest for cash or REIT shares. This will cause tax to be due on appreciation that occurred in the contributing partnership (although by selling their units over a period of time, the partnership unit holders may spread any tax over several years). Both holders of real estate partnership interest and REITs can benefit from the UPREIT. Real estate partnership unit holders transform their illiquid partnership interest into the more liquid REIT shareholder status. The REIT benefits by acquiring real property without having to generate capital to purchase the property.

16. Nevertheless, FFO should not be relied upon as an ultimate measure of a REIT's ability to pay dividends since it does not reflect recurring capital expenditures that are capitalized and not expensed. A reserve for these capital expenditures is therefore deducted from FFO. The result is cash available for distribution (CAD), a more accurate indicator of a REIT's ability to pay dividends.

17. FFO is defined as net income minus profit from real estate sales plus real estate depreciation. Adjusted FFO (AFFO) takes FFO and subtracts recurring capital expenditures, amortization of tenant improvements, amortization of leasing commissions, and rent straight lining. But controversy abounds as to definitions used in practice, and great attention must be paid to the details. To boost FFO, REITs may be capitalizing some expenses rather than treating them as current expenses. And REITs have been criticized for deeming certain costs nonrecurring, avoiding hits to their FFO. As Vanocur (1999) notes, "the figuring of FFO starts with net income as computed in accordance with GAAP. From that number gains or losses from debt restructuring and property sales are excluded. Real-estate-related depreciation and amortization is added back, and the total is adjusted for unconsolidated partnerships and joint ventures. Unlike earnings, FFO isn't an audited number, which gives REITs considerable leeway in how they treat costs."

For example, as noted in the *Wall Street Journal* of August 11, 1999, Archstone Communities Trust divided depreciable items into things such as carpets, roofs, and appliances that have a life of less than thirty years and those such as buildings and land improvements with a life of more than thirty years. Archstone treated depreciation of more perishable items as expenses instead of adding them back to cash flow, as most REITs have done.

Note also that the REIT Modernization Act of 1999, effective in 2001, allows a REIT to own as much as 100% of the stock of a taxable REIT subsidiary that provides services to REIT tenants and others. Previously, REITs could only own up to 10% of the voting stock of a taxable corporation, which made it difficult for hotel REITs to avoid potential conflicts of ownership and operating-control issues that arose when hotels had been required to lease properties to third parties. See *Wall Street Journal*, November 24, 1999.

18. In using debt instruments, and depending on the specific situation, the loan to value ratio might typically range between 60 and 75%.

19. For example, in Hilton's 1997 takeover of Bally Entertainment, total goodwill amounted to $1.3 billion, and annual goodwill amortization was $32.5 million.

20. PricewaterhouseCoopers, in privately commissioned research, estimated a correlation coefficient of -0.4 between changes in the airline cost index and changes in lodging demand for the 1979–97 period. The firm also estimated that a 1% increase in the price of crude oil causes a 0.06 to 0.09% decline in lodging demand.

21. However, the combination of better technology and faster than average unit expansion of the limited service formats that require relatively lower labor content has enabled the number of hotel industry employees per 100 rooms to decline from approximately 78 in the late 1980s to 74 by the late 1990s.

Chapter 5

1. Berger and Bruning (1979, p. 17).

2. The Flamingo Hotel was designed by Siegel to attract the rich and famous to the middle of the desert. The hotel started a building boom that was not to slow until the early 1980s, when more than 50,000 hotel rooms were available to host some of the largest business conventions in the world. Also see Puzo (1976).

3. Taxes are currently at a rate of 6.25% of gross winnings in Nevada and 8% in New Jersey, where a surcharge of 1.25% of gross revenues to be invested in urban development over twenty-five years also exists. In Detroit, the 18% tax on gross income is divided 55% to Detroit and 45% to Michigan.

4. However, the average length of stay of Atlantic City visitors is probably a little less than a day, and for many visitors just a few hours. In Las Vegas, the average length of stay is about 3.8 days.

5. Regulations vary widely by jurisdiction and change over time. See Braunlich, Cabot, Thompson, and Tottenham (1999), Cabot (1995), and the website www.CasinoLaw.com.

6. As Harden and Swardson (1996) note, Indian gaming began in 1975, when the Oneidas of New York began to use bingo as a fund-raising mechanism to pay for a fire department. The Oneidas argued that because they are an Indian nation, their sovereignty entitled them to run their own game. The Seminoles of Florida quickly began their own high-stakes bingo game and were challenged in *Seminole Tribe v. Butterworth*, a landmark 1981 case.

The Indian Gaming Regulatory Act (IGRA) of 1988 had its roots in two U.S. Supreme Court decisions. In *McClanahan v. Arizona Tax Commission* (1973), the Court pronounced that Indian tribes "have a right to make their own laws and be governed by them," which essentially recognized certain tribes as sovereign nations. And in *Bryan v. Itasca County, Minnesota* (1976), the Court said that states lack civil regulatory jurisdiction over Indian tribes and members on their reservations or trust lands.

In a later decision, *California v. Cabazon Band of Mission Indians* (1987), the Court decided that if a state didn't have a public policy against gaming activities and allowed various forms of gambling, the state could neither prohibit nor regulate gaming activities on tribal lands. Congress, then recognizing the sovereignty of Indian tribes, passed the IGRA. This act established an independent federal regulatory body (the National Indian Gaming Commission) and federal standards governing the operation of gaming on reservations.

Three categories of gaming activities have been defined:

Class I: Traditional social gaming activities for prizes of minimal value, the regulation of which is the responsibility of the tribal government.

Class II: Primarily bingo, but also lotto, pull-tabs, and card games. Such games are regulated by the National Indian Gaming Commission (NIGC).

Class III: All other games not otherwise classified – which means casino-type gaming. Such games must be approved by tribal ordinance and be conducted in conformity with a tribal-state compact entered into by the tribes and the states. The compact must be approved by the NIGC.

As of 1996, over 200 Native American tribes had set up 126 casinos in twenty-four states. Goodman (1995, pp. 111–113) describes background for the *Cabazon* decision in more detail.

7. In North Dakota, where low-stakes charity games are legal, the state receives 5%, the charity 65%, and the location owner 30% of the casino's gross win. Similar charity-designated games are also conducted in Canadian provinces. In Alberta, for instance, charities split 10% of their gaming profits with the provincial government, and the operator is entitled to 40%. See also Note 9 below.

8. However, as the U.S. Congress (1999) National Gambling Impact Study suggests, the Interstate Wire Act is fraught with ambiguity. For example, does the phrase "wire communications" include the Internet? What types of wagering and gambling are allowed?

And where does jurisdictional authority reside? Some argue that because the Internet didn't exist at the time of the statute's formulation, the intent of the law applies only to telephone communications. Complications also arise from interpretations of the U.S. Penal Code. For instance, Sec. 47.05 says that: "(a) A person commits an offense if, with the intent to further gambling, he knowingly communicates information as to bets, betting odds, or changes in betting odds or he knowingly provides, installs, or maintains equipment for the transmission or receipt of such information." Sec. 47.06 says, in regard to possession of gambling devices, equipment, or paraphernalia, that "(a) A person commits an offense if, with the intent to further gambling, he knowingly owns, manufactures, transfers, or possesses any gambling device that he knows is designed for gambling purposes or any equipment that he knows is designed as a subassembly or essential part of a gambling device. (b) A person commits an offense if, with the intent to further gambling, he knowingly owns, manufactures, transfers commercially, or possesses any altered gambling equipment that he knows is designed for gambling purposes or any equipment that he knows is designed as a subassembly or essential part of such device."

As noted by the *National Gambling Impact Study Commission Report* (1999), the countries with laws in place to extend Internet gambling licenses include Australia, Antigua, Austria, Belgium, Costa Rica, Curaçao, Dominican Republic, Finland, Germany, Honduras, U.K., and Venezuela. Updated licensing information is available at web site www.igamingnews.com. Also see Cukier (2000).

9. In Canada, for example, casino gaming has been legal since 1969, when the Canadian federal government's criminal code allowed provinces or charities to establish casinos using the games of roulette or blackjack. More recently, video lottery terminals and slot machines have been approved. Casino licenses are held either by provincial governments or by nonprofit organizations.

10. These numbers are also not to be confused with the gross amounts bet, or the handle, which is estimated by Christiansen (1998) to have been around $600 billion in 1997. See also Scarne (1978).

11. There is evidence to suggest that the majority of players consider gaming to be a form of entertainment. As the survey in the U.S. Congress (1976) indicates, 81% of respondents said that one of the reasons they bet at a casino is to have a good time. See Supplementary Table S5.1.

12. Judging by history, the industry has experienced only two important setbacks in the postwar period – in 1981 and in 1991 – and both episodes coincided with an economic recession. It seems likely, however, that new competition will probably heighten the industry's future sensitivity to changes in the overall economy.

13. In September of 1997, the Ninth Circuit Court of Appeals ruled unconstitutional a federal law banning the broadcast of gaming ads. This ultimately led to a June 1999 Supreme Court decision that struck down a federal law that had banned casino gambling ads on television and radio. See also Greenhouse (1999) and Ritter (1999).

14. As of 1985, for example, cash transactions above $10,000 have had to be reported to the Treasury Department.

15. Acting on the wishes of the legislature, the commission specified the following:

- Minimum size of table bets
- Numbers of tables and slots of different denominations and type allowed in each casino
- Hours of operation
- Number of square feet of public space relative to number of rooms

Table S5.1. *Reasons for gambling*

Reasons for betting[a]	%	Reasons for not betting[a]	%
To have a good time	81	Not available	48
For excitement	47	Don't know about it	27
Challenge	35	Not interested	26
To make money	35	Other things to do	23
To pass the time	23	Don't think about it	22
Something to look forward to	21	Odds against you	22
Chance to get rich	11	Don't want to lose money	16
Net activity reasons	94	Don't have the money	16
Net money reasons	43	Waste of money	14
		Illegal	10
		Not lucky	8
		Net money reasons	53
		Net activity reasosn	55
		Net moral reasons	8
		Net legal reasons	12

[a]Respondents chose one, two, or three reasons from a list of 11 reasons provided for betting and 18 reasons provided for not betting.
Source: U.S. Congress (1976).

- Numbers of security guards required
- Number of days per week that live entertainment had to be provided (in the first off-peak seasons there were days when there were more performers on stage than people in the audience)
- Various other aspects of hotel-casino operations, including limitations on marketing that are normally considered in the province of management.

16. Major public casino companies at the end of the 1990s include Aztar, Harrah's Entertainment, MGM Grand, Mandalay Resort Group (formerly Circus Circus Enterprises), and Mirage Resorts. Racing companies include Hollywood Park and Santa Anita Consolidated. Gtech is prominent in lotteries and the dominant slot machine manufacturer is International Game Technology.

17. There are, however, exceptions: In May 1989, the Atlantis (originally Playboy) hotel-casino next to the Atlantic City convention center went bankrupt. It failed for a number of reasons, but mostly because it was never able to overcome its initial design handicap of having the casino spread over three floors.

18. Multiples have generally ranged between five and nine in recent years. Also, in evaluating individual casino properties for the purposes of merger or acquisition, "casino" cash flow, which is EBITDA before corporate expenses, might be considered a more appropriate measure against which to apply a multiple than against EBITDA itself.

19. For this reason, when a management attempts to assess the profitability of, for example, "junkets" (in which travel, hotel, and other expenses are paid by the casino-hotel in return for a promise to gamble a certain minimum over a few days' time) it should use a formula including an estimate of the house edge, the average number of decisions per hour, and the average size of betting units. Similar criteria should be used in determining whether or not a bettor qualifies for "comps" (complimentaries), which may include any, or all, of free drinks and meals, shows, rooms, and transportation.

20. However, Binion's Horseshoe in downtown Las Vegas has a unique policy whereby the player's limit is as high as his first bet. Also, a group of very high-stakes players can "pool" their play.

21. *Gambling Times*, August 1983, p. 16. Also note that this example is a variation on the "Gambler's Ruin" formula. Assume that payoff odds are 1 to 1, that each bet is of one unit, and that the player keeps gambling until a certain goal is reached or the player goes broke. Then the chance that the goal is reached is represented as follows:

Let

p = chance of winning one bet

$q = 1 - p$

i = initial betting units

N = goal (where $N > i$)

Then, if p is less than 0.5, the probability of reaching the goal before going broke equals

$$1 - (q/p)^i / 1 - (q/p)^N$$

and if $p = 0.5$, the probability of reaching the goal before going broke equals i/N.

For instance, in craps, the win probability on the "pass line" bet is 0.493. If the goal is to turn $100 into $250, and the unit bet is $50, then $p = 0.493$, $q = 0.507$, $i = 2$ (initial two betting units), $N = 5$, and the probability, after applying the formula, is 0.383. If the goal was to reach $500 before going broke, the probability would be only 0.18. See *Win*, January–February 1993, p. 51.

22. Note that for slot machines, the coins-in, or slot handle, is obviously a known quantity and is reasonably well correlated with the slot drop (i.e, what falls into a slot machine's bucket after winners have been paid out). However, as explained later in the text, in table games, the handle is, under actual playing conditions, very difficult to calculate and may be quite different from the drop.

23. Interestingly, the definitions of hold percentage are somewhat different in Nevada and in New Jersey. New Jersey's definition includes all cash and markers, but Nevada's definition does not include markers that may be redeemed at the table where the credit slip originated. All other things being equal, New Jersey hold figures are normally lower by 3 to 4% than those of Nevada. The hold percentage, or the hold p.c. as it is also known, of course, should not be confused with percentages used to express casino advantages (expected values) for table games. Such casino advantages are stated as percentages of handle and not as percentages of drop.

24. If, however, as is more likely, players initially buy many more chips than they bet on each decision (some lose and some tend to walk away from a table without betting all the chips initially bought), then the ratio of handle to drop does not grow as rapidly as in this example.

25. Win rates, of course, also depend on game rules, which may vary (especially in Nevada) according to the discretion of management.

26. Consider another illustration: In craps, on the "pass line," the average cost per roll as a percentage of money bet is 0.42%. This is determined by taking the house advantage of 1.41% and dividing by the average number of rolls per decision, which is 3.38. The average cost per roll of the dice to the player, or conversely win per roll for the casino, can then be used to determine how long on the average it would take for the casino to generate a certain amount of revenue, or what minimum average pass bet at the table might be required to win a certain amount. If in one hour of play, for example, there are an average of 60 rolls, then 60 rolls per hour times 0.0042 cost per roll equals 0.252. For the casino to win $500 in that hour from just the pass line bets, the average pass line bet for the whole table would have to be $500/0.252 or $1,984.13.

27. Provost (1994, p. 59).

28. It is estimated that perhaps 20% of players may account for 80% of the upper-end business. See also Binkley (2000), who describes Harrah's sophisticated statistics-based marketing.

29. Junkets, in which rooms, meals, and travel costs may be picked up (i.e., "comped") by the casino, have diminished in popularity as the casinos have found that junkets are not as profitable as they had been thought to be. For instance, a casino wanting to earn at least $100 should know that if it costs $400 to bring a junket player in the door, it must – assuming a 20% hold (win/drop) – realize a minimum drop that averages $2,500. As noted in Stefanelli and Nazarechuk (1996, p. 135), a casino is generally "willing to comp guests up to one half of the amount it expects to win from them." Players are rated by: (a) buy-in amount to the game, (b) average bet, (c) largest bet, and (d) duration of play.

For table games, the comps rating, equal to the player's theoretical loss times percentage return, would be a function of:

(average bet) × (hours played) × (speed of game) × (casino advantage).

Generally, the number of decisions per hour would fall into the following ranges:

Baccarat: 50 to 110
Blackjack: 60 to 100
Craps: 75 to 145
Roulette: 25 to 35

30. The volume increase is a direct function of the credit extension itself and may also be indirectly affected by the exciting atmosphere that surrounds high-stakes tables, where smaller noncredit bettors may feel that they should become less conservative with their funds.

31. Credit play is, however, much less significant on most riverboat and Indian reservation casinos. Also note that prior to June 1983, gaming debts were not legally enforceable in Nevada. See Rose (1986) and AICPA (1984).

32. For instance, in 1983, receivables in Atlantic City casinos rose at about twice the rate of win and foreshadowed the potential for a noticeably slower growth of revenues (win) in 1984.

33. The cage, as noted in Eade (1996, p. 157), is the casino's operational nerve center, which is responsible for the custodianship of and accountability for the casino's bankroll, provides a vital link to the casino pit areas, deals with customer transactions, interfaces with every casino department, and is responsible for the preparation and maintenance of internal control forms.

34. Indeed, if it weren't for the Interstate Wire Act of 1956, which makes transmission of bets using phone lines a felony, wagering on the Internet would already be much larger.

Chapter 6

1. Actually, the oldest amusement park is Bakken, just north of Copenhagen, which began attracting visitors in 1583. See *Amusement Business*, March 3, 1996.

2. Indeed, the first true amusement park was Steeplechase Park at Coney Island, which was opened in 1897 by George Tilyou. Also, as Nasaw (1993, p. 85) notes, Luna Park, in competition with Steeplechase and Dreamland, in 1904 attracted 4 million people – a remarkable number for that time.

3. As Adams (1991, pp. 43–5) notes, the underlying concepts had also been proven in Tilyou's Steeplechase Park.

4. The 160-acre site for Disneyland was selected by the Stanford Research Institute.

5. In attempts to emulate Disney's concepts on a smaller scale, the Marriott Corporation, Taft Broadcasting, Six Flags, and others began a construction boom that lasted throughout most of the 1970s. A total of at least $500 million was spent in the construction of parks such as Busch Gardens Old Country, Great Adventure, Kings Dominion, Great America, and Canada's Wonderland. As of 1997, the largest corporate park operators after Disney in terms of total admissions were Anheuser-Busch (Sea World, Busch Gardens Tampa, FL, and Williamsburg, VA), Six Flags (partly owned by Time-Warner), Paramount (Kings Island, Kings Dominion, Canada's Wonderland), and Seagram (Universal Studios, Orlando and Los Angeles).

6. That was, of course, followed by another initial investment of $1.1 billion to open the EPCOT Center in 1981 as well as $500 million for the Studio Tour that opened in 1989.

7. A subset of the themed amusement business involves regularly scheduled state fairs and regional expositions. These fairs are, in essence, movable, impermanent theme parks that have operating characteristics similar to those of permanent facilities. According to compilations by *Amusement Business*, the industry trade journal, in 1999 the top fifty fairs attracted combined attendance of 45.5 million. But because only about 60% of all admissions are paid, the industry generates less than $200 million at the gate. Several times this amount, however, is derived from activities conducted within the fairs.

Waterparks, another subset, have also become popular in recent years. In 1999, an estimated 63 million people visited the nation's approximately 100 waterparks, according to *Amusement Business* estimates.

See also Lyon (1987).

8. A study by consulting firm Economics Research Associates indicates that in the year 2000, 340 parks worldwide generated a combined attendance of 545 million and revenues of $13.5 billion, with North America accounting for 49% of all revenues. The data include North American parks with attendance above 500,000 and "significant" parks elsewhere. In the 1990s, the number of parks and revenues approximately doubled, and attendance grew by 80%. See *Amusement Business*, January 10, 2000.

9. Location-based entertainment is a recent nomenclature that has been generally used to describe ride-simulator theaters and advanced video-game arcades built in urban or suburban shopping centers. However, LBE is a term that could as well be used to describe theme parks, movie theaters, themed restaurants, sports stadiums, or casinos. LBE companies generate revenues by selling and/or leasing systems and production equipment, by licensing film software to operators, or by owning and operating attractions.

10. A number of major European parks date to the early 1900s. As shown in Brown and Church (1987), Alton Towers in the United Kingdom was opened in 1924 and Kantoor (Duinrell) in the Netherlands in 1935.

Also, Asian parks are becoming important, especially in Japan, Indonesia, and Korea. Disney, for example, has a park project in Hong Kong.

11. Both traditional carnival-type games and electronic video games also generate high marginal profits.

12. Particularly in the case of smaller parks, it is conceivable, though not likely, that operation of the park turns out to be merely an interim holding action in anticipation of the maturation of higher-value alternative uses. In such instances, the park would be worth more dead than alive.

13. In 1983, Taft Broadcasting Company sold to Kings Entertainment Company theme parks that included Kings Island, Kings Dominion, Carowinds, and Hanna Barbera Land for $167.5 million. In 1984, Marriott's sold its 195-acre Santa Clara property to the city of Santa Clara for $101 million and the 325-acre Gurnee, Illinois park to Bally Mfg. for about $114.5 million. Also, in 1982, Six Flags parks (six facilities with 1982 attendance of approximately 12.6 million) were bought by Bally Mfg. for $147 million plus assumption of about $100 million in debt. Six Flags was subsequently again transferred to Wesray Capital Corp. by Bally Mfg. in 1987 for approximately $350 million plus assumption of $250 million of debt. Then, in 1994, Time Warner Inc. sold the properties to an investment consortium at a value of approximately $1.1 billion. The Six Flags facilities were ultimately bought by Premier Parks in April 1998 for $965 million.

Chapter 7

1. Smith (1995, p. 20) suggests that there is still no universally accepted operational definition of the words tourist or tourism even though both words have been a part of the language since the early 1800s. Also, the World Tourism Organization has grappled with guidelines and definitions. For statistical purposes, we can consider a tourist as a visitor whose visit is for at least one night and whose main purpose of visit may be classified as: (a) leisure and holidays, (b) business and professional, and (c) other tourism purposes.

2. Also, in Europe and North America more than 80% of tourism is domestic, whereas in the Pacific or Asia regions the domestic component tends to be much lower.

3. Beyond this, Kusler (1991) and Lindberg (1991) have also attempted to categorize ecotourists by type. Kusler's groupings, as described in (Fennell 1999, p. 56) include: do-it-yourselfers, ecotourists on tours, and school or scientific groups. The first category enjoys great flexibility, the second is highly organized, and the third sometimes involves relatively harsh site conditions. Lindberg, however, uses four basic tourist-type categories: hard-core nature, dedicated nature, mainstream nature, and casual nature. See also the Ecotourism Society's website at www.ecotourism.org and McLaren (1998), whose insights are valuable but whose conclusion against a capitalist and consumer-oriented economy is plainly misguided.

4. In contrast, *demand* for tourism services is derived from many different needs and segments, but the commercial implications of addressing each need and segment are, from experience, fairly well understood and can be more readily coordinated.

5. See note 9 below.

6. Additional tools that are sometimes used in tourism planning studies might also include input-output (I/O) transactions tables that indicate how a change in one factor input affects output of another. As described by Fletcher (1989) and also in a Fletcher article in Witt and Moutinho (1994), the tables can be broken down into many sectors and categories, possibly including types of visitors, purposes of visit, etc. Also, as Smith (1995) has indicated, the tourism forecasting models that might be used in conjunction with multiplier estimates include hypothesized behavioral and attitudinal relationships (expectancy-value models) that have been developed by psychologists. Most such models, according to Smith (1995), are based on work by Fishbein (1967).

7. Note also that the underlying theory follows what is known as the Heckscher–Ohlin theorem, which suggests that a country's factors of production, including labor, capital, and land/natural resources, rather than relative efficiencies of production determine its comparative advantage.

8. Such imports, related to foreign-guest preferences, might be for food, entertainment, electronics devices, types of cars, etc.

9. Cost-benefit analyses that focus on externalities are the province of a separate field of tourism study, ecotourism (or "green tourism"), which goes beyond the economist's prime concerns about money flows and outputs. Ecotourism attempts to understand tourism's full impact on a region's ecology, including "quality of life" issues. It is based on the notion, supported by Krippendorf (1987), that tourism development should be consistent with its environment and arise naturally from the activities that are natural to the area. See also Ryan (1991, p. 104).

Appendix B

1. It is possible that a project's cash flow timing is such that the NPV never falls to zero or that the NPV crosses the horizontal axis and drops to zero more than once, thereby producing multiple IRRs.

Appendix C

1. Economists familiar with the efficient-market hypothesis will recognize many of the concepts (a martingale, for instance) that are involved in money management. A martingale is any system of trying to make up losses in previous bets by doubling or otherwise increasing the amount bet. The pyramid or D'Alembert system is also popular.

2. Players should also be aware that the IRS requires bingo and slot-machine winners of over $1,200, and keno winners of over $1,500, to file form W-2G. In the case of lotteries and racetrack winners, witholding of 20% for federal taxes may begin at $1,000.

3. Estimates are approximate and assume application of basic strategy.

4. Silberstang (1980, p. 388) has slightly different figures of -1.36% for Player and -1.17% for Banker. Also see Thorp (1984).

5. Numbers are from Barnhart (1983) and differ from those of Scarne (1978).

Index